THE PLANNED DESTRUCTION OF AMERICA

MW00531789

James W. Wardner

Copyright © 1993 by James W. Wardner
All rights reserved
Printed in the United States of America
International Standard Book Number: 0-9632190-5-7
Library of Congress Catalog Card Number: 93-078170

Tables on pages 15 and 16 used with the kind permission of the authors of *The Truth In Money Book.*

Scripture quotations marked (NIV) are taken from the *Holy Bible, New International Version* ®. NIV®. Copyright © 1973, 1978, 1984 by International Bible Society. Used by permission of Zondervan Publishing House. All rights reserved.

Chart on page 105 (MNCs portrayed as American) taken from the book *America: What Went Wrong?* copyright 1992 by Donald L. Barlett and James B. Steele. Reprinted with permission of Andrews and McMeel. All rights reserved.

This book or parts thereof may not be reproduced in any form without permission of the author.

Published by:
Longwood Communications
1310 Alberta Street
Longwood, FL 32750
407-260-0016

To order additional copies or to contact James Wardner to speak to your group write:

James W. Wardner
P. O. Box 533438
Orlando, Florida 32838-3438
1-800-TYRANNY
1-800-897-2669

ACKNOWLEDGEMENTS

I wish to express my thanks to three women who gave me a willing ear, wise counsel and lots of late evenings of difficult and exacting work. To Carol, Sunny and Melissa,

Many Thanks

The Planned Destruction of America

DEDICATION

This book is dedicated to those Americans who love their country as I was taught to by my parents and who desire to know who has torn it apart and why.

The Planned Destruction of America

TABLE OF CONTENTS

Introduction 9
1. Money and Inflation 11
2. The Federal Reserve: Public or Private? 19
3. The Federal Reserve: Creator of
      Fictitious Money 32
4. The Federal Reserve: Manipulating
      the Economy 39
5. The Council on Foreign Relations 51
6 The Trilateral Commission 78
7. Multinational Corporations 100
8. The Media Blackout 118
9. Calculated Cover-ups 145
      Alaskan Oil 145
      MNCs and the Genocide of the
          American Indian 148
      Nicaragua: America Supports
          Communism—Again! 152
10. Who Are the Bilderbergers? 161
11. Unholy Alliances Are Killing America 174
      Appendix 185
      End Notes 189
      Order Form 203

The Planned Destruction of America

The House Stabilization Hearings of 1928 proved conclusively that the Governors of the Federal Reserve System had been holding conferences with the heads of the big European central banks. Even had the Congressmen known the details of the plot which was to culminate in the Great Depression of 1929–1931, there would have been nothing they could have done to stop it. The international bankers who controlled gold movements could inflict their will on any country, and the United States was as helpless as any other."

Eustace Mullins – *Secrets of the Federal Reserve*

"Let me issue and control a nation's money and I care not who writes the laws."

Baron Nathan Mayer de Rothschild

"We are grateful to the *Washington Post*, the *New York Times*, *Time* magazine and other great publications whose directors have attended our meetings and respected their promises of discretion [silence] for almost forty years....It would have been impossible for us to develop our plan for the world if we had been subject to the bright lights of publicity during these years."

David Rockefeller

When I first read these words, I realized I was getting a behind-the-scenes look at an area reserved for those who are meant to be in the know. However, as time passed and I shared my new knowledge and the burden of it with many others, I discovered that almost no one was aware that the Federal Reserve Bank of the United States is indeed a private bank!

Worse than that, I have found that once people understand that, they rarely, if ever, understand the massive implications of that fact. Worse yet, I have come to learn that television is nothing more than Pravda USA—a massive tool of propaganda to keep America asleep, believing things really are okay and are going to stay the same. However, things are not okay and they are not going to stay the same. America's destruction has been planned! The gears are set in place.

I pray that this book will be eye-opening and will motivate the apathetic to do something other than vegetate with their TVs.

James W. Wardner

Chapter 1

MONEY AND INFLATION

In 1984 I bought a dental practice in a poor town in southeastern Massachusetts. Fully one-half of this hamlet was on welfare. Since this little town was on the water, it was rediscovered after a *Boston Globe* article featured its proximity to Boston and idyllic placement on the ocean. Soon real estate was booming. Every available piece of land was being bought up as an "investment." Downtown Boston prices had skyrocketed in previous years over 30 percent annually. Now it was our turn. I never saw so much excitement. The realtors were ecstatic. I thought, wow, this will benefit my business too!

Suddenly, out of nowhere came the Tax Reform Act of 1986. It seemed the day this Act was signed, that little town died. It was absolutely amazing to see, one day, the absolute frenzy of the dollar-diluted marketplace; the next day, nothing. No business. No money. No people. No phone calls. Nothing! I was there; I actually saw it happen. With one stroke of a pen, that particular piece of legislation wiped out the life of a community. It had been only the beginning of a renaissance, a recovery. The Tax Reform Act assured that recovery did not occur. Soon after, the real estate market in Boston followed suit. The market ground to a halt. Business slowed, sales dropped, industry stopped hiring, people lost jobs, homes and businesses were put up for sale, and the First Bank of Boston collapsed.

At about the same time, I received word that the government had decided to do away with the interest deduction on student loans. I remember thinking, that would mean I would have to earn two dollars for every one dollar I pay off. If the interest is not deductible, it comes out of after-tax dollars! That means both principal and interest come out of net income after already taxed gross wages! If the U.S. Government really cared about education, why would it take away the interest deduction on a school loan? And why would the government: 1) make it so hard for students to get through school, 2) make it so hard to get out of debt and 3) make it so hard to have a successful, thriving business whereby to hire others? Every day was a struggle, not to get ahead, but to get by.

Let me remind you that at or about the same time these changes were being made in our tax system, another change was being implemented which has affected us all. In general all interest on everything purchased has been removed from the deductible category. This in essence made the price of goods higher. If you purchase an automobile for $15,000 at 9 percent interest, that $1,350 or more that was *deductible* and taken off your taxable income is now *taxable* income. Ultimately, you have less money in your pocket now than before the new laws. Interest and inflation are chewing up the average American. When I went through all my educational studies, I had a plan. I forecast the type of education, the cost, how much I might be making, and my ability to pay it off. What I did not forecast, nor could I forecast, was my government's plan to change laws, increase inflation, debunk the currency, stultify business, and manipulate the economy. No one told me what effect inflation would have on tuition or that U.S. Government planning would make it even more difficult to pay it back. The 1986 Tax Reform Act reformed the Savings and Loan industry as well. If the S&Ls could not make it, how could the small businessman? What I didn't realize at the time is, we are not meant to. It was about at this time that I realized something was very wrong in America.

Let's face facts. If we were to analyze honestly the American educational system, we would have to agree it is a colossal failure. The evolution of civilization should be such that things get better. We should learn from our mistakes, make corrections, evaluate, and change for the better. How? By teaching that which we had not known before.

America today is dead last compared to other civilized countries with respect to reading and mathematics. If what is not working now is no good (and it isn't), why don't we at least return to that which was better. In the 1950s and 1960s America excelled. Suddenly we're dead last? What happened? Why are practical matters not taught in school? Is the answer quite simply that we have been educated not to know?

Already, taxpayers work from January through June specifically for the running of the bureaucracy in Washington. Should our so-called representatives be responsive to us since we fund their machine? Yes! Are they? No! Can we control them? Rarely! Again, we ask, why? Isn't this a constitutional republic? What is going on?

Don't look to the government for help or an example. In 1990, at a time when the economy of the country was sinking below water, the Savings and Loans were going under, real estate prices were declining, unemployment was escalating, and government was out of control, congressmen voted themselves a raise. Even though 85 percent of the American public were totally against it, they did it anyway. What did we do shortly thereafter? We voted the incumbents right back into office with our blessing. The media said we needed "experienced" senators and congressmen. It is this kind of "experience" that is leading this country into financial and personal bondage, educational bondage, and servility.

Why is it in the best interest of the American government that we not comprehend what is going on? Why is it better for *them* to plan than for *us* to plan? Why is it that every time we *do* plan, they *change* the rules? Why is there never a tax law change in *favor* of the American voter except a token in an election year?

It is said that nothing happens in politics that was not meant to happen. I hope to be able to show you that much of America's demise has been planned! You and I are part of that plan—a plan that you were not asked about, a plan you will not get to vote on, a plan that affects your life each and every day, a plan that you fund by the sweat of your brow.

Do the men and women who shuffle around Washington care about your problems or concerns? It is my contention that with rare exception, they do not. As if I have to prove it; they themselves prove it daily. At a time when we, the taxpayers, are trying to pay the interest on a national debt of over $4 trillion, our poor, over-worked representatives vote themselves a raise. *We* will pay for their raises. (Since this was written the bank scam has been exposed.)

Our families will also pay dearly for every inflationary dollar *we* personally spend or borrow. We probably went into debt believing we could pay it back. We trusted the economy would stay on the same frequency long enough for us to get out of debt and obtain control of our finances. My friend, if you are enslaved by debt, you are likely contributing to the plan of those unseen forces around you and to your own demise. "The rich rule over the poor, and the borrower is servant to the lender" (Prov. 22:7).

Florida State Representative (R) Daniel Webster recently stated that legislators currently believe that all of the money taxpayers earn belongs to the state. Actually, taxpayers should be "thankful" they are left any exemptions at all.

Many people are at the food, clothing, and shelter stage of survival. Do you suppose the government will leave the citizens any exemptions for the basic necessities of life? Further spending by government, followed by further taxation of the people, will not work. People are the resource. Not just their money. Government has not realized that a man's time, his productive time, is one of our nation's greatest wealth-producing resources.

Don't think for a minute that all of the homeless are negligent bums. Once workers realize there are not enough hours in the week or enough jobs in the city to earn sufficient income to pay for necessities *and* the frivolous demands of the state—they give up! Many are the result of a government out of control which no longer cares about people but rather must feed itself in a self-sustained eating frenzy. As men lose their spirit to work, and as more employers lose their ability to hire, the government will grind to a halt.

Why do we as a nation, despite all logic, repeatedly travel this road of moral and financial bankruptcy and despair? Is it the people we elect into office? Do they dream up their own destructive and stupid legislation? Or are there other forces at work?

Suffice it to say, there are certainly enough questions to warrant investigation.

A friend of mine used to say, "The apple doesn't fall far from the tree." That is, the fruit of the tree (or the legislation) is pretty close in kind to the tree (or government) that birthed it. This is stated another way in Matthew 7:16–17: "By their fruit you will recognize them…every good tree bears good fruit, but a bad tree bears bad fruit. A good tree cannot bear bad fruit, and a bad tree cannot bear good fruit…."

Americans have become accustomed to adjusting their lives to the situation at hand. If we encounter a new tax law, we pay it. If our government wants to fight a war, we fight it. If cars and houses go up in price, we simply work harder to try to attain them. However, more and more of those things are out of reach. More Americans are driving an older car, living in a poorly constructed home, and saving less. Oh, yes, we can blame those dastardly credit cards and our lack of discipline for using them, but were those purchases based on realistic expectations? Certainly no one continues to buy, thinking the bills will never roll in. Most purchases are made, I believe, with the expectation that we will have the money to pay for those things we buy. Although self-control is necessary, we must realize that inflation has figured into the cost of our goods at such a rate as to make our once-realistic expectations suddenly unrealistic with our present finances. Our desires outweigh our knowledge. Naively, we buy and continue to buy. Suddenly, we realize we can't pay the bills any longer.

If you will spend just a few minutes analyzing these graphs, it will make a great difference in your comprehending the financial danger you are in. The Consumer Price Index (CPI) is a measure of the price of a typical consumer's expenditure on basic goods and services. If we compare one year's index with another, we can discover how much prices have moved up and how much the purchasing power of the dollar is declining. The following chart demonstrates that prices have been rising steadily since the mid-1950s.

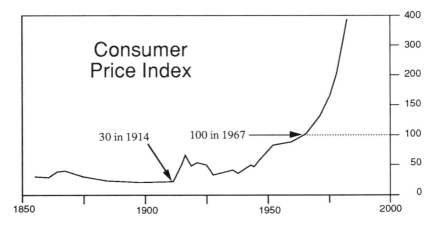

In 1979 prices were more than eight times higher than in 1900. In 1992 prices are more than fifteen times higher. It is obvious that the purchasing power of the dollar has decreased dramatically. Translated: An increasing number of dollars are needed to pay for the same goods and services (see charts below).

Purchasing power of a dollar based on the value of a dollar being 1 in 1914	
Year	Purchasing Power
1900	$1.20
1914	1.00
1920	.50
1925	.56
1930	.60
1967	.30
1975	.19
1977	.16
1979	.14
1981	.11
1982	.10
1983	.10 (May)

The Collapse of the 1914 Dollar

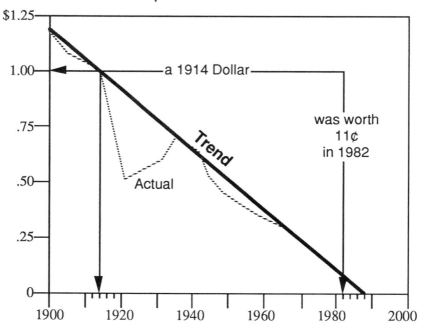

Money and Inflation

Since 1945 the money supply has been increased eleven times, and, accordingly, inflation has increased twelve times! There is therefore a direct relationship between the increase in dollars put into circulation and the amount of inflation. Note also that each individual has only so many man-hours of work available to him in his lifetime. That is, of course, if he can find employment. As inflation increases, it takes more and more man-hours to achieve the same goal—that is, purchase the same goods. Inflation has an equally destructive effect on a man's ability to pay for goods and services. He works longer and harder while his self-esteem suffers and his family's standard of living declines.

From 1945 to 1980 the dollar actually lost <u>92 percent</u> of its purchasing power, and in comparison to 1945, a dollar is now worth only eight cents! Soon the dollar will be absolutely worthless.

As it turns out, inflation without taxation is a powerful political force. Most of our congressmen are elected and reelected (incumbents are 95 percent successful) based on promises of securing more federal aid for their local voters. If an elected official proposes a bill to ensure large sums flowing into his district, he no doubt will be thanked by the votes of his admiring constituency for the "free" favors he has received from the federal government. Ultimately, those very people will have to pay for those "free" gifts.

The bureaucrats do not desire to incur the wrath of the voters due to higher taxes; therefore, these legislators encourage the Federal Reserve Bank to inflate the money supply. By printing extra paper, funds are suddenly more available—thus no need to raise taxes. The voters fail to understand that this sudden influx of money (paper) causes a great reduction in their purchasing power and their standard of living.

If the government can keep the voters always asking government to supply their needs, (according to nationally known financial counselor, Larry Burkett, eighty percent of all Americans receive government financial assistance in one form or another) this ensures government favor and control will continue. The bureaucrats are happy to oblige by printing more money in order to create public dependency. Meanwhile, the nation's wealth goes unprotected, our standard of living declines, goods cost more, and on it goes.

The stable of bought media analysts interview financial gurus who blame the economy on trends and blame us for lack of planning and lack of self-control. I used to believe that was true. The trouble is, my investigation showed conclusively that what we are being told is absolutely not true. In fact, the American people are being taken on one of the longest Trojan horse rides of history. Sadly, we are being duped by our own leaders, who have conspired against us. My friends, I am here to tell you that the declining American standard of living has been planned from the beginning. It is not an unusual blip on the economic screen. It is not an obscure "trend." Rather, it is the result of planning at the very highest levels of American government—a plan to fail, a plan to create insecurity and uncertainty, a plan to make the American people serfs in the New World Order.

Chapter 2

THE FEDERAL RESERVE:
PUBLIC OR PRIVATE?

T he greatest overall influence on the American standard of living, the economy, jobs, and the "good" feelings that can go along with a good economy or the "bad" feelings that accompany a poor economy, is the activity of the Federal Reserve Bank. This so-called central bank has been playing havoc with American lives for eighty years. The bank doubles the money supply routinely every ten years. This causes inflation and lowers the standard of living. Former Soviet Premier Nikita Kruschev said, "By a continuing process of inflation, governments can confiscate, secretly and unobserved, an important part of the wealth of their citizens."[1]

Who owns the Federal Reserve?

The Federal Reserve Act allowed the credit of the nation to fall into the hands of a few international bankers who now direct American policy and hold in their palms the destiny of the people. Lenin assured us in 1910, "The surest way to overthrow an established social order is to debauch its currency."[2]

This banking act was created in complete secrecy at Jekyll Island, Georgia. One of the designers, Frank Vanderlip, president of Kuhn,

Loeb's National City Bank of New York, later wrote:

"There was an occasion near the close of 1910 when I was as secretive, indeed as furtive, as any conspirator. I do not feel it is any exaggeration to speak of our secret expedition to Jekyll Island as the occasion of the actual conception of what eventually became the Federal Reserve System.

"We were told to leave our last names behind us. We were told further that we should avoid dining together on the night of our departure. We were instructed to come one at a time...where Senator Aldrich's private car would be in readiness, attached to the rear end of the train for the South.

"Once aboard the private car, we began to observe the taboo that had been fixed on last names. Discovery, we knew, simply must not happen, or else all our time and effort would be wasted...."[3]

The obvious question is, Why the need for secrecy, especially regarding public legislation? Those who met in secret were bankers. They understood what Karl Marx, in the *Communist Manifesto*, had proclaimed: "Money plays the largest part in determining the course of history."[4] Since bankers wrote their own legislation, it is the course of history that they desired to effect.

The name was designed to deceive. The Federal Reserve Bank is not federal, nor is it owned by the government. It is privately owned. The bank pays its own postage like any private corporation; its employees are not civil service; and its physical property is held under private deeds and is subject to local taxation. Government property is not.

To slip the private bank past the unwary American people, the stealthy planners of the bill titled it the Federal Reserve Act. Prior to that it had been called the Aldrich Bill and received much opposition. Congressman Charles A. Lindbergh Sr. had complained at the time:

> "It is a common practice of congressmen to make the title of acts promise aright, but in the body or text of the acts to rob the people of what is promised in the title."[5]

Thus, it was no surprise to discover that "the government does not own one dollar of stock in the Federal Reserve Banks....The first words of the [Federal Reserve] act are definite promises which the people assumed Congress made that the banks established were Federal Reserve—that is, *government* banks. That promise was a deliberate lie!"[6]

The Federal Reserve Act charade of 1913 was intended to pacify the American voters. They had been crying out for banking reform and held scores of elections alternating one set of politicians with another only to find themselves with the same programs and deeper in debt. It turns out that then, as now, government officeholders understood "that by joining with the [banking] interests to exploit the people, their reelection is more certain than if they serve people who elect them. By joining the exploiters their campaign expenses are paid, the support of the 'machines' and the capital press is assured, and if by chance they should lose they are appointed to some office that should suit them equally or better."[7]

Any close scrutiny of the revolving door between the various administration posts and high-ranking business officerships will prove this to be more than true today. The same people continue to show up in government, regardless of whether the nation votes Democratic or Republican.

Finance has always manipulated business and bought legislation on an enormous scale and generally strangles all enterprise that attempts to compete with it. The Federal Reserve Act, though, gave to a handful of private international bankers the privilege to inflate and deflate the economy and enlisted for its enforcer—the government. In fact, the Federal Reserve "...controls the times, dictates business, affects our homes and practically everything in which we are interested."[8]

There is a ruling elite in America, and they with their imperial wealth know what they want and how to obtain it. They achieve their desires through legislation. Lindbergh had claimed, "The Federal Reserve Act gives a power to the Federal Reserve Banks that makes the government impotent to protect the people...."[9]

Congressman Lindbergh had done his homework. He was absolutely certain that when the power to control the money of the United States went to what he called the private "money trust," it would be akin to having a known robber guard your home. He was not alone. On Tuesday, December 15, 1931, Louis T. McFadden, chairman of the House Banking and Currency Committee, proclaimed:

> "The Federal Reserve Board and banks are the duly appointed agents of the <u>foreign</u> central banks of issue and they are more concerned with their foreign customers than they are with the people of the United States. The only thing that is American about the Federal Reserve Board and banks is the money they use..."[10]

On Friday, June 10, 1932, McFadden again pleaded his case with his fellow elected colleagues:

"Mr. Chairman, we have in this country one of the most corrupt institutions the world has ever known. I refer to the Federal Reserve Board and the Federal Reserve Banks....

"Some people think the Federal Reserve Banks are United States Government institutions. They are not government institutions. They are private credit monopolies which prey upon the people of the United States for the benefit of themselves and their foreign customers; foreign and domestic speculators and swindlers; and rich and predatory money lenders. In that dark crew of financial pirates there are those who would cut a man's throat to get a dollar out of his pocket; there are those who send money into the States to buy votes to control our legislation; and there are those who maintain an international propaganda for the purpose of deceiving us and wheedling us into the granting of new concessions which will permit them to cover up their past misdeeds and set again in motion their gigantic train of crime."[11]

The twelve regional banks are also members of this private cartel. Before the Senate Banking and Currency Committee, while the Federal Reserve Bill was under discussion, attorney Alfred Crozier from Ohio observed:

"...the imperial power of elasticity of the public currency is wielded exclusively by these central corporations owned by the banks. This is a life and death power over all local banks and all business. It can be used to create or destroy prosperity, to ward off or cause stringencies and panics. By making money artificially scarce, interest rates throughout the country can be arbitrarily raised and the bank tax on all business and cost of living increased for the profit of the banks owning these regional central banks, and without the slightest benefit to the people. These twelve corporations together cover the whole country and monopolize and use for private gain every dollar of the public currency and all public revenues of the United States. Not a dollar can be put into circulation among the people by their government without the consent of and on terms fixed by these twelve private money trusts."[12]

The American people wrongly assume from the mind-manipulating press that we actually have something to say about how this country is governed. President Garfield, shortly before he was assassinated, had declared that whoever controls the supply of currency would control the business and activities of all the people. Whether we vote Republican or Democratic, the answer to

22

Americans has routinely been yes to more government, yes to more spending, and yes to more <u>control</u>.

After the National Banking Act of 1863 was passed, Lincoln stated:

> "The money pow7er preys upon the nation in times of peace and conspires against it in times of adversity. It is more despotic than monarchy, more insolent than autocracy, more selfish than bureaucracy. I see in the near future a crisis approaching that unnerves me and causes me to tremble for the safety of my country. Corporations have been enthroned, an era of corruption in high places will follow, and the money power of the country will endeavor to prolong its reign by working upon the prejudices of the people until the wealth is aggregated in a few hands and the republic is destroyed."[13]

Lincoln, like Garfield, was assassinated. As far back as 1835 there was an assassination attempt on President Andrew Jackson. Why? His distaste for the international bankers led him to exclaim:

> "You are a den of vipers. I intend to rout you out, and by the Eternal God I will rout you out. If the people only understood the rank injustice of our money and banking system, there would be a revolution before morning!"[14]

Some revealing information has recently surfaced regarding the John F. Kennedy assassination. Shortly before Kennedy's death, he had signed an executive order giving the government the responsibility to write paper money, conceivably taking that privilege away from the Federal Reserve Bank. Oops! Big mistake!

The question is, Who is running whom? For certain, the government does not control the Federal Reserve Bank. President Bush aligned every country of the UN to fight a battle against Saddam Hussein. He sent 20,000 troops and stealth fighters to Panama. He threatened Moammar Quaddafi from great distances, but he must get on his hands and knees and beg Alan Greenspan to lower interest rates one-half of 1 per cent. Nevertheless, Greenspan tells Bush (and now Clinton) what <u>he</u> will do. He answers not to the president, not to Congress, and least of all to the American people! Again, Congressman McFadden says:

> "Every effort has been made by the Federal Reserve Board to conceal its power but the truth is the Federal Reserve Board has usurped the government of the United States. It controls everything here and it controls our foreign relations. It makes and breaks governments at will."[15]

McFadden was one of the few truly great representatives of our century. He was a serious man, not a stooge of greed and power as so many were then and more are today. He was so serious he led an attempt to impeach President Herbert Hoover:

> "Whereas the said Herbert Hoover, President of the United States, has, in violation of the Constitution and laws of the United States, permitted irregularities in the issuance of the Federal reserve currency which have occasioned great losses to the United States and have deprived the United States of legal revenue and has permitted the Federal Reserve Board and the Federal Reserve Banks unlawfully to take and to use government credit for private gain and has permitted grave irregularities in the conduct of the United States Treasury, which violations make him guilty of high crimes and misdemeanors and subject to impeachment...."[16]

The result of the vote on impeaching Hoover was 361 to 8 with 60 not voting. Certainly no legislator would be so silly as to risk his professional career by impeaching the president most under the influence of the foreign bankers. These men were powerful. So powerful, in fact, that McFadden was smeared in their private press and driven from office.

Were Lindbergh and McFadden wrong? Even a member of the Federal Reserve Board itself, W.P.G. Harding, pronounced the unthinkable in testimony before Congress. He admitted that the Fed is an outright private banking monopoly. He revealed, "The Federal Reserve Bank is an institution owned by the stockholding member banks. The government has not a dollar's worth of stock in it."[17]

The privacy issue and illegal control of the money-making powers of government have surfaced again and again throughout the years. Honest elected representatives have sought to warn us, yet never does the banker-owned media address this issue. In 1952 Congressman Wright Patman repeated the menace of this private banking monopoly:

> "This international banking cartel, as will be shown, manages the credit of the United States for the profit and advantage of its foreign and domestic members. In so doing, the Federal Reserve exploits the entire producing strata of the American society for the gain of a select, non-producing few."[18]

Exposing the myth of government instrumentality, Congressman Patman declared:

> "These funds [interest from government obligations] are expended by the [Federal Reserve] system without an adequate accounting to Congress. In fact there has never been

an independent audit of either the twelve banks or the Federal Reserve Board that has been filed with the Congress where a Member [of Congress] would have an opportunity to inspect it. The General Accounting Office does not have jurisdiction over the Federal Reserve. For 40 years (1952) [now 81 years] the system, while freely using the money of the government (taxpayers), has not made a proper accounting."[19]

Again, in 1971, Representative John R. Rarick, in denouncing Nixon's plan for extreme deficit spending, exclaimed:

"The Federal Reserve is not an agency of government. It is a private banking monopoly."[20]

In my possession I have a copy of House Resolution Bill H.R. 1468 introduced March 19, 1991, by Philip Crane, 102nd Congress, 1st session. This bill was designed "to authorize and direct the General Accounting Office to audit the Federal Reserve Board, the Federal Advisory Council, the Federal Open Market Committee, and Federal Reserve Banks and their branches."[21]

Congressman Jerry Voorhis in his book *Out of Debt, Out of Danger* revealed there were as many as 15,000 privately owned commercial banks and branches of twelve privately owned Federal Reserve Banks.[22] Debt has literally bankrupted this country, and as of 1995 all of the money paid by all of the taxpayers will not even pay the interest on the national debt (owed to unconstitutional, unelected private international bankers). But what do you suppose became of H.R. 1468? You guessed it. It landed right where the buyers of power wanted it—in the cobwebs, unknown to the majority of enslaved, tax-paying American workers. The truth is not to be revealed!

Want more proof? A man injured by an automobile owned and operated by the Federal Reserve Bank of San Francisco sued for damages in a federal court. In the Ninth Circuit Court decision of *Lewis vs. United States* rendered April 17, 1982, the court declared "that since the Federal Reserve System and its twelve branch banks are private corporations, the Federal government could not be held responsible."[23]

Former Congressman Ron Paul writes an insightful newsletter exposing the government money defrauders. For years as a congressman he had tried to expose the central bankers who undermine the wealth of America. His statement, which appeared in the *National Educator* of April 1983, is revealing:

"As a member of the House Banking Committee, I have long believed that present economic difficulties are caused principally by our centralized banking system headed by the Federal Reserve, and by the use of irredeemable paper money.

"Article I, Section 8 of the Constitution grants Congress the exclusive power of coining money, not printing it. But seventy years ago, in 1913 Congress enacted the Federal Reserve Act establishing our present banking system. At the time we were still on a gold standard, and the harmful effects of the Federal Reserve System were meliorated by the continued use of gold and silver as coins and as backing for paper currency. Still, the Federal Reserve has succeeded in causing the worst depressions, inflations, recessions, unemployment, and interest rates in our history....

"I am convinced that there is no permanent solution to our severe economic problems that does not involve thorough monetary reform. This is why I have introduced four major pieces of legislation. The first bill, H.R. 875, would repeal the Federal Reserve Act of 1913, thus ending our 70-year experiment with paper money, an experiment that has obviously failed. To achieve that end, I have also introduced a bill requiring, for the first time in history, a complete audit of the Federal Reserve, H.R. 877. I believe that a thorough audit and investigation of the Federal Reserve would reveal enough damning information about the Fed that virtually all members of Congress would support its abolition...."[24]

In 1833 President Andrew Jackson ordered the considerable deposits of the federal government removed from the central bank of the United States and transferred to various state banks. Nicholas Biddle, head of the central bank, determined to undermine Jackson by ordering a sharp reduction in loans throughout the banking system. The inevitable result was a sharp contraction in business activity and an economic panic. Biddle was a Rothschild European banking representative. He purposely created a financial panic to blackmail the government into rechartering the bank. Jackson warned the American people:

"The bold effort the present bank had made to control the government, the distress it had wantonly produced...are but premonitions of the fate that awaits the American people should they be deluded into a perpetuation of this institution, or the establishment of another like it."[25]

Jackson told his vice president, Martin Van Buren, "The Bank, Mr. Van Buren, is trying to kill me...."[26]

Do you suppose he meant figuratively? Apparently not, since

shortly thereafter an attempt was made on his life. The would-be assassin, Richard Lawrence, claimed that he had been "in touch with the powers in Europe, which had promised to intervene if any attempt was made to punish him."[27]

The Federal Reserve is inherently evil. It was designed to alter, inextricably, the financial freedom and enterprise and hope of the American people. It was designed to give ultimate power to a very small group of evil men. These are men who desire subservient behavior and ruthless power. The New World Order will be ushered in by a similar "quake" as that which nearly toppled Jackson. Some years ago Secretary of the Treasury George Humphrey declared:

> "We are on the verge of something that will curl a man's hair to think about it....It will make the 1930s look like rip-roaring prosperity."[28]

If you are interested in alerting government to the corrupt Federal Reserve, consider the dialogue at the House Hearings of 1947. Governor of the Federal Reserve, Marriner Eccles, was asked: "Chairman Eccles, when do you think there is a possibility of returning to a free and open market, instead of this pegged and artificially controlled market we have now?"

Eccles: "Never. Not in your lifetime or mine."[29]

The principles imbued in the Federal Reserve Act were the creation of Paul Warburg, a partner of Kuhn, Loeb Company. Typical of the monied fraternity, he married money as well. In 1895 he married the daughter of Solomon Loeb. Warburg's salary in 1902 was $500,000 a year.

Eustace Mullins, in *Secrets of the Federal Reserve*, states:

> "Because the Federal Reserve Bank of New York was to set the interest rates and direct open market operations, thus controlling the daily supply and price of money throughout the United States, it is the stockholders of that bank who are the real directors of the entire system....Of the initial 203,053 shares issued, the Rockefeller Kuhn, Loeb-controlled National City Bank took the largest number of shares of any bank, 30,000 shares."[30]

The banking house of Kuhn, Loeb Company had been identified by Senator Robert L. Owen as the representative of the European Rothschilds in the United States. Colonel Elisha Ely Garrison, in *Roosevelt, Wilson and the Federal Reserve Law* wrote: "Paul Warburg is the man who got the Federal Reserve Act together after the Aldrich Plan aroused such nationwide resentment and opposition. The mastermind of both plans was Baron Alfred

Rothschild of London."[31] Senator Nelson Aldrich was maternal grandfather to the Rockefeller brothers.

The Aldrich Plan had been objected to on the following points:

1) It entirely lacked adequate government or public control.

2) Voting control was in the hands of the large banks.

3) Extreme danger of inflation was inherent in the system.

4) The bill had dangerous monopolistic aspects.

In fact, the Aldrich Plan and the Federal Reserve Act bills were almost identical. Aldrich was one of the secret planners at Jekyll Island. He was rewarded handsomely for his efforts. When he entered the Senate in 1881, he was worth $50,000. When he left in 1911, he was worth $30 million!

Aldrich wrote in July 1914:

> "Before the passage of this Act [Federal Reserve], the New York bankers could only dominate the reserves of New York. Now we are able to dominate the bank reserves of the entire country."[32]

In 1914 Paul Warburg supposedly retired from Kuhn, Loeb in order to serve on the Federal Reserve Board. He was asked to appear before a Senate subcommittee but stated that it might impair his usefulness on the board if he were required to answer any questions. Warburg was confirmed, yet he did not resign his directorships in other companies; namely:

> American Surety Company
> Baltimore and Ohio Railroad
> National Railways of Mexico
> Wells Fargo
> Westinghouse Electric Company
> American I.G. Chemical Company (I.G. Farben)
> Agfa Ansco Corporation
> Westinghouse Acceptance Company
> Warburg Company of Amsterdam
> International Acceptance Bank (Chairman of the Board)

Warburg also authored the War Finance Corporation, which allowed Kuhn, Loeb and J.P. Morgan to finance World War I. In fact, the Federal Reserve Act and the new income tax law had been delivered "just in time" to finance a European war. Without them, the war could not have occurred. 1914 was a busy year for the owners of Kuhn, Loeb. That was the year they bought controlling interest in the *New York Times* to promote their own agenda.

Warburg served as governor of the Federal Reserve Board from 1914 to 1918. In 1918 J.P. Morgan gave up his seat on the Federal

Advisory Council, which Warburg promptly filled and there remained for the next ten years. It should not be surprising to anyone that the great J.P. Morgan would move aside for the "unknown" Paul Warburg. Throughout his American career, J.P. Morgan had been a front for the House of Rothschild. A story in the *New York Times* (May 27, 1905) noted that Baron Alphonse de Rothschild, head of the French house of Rothschild, possessed $60 million in American securities even though Rothschild reputedly was not active in American finance. This explains why the supposedly wealthy and powerful J. P. Morgan had only $19 million in securities when he died in 1913, $7 million of which he owed. The tremendous surplus of American securities that were manipulated by Morgan were actually owned by his employer, Rothschild.

Further confirmation comes when we realize that another of the Federal Reserve Bank's primary stockholders was J.P. Morgan's First National Bank (15,000 shares). In 1955 First National Bank merged with Kuhn, Loeb's National City Bank and thereby owned the controlling block of the Federal Reserve Bank of New York, the dictator of the entire system. Author Eustace Mullins states, "An examination of the principal stockholders in these banks, in 1914 and today, reveals a direct London connection."[33]

British maneuvering in the American economy is nothing new. As early on as 1835, Baron James de Rothschild of Paris was the principal investor in the Bank of the United States. Baron Nathan Mayer de Rothschild once arrogantly exclaimed, during a party in his mansion, "I care not what puppet is placed upon the throne of England to rule the Empire on which the sun never sets. The man that controls Britain's money supply controls the British Empire, and I control the British money supply."[34]

Rothschild is also reputed to have said :"Let me issue and control a nation's money, and I care not who writes the laws."[35]

The central banks of not only the United States, but also England, France, Germany, Italy, and Austria are privately owned and Rothschild controlled. So much for political elections!

Napoleon once said:

> "When a government is dependent for money upon bankers, they and not the leaders of the government control the situation, since the hand that gives is above the hand that takes....Money has no motherland; financiers are without patriotism and without decency; their sole object is gain."[36]

Money knows no nationality. This was proven dramatically during World War I. While Paul Warburg was financing the Allies, his brother Max was financing the enemy—Germany.[37] Max was also head of the German Secret Service. It was Max, who as head of the S.S., allowed Lenin to travel from exile in Switzerland through Germany to Russia (with plenty of American money). This, of course, led to the Bolshevik Revolution and to the loss of sixty million lives.

According to Colonel Ely Garrison and the United States Naval Secret Service Report on Paul Warburg, the Russian Revolution had been financed by the Rothschilds and the Warburgs.[38] Kuhn, Loeb partners held the highest governmental posts in the United States during World War I, while in Germany Max and Fritz Warburg, and Philip and Ludwig Schiff (brother of Jacob Schiff—Kuhn, Loeb USA) moved in the highest councils of government.[39]

It was also Max who headed the German delegation at the Versailles Peace Conference. Naturally, Max was pleased to find his brother Paul as Woodrow Wilson's chief financial advisor. Indeed, Baron Edmond de Rothschild served as the genial host to the leading members of the American delegation. He even turned his Paris mansion over to them.

With control of international finance, the Rothschilds bought control of Reuters International News Agency, based in London, Havas of France, and Wolf in Germany, and thereby control the dissemination of all news in Europe. This is only to show that there is slightly more behind the scenes than the bankers would have us believe. Actually, they must marvel at our stupidity!

After the war the bankers at the Peace Conference convinced President Wilson that they needed an international government (League of Nations) to facilitate their international monetary operations. Properly brainwashed, Wilson was surprised to have American citizens boo him as he campaigned to have them turn over their hard-won independence to an international banking dictatorship. Mullins suggests: "It is entirely logical to say that the American people suffered that depression [1929] as a punishment for not joining the League of Nations."[40]

The House Hearings on the Stabilization of the Purchasing Power of the Dollar in 1928 proved conclusively that the Federal Reserve Board worked in close cooperation with the heads of European central banks and that the Depression of 1929–1931 was planned at a secret luncheon of the Federal Reserve Board and those heads of European central banks in 1927. This was the same time that Paul Warburg was on the Federal Advisory Council. During the hearings a Mr. Steagall asked: "Is it true that action [transfer of gold] stabilized the European currencies and upset ours?" Adolph Miller, governor of the Federal Reserve Board, replied: "Yes, that was what it was <u>intended</u> to do."[41]

There has never been a court trial on the legality or constitutionality of the Federal Reserve Act. In 1935 the National Recovery Act was ruled unconstitutional by the Supreme Court on the grounds that "Congress may <u>not</u> abdicate or transfer to others its legitimate functions...." Nevertheless, this is exactly what Congress has done in the case of the Federal Reserve.

Chapter 3

THE FEDERAL RESERVE:
CREATOR OF FICTITIOUS MONEY

The *Olympic Herald*, February 16, 1982, revealed that Senator Jack Metcalf, a Washington state legislator, introduced Senate Resolution No. 127 which challenged the constitutionality of delegating the power to create money to the Federal Reserve System. "The Federal Reserve System is nothing more than a group of private banks which charge interest on money that never existed," Metcalf declared. The senate report and full text of *Information Prepared for Washington State Senate in Consideration of State Concurrent Resolution #127* is as follows:

> Sen. Sellar: Senator Metcalf, are you contending that inflation and interest rates are directly related?
>
> Sen. Metcalf: Yes, they are. If you are willing to loan money at 5 percent, but anticipate 10 percent inflation rate, you will ask 15 percent interest instead of 5 percent. What may be worse, you will fear further inflation so tend to ask a little more just in case. When everyone anticipates inflation, it is self-fulfilling.
>
> Sen. McCaslin: Reading your Resolution, are you really telling us that the Federal Reserve Banking System is a private banking system?
>
> Sen. Metcalf: Like most Americans, I believed the Federal

Reserve was a part of the Federal Government. It is not! It is a federally chartered private banking corporation which has by law—not by the Constitution, but by law—been given the power to control and issue the money used in the U.S.

Sen. Guess: How does the Federal Reserve create money?

Sen. Metcalf: This will have to be an over-simplification; the actual operation is very complicated. However, this is an accurate summary of what happens.

The Federal government is going into debt about a billion dollars a week. (Now a billion dollars a day!) Where does that money come from? The government prints a billion dollars' worth of interest-bearing U.S. Government bonds, takes them to the Federal Reserve, the Federal Reserve accepts them and places $1 billion in a checking account. The government then writes checks to a total of $1 billion.

The crucial question is: "Where was that $1 billion just before they touched the computer and put it in the checking account?" The answer: "It didn't exist." We, the people, allowed a private banking system to create money at will—out of absolutely nothing—to call it a loan to our government and then charge us interest on it forever.

Sen. Quigg: Are you saying the Federal Reserve Act gives to the national banking system as a whole the power to create money, in addition to what you have said about the Federal Reserve specifically?

Sen. Metcalf: Yes, the Fractional Reserve System implemented under the Federal Reserve Act of 1913 allows the banking system, as a system, to create money to expand the money supply. The authority to expand or contract the money supply by changing reserve requirements, given to a private banking system, puts our whole money system in fearful jeopardy. I would urge you to remember the quote from Thomas Jefferson that I placed on your desks in the last session.

> I believe that banking institutions are more dangerous to our liberties than standing armies. Already they have raised up a money aristocracy that has set the government at defiance. The issuing power should be taken from the banks and restored to the government, to whom it properly belongs.

Jefferson emphasized repeatedly that no private bank—whether chartered by the federal or a state government—

should ever be permitted to issue currency or control credit; for once entrusted with such power, they become superior to the nation itself.

Sen. Vognild: Do you contend that we, the people, are paying interest to a private banking system for use of our own government money?

Sen. Metcalf: Yes, and you bring up the most crucial point. I mentioned the creation of "checkbook money" by the Federal Reserve. As these checks from the $1 billion of newly created money go out all over America, they become our money in circulation. Why are we paying interest to a private banking system for use of our own money? By what logic does any private group collect a tax from the people for the use of our own money? And, remember, the Federal Reserve System, which receives the interest, is allowed to set the rate of interest they receive!

Sen. Lysen: The Federal Reserve Act delegates to the Federal Reserve the power to create money. Are you contending that Congress does not have the constitutional authorization to delegate that power?

Sen. Metcalf: Now, we are down to the crux of the matter. We are all aware that power granted to a body may or may not be delegated to another body, agency, or institution. Our most basic document, the U.S. Constitution, states in Article 1, section 8:

> The Congress shall have the power to coin money and regulate the value thereof.

Nowhere is there the slightest hint of authorization to delegate that power even to another governmental institution—much less to a private banking system. That is absolutely outside the most broad interpretation possible.

The Constitution does not grant the authority to delegate the power to create money, and this is the heart of the resolution introduced in the Senate. This resolution, SCR 127, declares it the intent of the State of Washington to cause an action to be filed in the U.S. Supreme Court challenging the constitutionality of the delegation of power embodied in the Federal Reserve Act of 1913. This action is a matter of monumental importance to the people of this state and of this nation, especially at this time of high interest rates and budget deficits at all levels—federal, state, and in the businesses and homes all across this land.

Sen. Fleming: Has there never been an independent audit of the Federal Reserve?

Sen. Metcalf: It does seem incredible, but the Federal Reserve has never been subject to an independent audit. On several occasions, members of Congress and the U.S. Senate have requested such an audit, but a way has always been found to avoid it. Our action here must result in that audit.

As if this news isn't bad enough, the bank itself continues to purchase for itself new monarch-type privileges. One of the best scams of late is described in *The Most Secret Science* by Lieutenant Colonel Archibald Roberts:

"Without going into a lot of detail, I'd like to just comment on an amendment to the Federal Reserve Act—*The Monetary Control Act of 1980*... Many people are deeply concerned about the ramifications of that Act. Congressman Ron Paul was very much concerned about it and Congressman Paul did some homework after the passage of the Monetary Control Act of 1980 and he found that one of...the powers granted to the Fed that year, was <u>the power to monetize foreign debt</u>. <u>That means to use the assets of America to buy up foreign debts</u>. And, you might say, 'Why? What is going on there?' Just a couple of quotes, if you will permit me to read, from Congressman Ron Paul's newsletter. He said:

"'In 1980, radical changes were made in the Federal Reserve Act, the Monetary Control Act of 1980, allowing a massive increase in the power of the Federal Reserve System. Among those powers is the <u>authority of the Fed to use the debt of foreign nations as collateral for the printing of Federal Reserve notes</u>. That's what is happening in America. This is of the greatest significance in light of the $850 billion debt owed to the West by Third World and Communist nations. To begin with, the foreign bonds of the Fed purchases are bought with paper money backed with our own debt. Then we turn around and use the newly purchased foreign bonds as collateral to print up more Federal Reserve notes. This is responsible for the dramatic increase in the money supply recently. This system of money creation is unbelievable to rational human beings. <u>It will surely lead to a disastrous end to the American dollar</u>.'"

"Congressman Paul published a letter in June of 1982 wherein he delineated $3.3 billion of foreign debt that had been monetized up until that time. After he published the letter, six months or so later, I had a telephone conversation with him, and I said, 'Congressman, we really need you to update that letter. Tell us what further foreign monetization has taken place.'" He told me something that was unbelievable. He said, "'<u>I am a member of the House Banking and Currency Committee and the Fed will not answer my questions</u>.'" This went on for months and months. He couldn't get the information as to how the Fed was using the American money system and, essentially, saddling the American taxpayers with foreign debts. He has gotten the information now, and now it is up to about $9 billion.

Just one further quote from Congressman Paul's newsletter:

"'Mexico owes $81 billion and Argentina $39 billion. This is only a small fraction of the total debt owed to Western governments and Western banks. Eastern bloc Communist nations and Third World nations owe over $850 billion and reasonable people do not expect that this sum will ever be repaid. The race now going on is to finance all this debt to governments, principally the United States, and bail out the international banking system.'"

"This, then, seems to be one of the purposes of the Monetary Control Act of 1980—an extension of Federal Reserve power. He says, '<u>The default which many pretend can be avoided is inevitable</u>. The only question that remains is, shall it be the bankers or the innocent, uninformed American citizens?'"[42]

Dear reader, are you as amazed as I was to learn that:

1) Not only is the Federal Reserve Bank a <u>privately owned</u> corporation in which the government has not three cents worth of equity, but

2) the money it does loan is made out of nothing?

Money is nothing more than a computer entry, and that number, for example, $10 billion, is what we the taxpayers pay interest on. This is the reason America is broke. This is the reason why many people cannot afford to buy a home. This is the reason for the homeless, the poor, the under-educated, the malnourished. This is the most immoral system which ever landed on this continent. The 247 million people of this nation are going slowly, insidiously toward a great waterfall of financial destruction while a handful of bankers have money they can only weigh.

Many years ago John C. Calhoun said that we had given the banks the government credit for nothing, only to borrow it back again at interest. Commenting on U.S. economic problems, *The Nation,* (December 11, 1982) reported: "The blame for all this lies at the door of the Federal Reserve System working as usual on behalf of the international banking system."[43]

Remember it was the Congress of 1913 that blessed this wicked system. Is it any wonder that today America's representatives are selling out our Constitution, our rights, and our sovereignty in the name of the New World Order? Where is the righteous indignation of a nation headed rapidly toward abysmal poverty and destruction?

The following international investment banks are the principal stockholders of the Federal Reserve system:

Rothschild Bank of England
Rothschild Bank of Berlin
Lazard Brothers Banks of Paris
Israel Moses Seiff Banks of Italy
Warburg Banks of Hamburg and Amsterdam
Lehman Brothers Bank of New York
Kuhn, Loeb Bank of New York
Chase Manhattan Bank of New York
Goldman, Sachs Bank of New York

These banks are fanatical devotees of inflation and totally devoted to the secret use of financial influences in political life.

Only three years after the Federal Reserve System had been in operation, President Woodrow Wilson admitted:

"...The growth of the nation...and all our activities are in the hands of a few men... We have come to be one of the worst ruled; one of the most completely controlled and dominated governments in the civilized world...no longer a government by conviction and the free vote of the majority, but a government by the opinion and duress of small groups of dominant men."[44]

With no exposure or change since 1913, can you imagine what the meaning of that is for us today?

A communique sent from the Rothschild investment house in England to an associate banking firm in New York read: "The few who understand the system...will either be so interested in its profits or so dependent on its favors that there will be no opposition from that class, while on the other hand, the great body of people, mentally incapable of comprehending...will bear its burdens, without complaint."[45]

Chapter 4

THE FEDERAL RESERVE: MANIPULATING THE ECONOMY

D r. Carl Sandberg said: "From those not previously familiar with these things, have come expressions of interest and enthusiasm, but also reluctance to accept as truth the fact that our government without getting *anything* whatsoever in return, gives the Federal Reserve notes to private bankers for them to loan out at interest, even back to the government itself. To them this seems so senseless as to be unbelievable."[46]

The volume of money in this nation and even the speed at which it moves is determined by the Federal Reserve Board. Our money system is a debt money system. Before a dollar can circulate, a debt must be created. The Fed, in fact, is absolute master of all industry and commerce. That is why there are more bankruptcies, bank failures, and downward trends now than even occurred during the Great Depression. (All one has to do is consult the Congressional Record to understand that Congress proved that these private bankers created the Depression and made a lot of money in the process!)

Not only did the international bankers confiscate our currency, they did better than that, they got the real thing—gold! At a time when the dollar has lost an incredible 92 percent of even its 1963 purchasing power, gold is still gold. In 1964 it took $35 to equal one gold ounce, in 1988 $50, in 1993, approximately $330.

Here are some amazing facts from *"... Good As Gold?" How We Lost Our Gold Reserves and Destroyed the Dollar* by Christopher Weber:

Fact 1: From 1958 to 1968, 52 percent of the nation's gold reserves left this country.

Fact 2: These shipments were made <u>with</u> the knowledge and acquiescence of government officials.

Fact 3: For 35 years, the government has failed to conduct a physical inventory of its gold.

Fact 4: Inquiries into the history of America's gold reserves and the policies behind that history have been consistently stonewalled.[47]

Christopher Weber has contributed to *A Case for Gold, a House Minority Report of the U.S. Gold Commission*. This report stated that at its peak in 1949, Fort Knox held 702 million ounces of gold. By 1971 only 291 million ounces were left, a loss of over 58 percent. Not only have we lost nearly 60 percent of our "good delivery" gold, but 90 percent of what remains is coin melt. This means that only 10 percent of the 264 million ounces held by the Treasury is considered "good delivery" gold. The rest is tainted with nearly 10 percent copper coin melt. In other words, the gold of America, at $35 an ounce, has been sold to foreign bankers. Here are some excerpts from Weber's book:

The post-1933 history of the gold stock of the United States presents a great mystery: Why did what happened happen? That question we cannot now answer with surety. Yet there are basic facts we know that enable us to construct some not-implausible hypotheses. The two salient facts are these:

First, the policy the government stubbornly followed with respect to the gold stock was both illegal and impossible, and has never been adequately explained or justified.

Centralization of the gold stock in Fort Knox and other government depositories began, in 1933, with the unconstitutional confiscation of privately held gold—predominantly the gold coinage that comprised (with silver dollars and fractional coins) the constitutional money of the country. The rationalization the government offered for this looting of its own citizens was that gold was "too important" to the stability of the monetary and banking systems to be left in private hands, but needed conservation and control by the national Treasury....

Second, the policy the government stubbornly followed with respect to the gold stock seriously undermined the domestic monetary stability, international monetary position, and national sovereignty of the United States.

Besides seriously weakening the United States economically, all of this created the apparent "need"—now the subject of widespread discussion in the international economic press—for a new world "reserve currency" and world central bank with supranational powers that would override American sovereignty, at least in the areas of money and banking.

These facts are undeniable, but they are nevertheless subject to varying interpretations.

1. One possible interpretation of events is that the officials responsible for the immense losses of gold during the period 1951-1971 simply erred. They honestly—if somewhat ignorantly—believed that they could maintain a gold price of $35 per ounce, even while emitting Federal Reserve Notes vastly in excess of that ratio. This may be styled "the stupidity theory" of the gold loss.

Where politicians and bureaucrats are concerned, such an explanation always has appeal. Here, however, the facts tend to undermine it. The individuals who oversaw the outflow of United States gold were not amateur economists, but rather professional financial operators who moved from successful careers on Wall Street to the Treasury Department, and back, without missing a step. Their rationalizations for what they did while serving in the Treasury were extraordinary in that they gave every "answer" for the chronic losses of gold except the correct answer, as if they knew precisely what the correct answer was but were determined (for some reason) not to admit it to the American people. When private citizens began to question what was going on, these same officials then turned to evasion, cover-up and "stonewalling" as if they had something less than honorable to conceal. And the whole affair transpired over some two decades, certainly long enough for even bureaucrats to learn the lessons of their yearly failures, *unless they viewed what was happening not as a failure but somehow as a success*.

2. This raises the second possible, and arguably more plausible, interpretation of the facts: that those responsible for the immense losses of United States gold were fulfilling some

plan other than the maintenance of American monetary stability. This may be styled "the ulterior-motive theory" of the gold loss.

An explanation of this kind also has great appeal where politicians and bureaucrats are involved. Here, moreover, it tends to fit and explain the facts better than "the stupidity theory" does. A strong and consistent undercurrent in the history of international finance and banking during the twentieth century has been the attempt by certain groups—predominantly centered in Europe, but with their allies in the United States—to create a "one world" *fiat* (irredeemable) paper currency and a "one world" central bank politically independent of, if not actually superior to, any nation or combination of nations. To achieve this goal certain preliminaries were required: (1) To drive the world, and particularly the United States as the world's leading free-market economy, from the pre-World War I "gold-coin standard" based on a single national paper currency. That was accomplished by the 1922 Genoa and the 1944 Bretton Woods Agreements, which elevated the Federal Reserve Note to the status of the unique "world reserve currency" under a form of the "gold-exchange standard"; (2) To destroy this national paper currency as a viable "world reserve currency," so as to justify the creation of a new "reserve" currency independent of any particular nation. That was accomplished by the systematic inflation of the Federal Reserve Note during the post-World War II period, destroying over 90 percent of its purchasing power, and creating monetary chaos world wide; (3) To prevent the United States from frustrating the establishment of a true "world currency" by itself returning, unilaterally, to a domestic "gold standard" of the pre-1933 type. This was accomplished by the looting of Fort Knox and other depositories as an adjunct to the destruction of the Federal Reserve Note; and (4) To force the United States into the "one-world" currency-and-banking scheme, with a concomitant loss of economic and political sovereignty. This has yet to be accomplished, but is the subject of strenuous and strident propaganda in the international press even as these lines are being written.

Whether these steps were accomplished through the knowing, intentional action of those officials of the United States government who oversaw and allowed the 1951–1971 drain of gold is as yet unknown, and must be considered supposition, not fact. It is a supposition well-based on facts, and supposition that the facts support more completely and convincingly than some other alternative hypotheses. The explanation—that American officials purposefully sacrificed the interest of the United States to the agenda of foreigners bent on subordinating this country to a *supra*national financial oligarchy—is of course, distasteful. Yet the truth must be faced, palatable or not.[48]

The words of Senator Elihu Root, who denounced the Federal Reserve bill just days before it was passed, now ring true: "Long before we wake up from our dreams of prosperity through an inflated economy, our gold, which alone could have kept us from catastrophe, will have vanished and no rate of interest will tempt it to return."[49]

Now you are beginning to get the picture. We have an unconstitutional, private bank which creates money completely out of thin air and at the same time transfers our real wealth to foreign, private banks in France, England, and Germany. But wait, that is not all! There is more yet! The Fed's commercial banks also have the ability to create money. They do this by literally creating new money when making loans. This is called "fractional" reserve banking, which means that the total of all the reserves held by all the banks is only a small fraction of new bank deposits created and loaned at interest. (If you ask your local banker what fractional reserve banking is, more than likely he has never heard of it, even though the bank uses the system every day.)

What does all this mean? We stated that the private bankers control the local economy. How? One easy way is by the "reserve" requirement they place on their commercial banks. To stimulate business activity, the reserve requirement will be lowered, allowing more money to be loaned into the system. The numbers work like this:

If the reserve requirement is 15 percent, the money supply can be expanded to:

1/.15 X 1 billion = $6.667 billion

The amount of new money in the system is the original one billion of "reserves" given the commercial banks by the Fed expanded to 6.667 billion!

At a 10 percent reserve requirement:

1/.10 X 1 billion = $10 billion

Now, I know as you do that you cannot get $10 billion out of one billion. At least you and I can't. I spent an hour trying to convince one of my professional friends how this worked, and he thought I was off the deep end as he tried to show me using real money how this could not be! The trouble is, the private owners of the Federal Reserve Bank are not using real money. They are using computer entries and a design that could have been created only by bankers for bankers. As money expands in this way, it gets easier to understand why we have an eight cent dollar. It is so unbelievable, I strongly recommend *The Truth in Money Book* by Thoren and Warner for a simpler, more easy to understand explanation.

In his enlightening treatise on money *The Most Secret Science*, Lt. Col. Archibald C. Roberts voices the paradox of the matter:

"We have a situation here where—if one of you deposits $100 in a bank account and if you write checks upon that deposit twice—if you do it in my county, I have to come around and put you in jail and lock you up! You have committed a felony. Yet the very same bank in which you deposited that $100 can write checks on that same $100 not once, not twice, but five or ten times, even 20 times and can do so with impunity. This is called the fractional reserve system! We penalize one man who writes checks on the same money twice and send him to jail. We glorify the banker who writes checks on the same money ten times and send him to Congress."[50]

The main difference between the activity of the blue-collar worker and the banker is that the banker even charges interest for lending the same money ten times.

From the original printing of the *Federal Reserve System, Its Purpose and Function*, written by the bank itself, we read, "Since the Federal Reserve authorities have the power to increase or decrease the supply of reserve funds and written limits to increase or decrease reserve requirements, they are able to exercise considerable interest over the amount of credit, in the aggregate that banks may be in a position to extend."[51]

If you are a small businessman, a farmer, an entrepreneur, someone expanding a home business, or even a middle-size company, you will find throughout the years a rather whimsical pattern to a banker's ability to loan money. They may not loan at all. They may loan but at high interest rates. They may loan plenty of money at relatively low interest rates. What many people are now beginning to discover, our founding fathers knew from history.

Thomas Jefferson said: "I believe that banking institutions are more dangerous to our liberties than standing armies... The issuing power should be taken from the banks and restored to our government, to whom it properly belongs."[52]

James Madison agreed: "History records that the money changers have used every form of abuse, intrigue, deceit, and violent means possible to maintain their control over governments by controlling the money and its issuance."[53] According to Sir Josiah Stamp, "If you want to continue the slaves of bankers and pay the use of your own slavery, let bankers continue to create money and control credit."[54]

That the bankers increase or decrease the money supply is totally dependent on what *they* want. By virtue of their power, they can defeat or make a president.

As the bankers get richer, what do you suppose they buy? They buy things that make them even *more* money. For example, all of the oil companies are owned by the banking establishment. What else? Well, think of businesses that are extremely profitable: gold mining, diamond mining, oil production, gas production, car manufacturing, food production, etc.

Now, if you can, consider how much money is being made by private bankers at the expense of this country's taxpayers. They receive $400 billion a year in interest by loaning to the American government, in addition to all of the money made in the sale of gas and oil, member banks' profits, owned commercial banks' profits, and unknown amounts of sales in gold, diamonds, copper, silver, and so forth.

Obviously to those of us who are just getting by, this kind of wealth requires the creative side of our brain even to imagine. These people make Donald Trump look like a street beggar by comparison!

This kind of wealth is limitless and has by now bought up most of the valuable money-producing assets and companies and real estate in our country and in the world. What's their next priority?

The answer is power. Greed leads to power. These men involved in the "money trust" are so powerful that they buy legislation. They control the U.S. Government by power. They have unlimited money (created out of nothing but paid by the American citizen) to effectively lobby any right of passage they desire. If you follow the banking enactment laws alone from 1911 through 1980, you will find a series of laws enabling bankers to have more power and more control—accountable to no one.

1. The Banking Act of 1933 legislated that all earnings of the Federal Reserve Banks must go to the banks themselves. A provision that the government must share in the profits was

removed. The increase in assets from $143 million in 1913 to $45 BILLION in 1949 went entirely to the banks' private stockholders.

2. The Banking Act of 1935 allowed a banking house on the Stock Exchange to be involved in investment banking as well.
3. The Banking Act of 1935 extended the terms of office of the Federal Reserve Board of Governors to fourteen years, or three and a half times the length of a presidential term. This means a president who might be hostile to the board could not appoint a majority to it who would be favorable to him. The monetary policy set in place would go on regardless of his wishes.
4. The 1980 Monetary Control Act gave the Fed control of all depository institutions. This was passed because many honest banks—430 member banks—had left the Federal Reserve in an eight-year span, including 15 major banks in 1977 with deposits of more than $100 billion, and another 39 banks in 1978.

As an employer, you must hire without discriminating as to religion, race, sex, etc. However, with one stroke of the pen, the banking establishment has the ability to put literally millions out of work with no regard to discrimination at all and with no penalty to pay for doing it. Not only do they not answer to presidents or Congress, but we cannot even vote them out of office.

To get a vivid perception of how preposterous this whole scam is, let's take a real example.

To fight World War II, we gave the bankers $250 billion in U.S. bonds that we might use our own nation's credit. In addition, we permitted them to place "credit" in their "reserve" accounts for a matching $250 billion. This gave them nearly $1.3 trillion in bank credit (remember fractional expansion). This credit is to the bankers what your deposits are to you. They can lend it or use it to buy investment obligations (U.S. bonds, corporation stocks and bonds, etc.). It is cash to them! At the time of World War II, the Federal Reserve system had assets of only $52 billion with no productive know-how or ability to produce goods or services. The United States had nearly $600 million in assets and $1 trillion in productive capacity. What happened was, the rich man (U.S.) borrowed from the poor man (Federal Reserve).

At the end of the war, the bankers were $1,500 billion richer while the rich man (the U.S.) came out $250 billion in debt to the bankers. Could Congress be so stupid? Is it possible that they have truly given the nation's wealth and productive capacity (i.e., farms, ranches, industries, businesses) over to a private group of madmen? Yes, your Congress did this. Incredible!

Let's take some points one by one:

1. Neither the meetings nor the minutes of the Fed's meetings are open to the public.
2. The members of the board, once approved, face no constitutional checks and balances thereafter.
3. The Fed controls the entire nation's money supply.
4. The Fed <u>at its own discretion</u> can influence both the United States and the world economy.
5. Insiders at the Fed have advance information regarding major shifts in economic climate. They determine it!
6. If the Fed contracts the money supply as it did in 1929, 1934–36, 1953, 1955–57, 1960, 1966, and much of the 1970s and late 1980s, the effect on you and me is less money in circulation, thus higher interest rates and fewer loans.
7. This translates to decreased business activity, unemployment, bankruptcies, and delayed or no economic recovery.
8. The private Federal Reserve proponents argued in 1913 that the bank was needed to <u>prevent</u> our nation's boom-and-bust cycle. Yet, if anything, just the opposite has happened.
9. In 1952 William McChesney Martin, then chairman of the board of governors of the private Fed bank, said, "One of the fundamental purposes of the Federal Reserve Act is to protect the value of the dollar."[55] Anyone old enough to remember the $1,995 VW knows that it is time to do away with this bank because it has been <u>useless</u> in saving the value (buying power) of the dollar.

Although many people today decry how the government is overspending, it is actually *overborrowing*. Every penny that the government spends in excess of its tax receipts has to be borrowed at interest. By 1995, since all of the taxpayers' money will go only toward paying the private bankers the interest (not the principal) on the debt, <u>all</u> expenses of the federal government will <u>have</u> to be borrowed on credit and at interest on money created out of nothing— and good-bye America. It will be a mother ship sinking into the sea.

Could the federal government print the money itself at <u>no</u>

interest? Yes! Then why doesn't it? It is my belief that it is because most of the elected and nonelected (appointed) administrators of our government have already been "bought" to implement the new one-world system. The present money system demands that the government stay addicted to continued borrowing. Our government officials understand this. They have sold out the American people. They are truly traitors. Make no mistake about it!

Henry Ford understood the system. He put it this way: "If the American people knew the corruption in our money system, there would be a revolution before morning."[56] Ford saw the plan. He pointed out that "The one aim of these financiers is world control by the creation of indistinguishable debts." [57]

This is as good a time as any to come head-on with how we are being brainwashed by the media. In probably the best book on the subject, *The Truth in Money Book* by Thoren and Warner, the authors shed light on the true nature of this evil system: "It is a tragedy that cycles of prosperity and depression are thought and taught to be natural phenomena which are inescapable. The fact is that they are directly attributable to the policy manipulation of the amount of money and credit in the monetary system.

"Prosperity doesn't cause inflation any more than a windmill causes the wind to blow. Policy decisions restricting the flow of money causes depressions. The idea that depressions are necessary to counteract prosperity is one of the most fantastic misconceptions of present economic thinking."[58]

Thoren and Warner emphasize, "... there is absolutely nothing about meeting people's needs and aspirations that causes inflation. The cause of inflation isn't prosperity but the lack of debt-free money in our monetary system."[59]

Thus, all this discussion in the press and on TV regarding economic trends is nothing more than propagandized hogwash meant to deceive the public into ignorance.

The *Truth in Money Book* explains, "... the most popular misconception about monetary inflation is the theory that price levels vary in proportion with the amount of money which is in circulation. The theory is true, but *only* if the economy is practically debt-free."[60]

The old theory of inflation being "too much money chasing too few goods" just isn't true. In fact, we have an ever-expanding amount of money in circulation, yet we have masses of unsold goods in stores, warehouses, and automobile yards all over this country. Yet people don't have enough money to pay for these goods. So where is all the money going? It is going to usury!

Since more money passes through our hands, it *seems* that prices are inflated. That is, the quantity of money being borrowed into the system is increasing. However, what inflation really means is that the value of our money is deflated, i.e., the quality is declining, and its purchasing power is decreasing.

The very method by which our dollars are created takes the life out of the economy. Any charge by a private lender for the use of money he is allowed to create *out of nothing* is called usury.

Since all of the original principal borrowed, plus all of the usury, can never be repaid in a debt-money system (Federal Reserve), more borrowing is required to pay the unpayable usury. Increasing prices are the only way to pay the increasing usury charges. Since more and more debt-dollars are demanded to pay for the same goods and services, the value, or purchasing power, of each dollar declines.

Although America has been forced into economic submission by the money lenders, usury, which leads to economic slavery, is nothing new. In the Old Testament, Nehemiah proclaimed usury evil.

Others were saying, "We are mortgaging our fields, our vineyards and our homes to get grain during the famine." Still others were saying, "We have had to borrow money to pay the king's tax on our fields and vineyards. Although we are of the same flesh and blood as our countrymen and though our sons are as good as theirs, yet we have to subject our sons and daughters to slavery. Some of our daughters have already been enslaved, but we are powerless, because our fields and our vineyards belong to others." When I heard their outcry and these charges, I was very angry. I pondered them in my mind and then accused the nobles and officials. I told them. "You are exacting *usury* from your own countrymen!" (Neh. 5:3–7, italics added).

In the book of Ezekiel, usury was considered one of Jerusalem's sins.

"In you [Jerusalem] men accept bribes to shed blood; you take usury and excessive interest and make unjust gain from your neighbors by extortion. And you have forgotten me," declares the Sovereign Lord (Ezek. 22:12).

What was Christ's first act of civil disobedience? The Gospel of John states, "So he made a whip out of cords, and drove all from the temple area...he scattered the coins of the money changers and overturned their tables" (John 2:15).

Lastly, the Lord states He will always remember the unjust money lenders:

49

"Hear this, you who trample the needy and do away with the poor of the land, saying, 'When will the New Moon be over that we may sell grain, and the Sabbath be ended that we may market wheat?'—skimping the measure, boosting the price and cheating with dishonest scales, buying the poor with silver and the needy for a pair of sandals, selling even the sweepings with the wheat" (Amos 8:4–6).

The widespread belief that money must be entrusted to and administered by only high-powered experts has resulted in terrible abuse by a few and the greatest loss of freedom ever experienced in America. Inflation is the price of monetary ignorance; depression the result of monetary abuse. In 1976 the staff of the Committee on Banking, Currency, and Housing of the House of Representatives, 94th Congress, 2nd session, wrote *Federal Reserve Directors, A Study of Corporate and Banking Influence.*

In the foreword, Chairman S. Reuss (D-Wis.) writes: "This Committee has observed for many years the influence of <u>private interests</u> over the essentially public responsibilities of the Federal Reserve System." The study makes clear "it is difficult to imagine a more narrowly-based board of directors....Only two segments of American society—banking and big business—have any substantial representation...."

"Until we have basic reforms, the Federal Reserve System will be handicapped in carrying out its public responsibility....The System's mandate is too essential to the nation's welfare to leave so much of the machinery under the control of narrow private interests. Concentration of economic and financial power in the United States has gone too far." The committee noted in a section of the text titled *The Club System,* "This 'club' approach leads the Federal Reserve to consistently dip into the same pools—the same companies, the same universities, the same bank holding companies—to fill directorships." The Committee on Banking concludes:

"In summary, the Federal Reserve directors are apparently representatives of a small elite group which dominates much of the economic life of this nation."[61]

Until the government takes back its constitutional duty to create debt-free money, we will continue to embrace the most subtle and debilitating form of tyranny. It is this very tyranny to which almost every other great nation has fallen. The bankers know their history better than you do. So does God.

"Is it not the rich who are exploiting you? Are they not the ones who are dragging you into court? Are they not the ones who are slandering the noble name of him to whom you belong?" (James 2:6–7)

Chapter 5

THE COUNCIL ON FOREIGN RELATIONS

Now that the dust has settled and the smoke has cleared, Bill Clinton's administrative picks should give us some idea of the direction he is taking us. We already know two: homosexuals in the military and higher taxes and the destruction of the middle class. Here are just a few of his picks: (Note: the names are not important, but the organization is.)

Secretary of State: Warren Christopher (number two man in the Carter State Department)

Deputy Secretary of State: Clifton R. Wharton Jr. (former trustee and chairman of the Rockefeller Foundation, Director of the Ford Motor Company, Director of the New York Stock Exchange, and Director of the Council on Foreign Relations)

Secretary of Defense: Representative Les Aspin (chairman of the House Armed Services Committee)

National Security Advisor: Anthony (Tony) Lake, a Carter State Department policy planning chief

Deputy National Security Advisor: Samuel Berger (deputy director of policy planning in the Carter State Department)

CIA Director: R. James Woolsey (advisor on disarmament to both Republican and Democratic Presidents)

Chairman of the Foreign Intelligence Advisory Board: William J. Crowe Jr.

Secretary of Treasury: Lloyd Bentsen

Deputy Secretary of the Treasury: Roger Altman

Secretary of Health and Human Services: Donna Shalala (She lobbied the Defense Department to drop its ban on homosexuals in the military. She now has a budget of $590 billion with which to continue her work.)

Secretary of Housing and Urban Development: Henry Cisneros (Cisneros is a member of the board of trustees of the Rockefeller Foundation and deputy chairman of the Federal Reserve Bank of Dallas.)

Secretary of the Interior: Bruce Babbit

Under Secretary for Political Affairs: Peter Tarnoff (current president of the Council on Foreign Relations)

Assistant Secretary of State for East Asian and Pacific Affairs: Winston Lord (He served under Republican Nixon as special assistant to Henry Kissinger on the National Security Council. Last year, Lord chaired the Carnegie Endowment National Commission on America and the New World, a report which recommended reductions in American defense spending concurrent with increased American expenditures for UN "peacekeeping".)

Aid Coordinator to the Commonwealth of Independent States: Strobe Talbott

Deputy Director, Office of Management and Budget: Alice Rivlin

Chairman, Council of Economic Advisors: Laura Tyson

U.S. Ambassador to the United Nations: Madeleine Albright (She is director of the world-government-promoting Atlantic Council. She was responsible for foreign policy legislation during the Carter years.)

What is the common denominator of all of these names? They are *all* members of the Council on Foreign Relations. (Bentsen is a former member of the CFR.)

Just in case you think this Democratic or "liberal" administration will be better, or different than that of so-called conservative George Bush, don't bet on it! George Bush had completely saturated his own administration with members of the Council on Foreign Relations.

What is the Council on Foreign Relations, and why is our government full of its members?

Ever since 1868 an organization was formed in England which

affects our politics today. The Royal Colonial Institute was formed in Great Britain by the upper-class oligarchy to further the cause of English colonialism and imperialism in order to preserve the tradition and longevity of the ruling class. After 1870 it became more obvious that acquisition of colonies would lead to fantastic profits for individuals and companies and favorable support from the government by contributing part of the profits to politicians' expenses. The single most significant change in this "new" imperialism was that it was justified on grounds of moral duty and of social reform.

An Englishman, Cecil Rhodes, had exploited the diamond mines and gold fields of South Africa (a British colony) and monopolized these mines as the De Beers Consolidated Mines and the Consolidated Gold Fields with the help of England's Lord Rothschild. Just to keep things in perspective for 1992, in the 1890s Rhodes had a personal income of $5 million a year! He spent his money to further his desire "to federate the English-speaking peoples and to bring all the habitable portions of the world under their control."[62] In order to accomplish this goal, Rhodes organized a secret society in 1891 which utilized the Rhodes Trust to fund the extension of the British empire. This is the same trust from which the Rhodes Scholars are funded, i.e., Bill Clinton.

The dominant trustee of the Rhodes Trust was Lord Alfred Milner. Milner recruited young men who were able to win influential posts in government and international finance. In 1909–1913 they organized semisecret groups known as Round Table groups in the chief British dependencies and the United States. These continue today in eight countries. By 1919 they founded the Royal Institute for International Affairs (RIIA), also known as Chatham House. The RIIA was a front organization and had as its nucleus the Round Table group. Other similar Institutes of International Affairs were established in the chief British dominions and in the United States, where it is known today as the Council on Foreign Relations (CFR). The CFR, established in New York on July 29, 1921, was a front for J.P. Morgan and Co. (in itself a front for Rothschild banking) in association with this country's American Round Table Group. J.P. Morgan's personal attorney and millionaire in his own right, John W. Davis, was the founding president of the CFR. The founding vice president, Paul Cravath, also represented Morgan interests.

Since 1925, substantial contributions from wealthy individuals and foundations and firms associated with the international banking fraternity have financed the activities of the Round Table group known as the Council on Foreign Relations. The Carnegie United Kingdom Trust, J.P. Morgan, the Rockefeller and Whitney families, Lazard Brothers, and Morgan, Grenfell, and Company have all financed the imperialistic purposes of this club. All of these have links with the international banking family, the Rothschilds.

Let there be no doubt about it. "The power and influence of the Rhodes-Milner group in British imperial affairs and in foreign policy since 1889, although not widely recognized, can hardly be exaggerated."[63] In the twentieth century, there has grown up a power structure between London and New York which penetrates deeply into university life, the press, and the practice of foreign policy. Most of the respected newspapers in this country are closely allied with these men of wealth—that is, the Anglo-American establishment or the "Establishment". Carroll Quigley, in his text *Tragedy and Hope*, asserts that "The American branch of this 'English Establishment' exerted much of its influence through fine American newspapers (*The New York Times, New York Herald Tribune, Christian Science Monitor*, the *Washington Post* and what was the *Boston Evening Transcript*). In fact, the editor of the *Christian Science Monitor* was the chief American correspondent (anonymously) of The Round Table...."[64] It is no coincidence that such Wall Street luminaries as John W. Davis, Lewis Douglas, Jack Whitney, and Douglas Dillon were appointed to be American ambassadors in London.

In 1925 a third network of Institutes of International Affairs was organized by the same people with the same motives. The Institute for Pacific Relations was established. The countries of new addition were China, Japan, France, the Netherlands, and Soviet Russia. Pacific councils were also set up in Canada, Australia, and New Zealand. Financing came from the same international banking groups and their subsidiary commercial and industrial firms. The sphere of influence of the Round Table was now worldwide. In contemporary times the CFR (Round Table) has expanded its spiderweb to include a number of affiliated organizations, called the Committees on Foreign Relations, made up of local leaders in thirty-seven cities around the nation. It was out of the council's Atlanta committee, a group reflecting that city's power elite, that Jimmy Carter was recommended for membership on the Trilateral Commission (April 13, 1973).[65] He was also a member of the CFR.

To understand where the CFR (Round Table) derives its influence for foreign affairs, one must look carefully at its development and foundations. Consider how government (which is heavily influenced by the CFR today) responds to the needs of the individual citizen, and I believe you will see an extension of the Round Table into modern society. The philosophy of the Round Table CFR can be gathered from a sample of one of its earliest members. This was at a time when for propaganda purposes the term British Empire had been changed to the Commonwealth of Nations. Lionel Curtis wrote: "The rule of law as contrasted with the rule of an individual is the distinguishing mark of the Commonwealth....In a commonwealth rulers derive their authority from the law....The idea that the principle of the Commonwealth implies universal suffrage betrays an ignorance of its real nature. That principle simply means that government rests on the duty of the citizens to each other, and is to be vested in those who are capable of setting public interests before their own....

"The task of preparing for freedom the races which cannot as yet govern for themselves is the supreme duty of those who can. It is the spiritual end for which the Commonwealth exists, and material order is nothing except as a means to it....Personally, I regard this challenge to the long unquestioned claim of the white man to dominate the world as inevitable and wholesome, especially to ourselves....The world is in the throes which precede creation or death. Our whole race has outgrown the merely national state...."[66] This Round Table disciple had the fanatical conviction that with the proper spirit and the proper organization the ruling elite could predictably establish the Kingdom of God on earth.

It is absolutely critical to understand that the CFR is not a group of bored financiers who would prefer yachting to politicking. It is through their biased philosophy that they are actually able to control the daily activities, expenses, costs, inflation, and government regulations that achieve their end. If their end is the establishment of the kingdom of heaven on earth, who will rule? They are not God, but they think their standards, laws, and rules of government are best.

To what extent have we already experienced and will further experience their altruism? The Constitution enforces a government that was meant to exert virtually no influence on business, education, religion, and most other features of national life. The idea of free enterprise has been that everyone has an equal opportunity in the marketplace. J.P. Morgan and John D. Rockefeller, on the other hand, were powerful monopolists. A monopolist seeks to eliminate competition. Rockefeller once stated: "Competition is a sin." He understood that with government meddling, a monopolist achieves dominion over the government and the government sails to the wind of the monopolist. By controlling government through the CFR, the power brokers are able to control America's economy, politics, law, education, and day-to-day subsistence.

In his book *Confessions of a Monopolist*, Frederic Howe laid out the strategy of utilizing government: "This is the story of something for nothing—of making the other fellow pay. This making the other fellow pay, getting something for nothing, explains the lust for franchises, mining rights, tariff privileges, railway control, tax evasions. All these things mean monopoly and all monopoly is bottomed on legislation."

He went on: "These are rules of big business. They have superseded the teachings of our parents and are reducible to a simple maxim: Get a monopoly; let society work for you; and remember that the best of all business is politics, for a legislative grant, franchise, subsidy, or tax exemption is worth more than a Kimberly or Comstock lode, since it does not require any labor, either mental or physical, for its exploitation."[67] When the Federal Reserve was being considered in 1912, a J.P. Morgan partner CFR told Congress: "I would rather have regulation and control than free competition."[68]

Concerns over the purposes of the CFR and its alter-ego, the Trilateral Commission, are ongoing. On March 17, 1980, presidential candidate Ronald Reagan was asked if he would allow Trilateral Commission members in his cabinet. "No," he replied. "I don't believe that the Trilateral Commission is a conspiratorial group, but I do think its interests are devoted to international banking, multinational corporations, and so forth. I don't think that any administration of the U.S. Government should have the top nineteen positions filled by people from any one group or organization representing one viewpoint. No, I would go in a different direction."[69]

Soon thereafter, of the 59 people Reagan named to a transition team designated to select, screen, and recommend appointees for administrative posts, 28 were CFR members, at least 10 were Trilateralists, and 10 belonged to the secret Bilderbergers. As president, he appointed over 80 individuals to his administration who were members of the Council on Foreign Relations, the Trilateral Commission, or both. Note especially his running mate, Trilateralist George Bush. Reagan appointed to the highest offices in government: 64 CFR members, 6 Trilateral members, 6 both CFR and Trilateral members, and 5 former members of the Trilateral Commission. Examples from the Reagan administration include:

Vice President - George Bush CFR
Treasury Secretary - Donald Regan CFR
Secretary of State - Alexander Haig CFR
Secretary of State - George Pratt Schultz, director of the CFR.
    This member of the Pratt family is related to the Standard
    Oil fortune (Rockefeller). Mrs. Harold Pratt had donated
    the Pratt House to the CFR.
Deputy Secretary of State - John C. Whitehead CFR
Secretary of Defense - Casper Weinberger Trilateral
    Commission
Deputy Secretary of Defense - Frank Carlucci CFR
Ambassador to China - Winston Lord, president of CFR
Commerce Secretary - Malcolm Baldrige CFR
Labor Secretary -William Brock CFR
Federal Reserve Board Chairman - Alan Greenspan CFR[70]

Was Reagan a true conservative? Not when it came to spending money. He chalked up more government debt than all the presidents before him combined. Was Reagan a true anti-Communist? Not when it came to spending money. When Communist Poland defaulted on its interest payments to American banks in 1982, Ronald Reagan had the U.S. taxpayers pick up the tab. The American taxpayer-subsidized Export-Import Bank was also used to grant more than $200 million in credits to Communist Mozambique, specifically when pro-Western forces were fighting for liberation. You didn't hear about this in the media.

Things were little different during the Carter years. His southern style was also injected with the CFR shadow government, only by then the financial powers had produced the Trilateral Commission as well. In June 1976 the *Los Angeles Times* described a "task force" that had helped Jimmy Carter (then a candidate) prepare his first major foreign policy speech. The "advisors" enumerated were Zbigniew Brzezinski, Richard Cooper, Richard Gardner, Henry Owen, Edwin O. Reischauer, Averill Harriman, Anthony Lake, Robert Bowie, Milton Katz, Abram Chayes, George Ball, and Cyrus Vance. The names are unimportant. What is significant is that every man listed was a member of the CFR![71]

In the CFR's Fall 1984 issue of *Foreign Affairs,* Richard Cooper laid out the CFR plan for a one-world currency and one-world bank. "... I suggest a radical alternative scheme...the creation of a common currency for all the industrial democracies, with a common monetary policy and a joint Bank of Issue to determine that monetary policy."[72] In 1974 Richard Gardner wrote an article for

Foreign Affairs called "The Hard Road to World Order." Gardner lamented: "We are witnessing an outbreak of shortsighted nationalism that seems oblivious to the economic, political, and moral implications of interdependence." He asserted that "an end run around national sovereignty, eroding it piece by piece, will accomplish much more than the old-fashioned frontal assault."[73]

Carter appointed more than 70 men from the CFR and over 20 members of the Trilateral Commission (TC) to the highest unelected offices of government. Examples are:

> Secretary of State - Cyrus Vance CFR/TC (nephew of John W. Davis, founding president of the CFR and the J.P. Morgan Bank)
>
> Secretary of Defense - Harold Brown CFR/TC
>
> Federal Reserve Chairman - Paul Volcker CFR/TC
>
> Deputy Secretary of State - Warren Christopher CFR/TC
>
> Under Secretary of State - Richard Cooper CFR/TC
>
> Assistant Secretary of State - Richard Holbrooke CFR/TC
>
> Under Secretary of Treasury - Anthony M. Solomon CFR/TC
>
> Deputy Secretary of Energy - John Sawhill CFR/TC
>
> Special Assistant to the President - Hedley Donovan CFR/TC
>
> Ambassador at Large - Henry Owen CFR/TC
>
> Treasury Secretary - W. Michael Blumenthal CFR/TC
>
> HEW Secretary - Joseph Califano CFR/TC
>
> SALT Negotiator - Paul Warnke CFR/TC[74]

In his own memoirs, interestingly enough, Carter does not even mention the Trilateral Commission.

Of major impact on the Carter administration was the National Security Advisor, Zbigniew Brzezinski. In his book *Between Two Ages* (1970) Brzezinski states: "In the economic-technological field some international cooperation has already been achieved, but further progress will require greater American sacrifices. More intensive efforts to shape a new world monetary structure will have to be undertaken with some consequent risk to the present relatively favorable American position."[75]

In other words, in order to induce a truly international, global system of technocracy and currency, it was expected that the American standard of living would be forced to decline. Is that not exactly what has occurred between 1970–1993? Does this mean that the continuing recession and slide of the dollar, the decline of America as a world power, socialization, and decreased standard of living were planned by our own State Department? Yes! That is exactly what it means.

As if the American citizen isn't systematically burdened enough, Brzezinski suggests "a greater sense of community within the developed world...might also eventually lead to the possibility of something along the line of a global taxation system."[76]

The money trust CFR always backs both the Democratic and Republican party candidates. Although Hubert Humphrey (Democrat) was a CFR member, Richard Nixon (Republican) was able to garner CFR support as well.

Nixon had traveled with Christian Herter CFR to Europe as part of the committee that laid the blueprint for the Marshall Plan. Herter had married into the Rockefeller family.

In 1961 Nixon joined the CFR.[77] Thereupon, Nixon, a lawyer, was initiated into the law firm of Nelson Rockefeller's personal attorney. He lived in New York City in the same building as Rockefeller.

In October 1967, Nixon wrote an article for the CFR titled "Asia After Vietnam." He hinted of the probable open door to Communist China. He also wrote of the need in Asia "to evoke regional approaches to development needs and to the evolution of a new world order."[78] Nixon, in 1967, was—a globalist!

In the early 1970s Anthony Lukas in the *New York Times* and John Franklin Campbell in *New York* magazine wrote feature articles suggesting that the CFR was a has-been collection of foreign-policy fossils, no longer welcome in Washington; especially with "right-wing" Nixon in office.

Apparently Nixon didn't read the article. He appointed 110 CFR members to the highest unelected offices in the land.

Henry Kissinger was appointed Richard Nixon's national security advisor. Before joining Nixon's staff, Kissinger had been Nelson Rockefeller's chief advisor on foreign affairs. In his book *White House Years* Kissinger called Rockefeller "the single most influential person in my life."[79] The *New York Times* called Kissinger "the Council's most influential member," and a council insider has stated, "His influence is indirect and enormous—much of it through his Rockefeller connections."[80]

A sample of Nixon-appointed CFR members:
> Commerce Secretary - Peter G. Peterson (replaced David Rockefeller as Chairman of CFR in 1985)
> Federal Reserve Board Chairman - Arthur Burns CFR
> HEW Secretary - Eliot Richardson CFR
> Housing Secretary - James Lynn CFR
> Foreign Policy Consultant - George Ball CFR

Chief Economic Aide - Dr. Paul McCracken CFR
UN Ambassador - Charles Yost CFR
NATO Ambassador - Harlan Cleveland CFR
Ambassador to the USSR - Jacob Beam CFR
Director of Arms Control & Disarmament Agency - Gerard Smith CFR
Defense Secretary - Melvin Laird CFR
Treasury Secretary - David Kennedy CFR
Treasury Secretary - George Schultz (joined the CFR in later years)

To top it all off, Nixon was a conservative, right? Wrong! What one finds is an inexorable onslaught of the same kind of CFR (Round Table) politics throughout both Democratic and Republican administrations.

In 1971 syndicated columnist James Reston CFR exclaimed: "The Nixon budget is so complex, so unlike the Nixon of the past, so un-Republican that it defies rational analysis....The Nixon budget is more planned, has more welfare in it, and has a bigger predicted deficit than any other budget in this century."[81]

James Perloff in *The Shadows of Power* reminds us: "Nixon was no more conservative on foreign policy than domestic. His administration permitted the Soviets to discharge their $11 billion World War II debt at less than ten cents on the dollar, and then receive millions of tons of our grain at subsidized rates...."[82]

"Even though the Chinese Communists had been killing literally millions in the Cultural Revolution, Richard Nixon began a new era of friendly relations with them, fulfilling a step long called for by CFR study groups and publications."[83]

Although JFK preached a "New Frontier," he also became entwined in the net of the Round Table. The CFR dominated Kennedy's State Department, his Cabinet, and Secretary of State Dean Rusk's staff.

Anthony Lukas of the *New York Times* reported:

"Of the first 82 names on a list prepared to help President Kennedy staff his State Department, 63 were Council members. Kennedy once complained, 'I'd like to have some new faces here, but all I get is the same old names.'"[84]

Some of Kennedy's CFR appointees included:
Secretary of State - Dean Rusk CFR
Secretary of Treasury - Douglas Dillon CFR
National Security Advisor - McGeorge Bundy CFR
Deputy National Security Advisor - Walt Restow CFR

CIA Director - John McCone CFR
Deputy Secretary of Defense - Roswell Gilpatrick CFR
Assistant Deputy Secretary of Defense - Paul Nitze CFR
Under Secretary of the Treasury - Henry Fowler CFR
Under Secretary of State - George Ball CFR
Assistant Secretary of State for Far Eastern Affairs - Averill Harriman CFR
Special Assistant to the President - Arthur Schlesinger Jr. CFR
Special Assistant to the President - Jerome Wiesner CFR
Chief of Protocol - Angier Duke CFR
Chief of U.S. Disarmament Administration - John McCloy CFR[85]

The not-so-conservative John Kenneth Galbraith has been quoted as saying, "Those of us who had worked for the Kennedy election were tolerated in the government for that reason and had a say, but foreign policy was still with the Council on Foreign Relations people."[86]

Just as an aside: If you want to entertain the idea that there was a conspiracy at the very top to assassinate Kennedy, you might be interested to note that there were two members of the CFR on the Warren Commission—John McCloy (CIA head) and Allen Dulles. Dulles had been fired by the president after the Bay of Pigs fiasco. Yet he suddenly ended up deciding who really shot JFK.

After World War II, General Eisenhower returned home to become U.S. Chief of Staff. Even though he had no academic background, he was made president of Columbia University in 1948. He proceeded to join the CFR, was on the editorial advisory board of its publication, *Foreign Affairs,* and chaired a council study on aid to Europe.

In the 1952 issue of *Foreign Affairs,* McGeorge Bundy exulted over the nomination of both "Ike" and Adlai Stevenson, Ike's Democratic opponent (also CFR). Again, the Round Table Establishment had succeeded in controlling both parties!

As the president, "Ike" drew his staff also from the CFR-Round Table-Establishment club. One example of his appointees is John Foster Dulles, secretary of state. Dulles had been a founding member of the CFR; he was an in-law of the Rockefellers, chairman of the board of the Rockefeller Foundation, and chairman of the board of the Carnegie Endowment for International Peace, where his choice for president of that body had been Alger Hiss, a known Communist. He had been a delegate to the founding UN conference and a member of Truman's Democratic State Department. (Eisenhower was Republican.) As long as the public doesn't know, the CFR doesn't care!

Eisenhower had also tried to recruit John J. McCloy. McCloy had declined since he was already chairman of the CFR and chairman of the Chase Manhattan Bank (Rockefeller).

Although you've never heard of McCloy, take a moment to look at his *unelected* positions. He has been called by nine different presidents both Republican and Democratic for special assignments. He has been:

> President of the World Bank
> Attorney for Rockefeller's Standard Oil
> Chairman of the Board - Ford Foundation
> Chairman of the Board - Rockefeller's Chase Manhattan Bank
> Chief of the U.S. Disarmament Administration
> Director on the boards of a dozen blue-chip companies
> He supervised construction of the Pentagon, served on the Warren Commission, shared a box with Hitler at the 1936 Olympic Games, and was seen swimming with Khruschev. From 1953 to 1970 he was the CFR's chairman of the board.

During the Eisenhower presidency (1953–1961), Congress established the Reece Committee to investigate tax-free foundations (Rockefeller, Ford, Carnegie). The committee's report found:

"In the international field, foundations, and an interlock among some of them and certain intermediary organizations, have exercised a strong effect upon our foreign policy and upon public education in things international. This has been accomplished by vast propaganda, by supplying executives and advisors to government, and by controlling much research in this area through the power of the purse. The net result of these combined efforts has been to promote 'internationalism' in a particular sense—a form directed toward 'world government' and a derogation of American 'nationalism.'"[87]

They observed that the major foundations "have actively supported attacks upon our social and government system and financed the promotion of socialism and collectivist ideas." The Reece Committee clearly declared that the CFR was "in essence an agency of the United States Government" and that its "productions are not objective but are directed overwhelmingly at promoting the globalist concept."[88]

Harry Truman succeeded FDR in the spring of 1945. Six statesmen had careers which peaked during the Truman era:

> Secretary of State - Dean Acheson CFR
>
> Under Secretary of State - Robert Lovett (Later Secretary of Defense) CFR
>
> Marshall Plan Administrator - Averill Harriman CFR
>
> High Commissioner to Germany - John McCloy CFR
>
> State Department Advisor - George Kennan CFR
>
> Ambassador to the USSR - George Kennan CFR
>
> State Department Advisor - Charles Bohlen CFR

All six were members of the CFR. In the book *The Wise Men,* it is said that these men "left a legacy that dominates American policy to this day."[89]

Truman's predecessor, Franklin Delano Roosevelt, had a prototypical CFR background. His family had been in New York banking since the eighteenth century. His uncle, Franklin Delano, was on the Federal Reserve Board. FDR had attended Groton and Harvard. In the 1920s he had pursued a career on Wall Street. He had been on the board of directors of eleven different corporations. His son-in-law, Curtis Dall, wrote a book titled *FDR: My Exploited Father-in-Law* in which he discusses the true nature of FDR's wisdom:

"For a long time I felt that FDR had developed many thoughts and ideas that were his own to benefit this country, the U.S.A. But, he didn't. Most of his thoughts, his political 'ammunition' as it were, were carefully manufactured for him in advance by the CFR-One World Money group. Brilliantly with great gusto, like a fine piece of artillery, he exploded that prepared 'ammunition' in the middle of an unsuspecting target, the American people—and thus paid off and retained his internationalist political support."[90]

Prior to his White House tenure, FDR lived next door to the CFR's headquarters in New York City. Literally in the shadow of the CFR, he was prepared for his presidency.

While in the White House, FDR propelled the CFR menu forward:

1. He took America off the gold standard, setting the stage for decades of inflation.
2. He established the New Deal—borrowing for generations thereafter from the international bankers.
3. His Agricultural Adjustment Administration paid farmers to destroy crops and livestock in order to raise prices.
4. The Export-Import Bank was established in 1934,

subsidized by the American taxpayers.

5. The National Recovery Administration (NRA) was designed to regulate and <u>control</u> business. Typically, big business created and controlled the NRA's operating standards, prices, and wages and strangled their smaller competitors out of business.

James Warburg CFR was one of FDR's appointees. He was the son of Paul Warburg, one of the architects of the Federal Reserve Bank. James Warburg once told a Senate committee: "We shall have world government whether or not you like it—by conquest or consent."[91]

Does the CFR care if the candidate is a Republican or Democrat? In 1940 FDR's Republican opponent was Wendell Willkie CFR. Although Willkie lost the election, he became an international emissary for FDR.

When the war broke out during FDR's Presidency, the CFR made itself an adjunct of the U.S. Government. It became involved in the War and Peace Studies Project, which worked in secret and was funded by the Rockefeller Foundation (not for patriotic purposes). A State Department staffer, Harley Notter, wrote a letter of resignation to his CFR superior exclaiming that his dissatisfaction resulted from "relations with the Council on Foreign Relations. I have consistently opposed every move tending to give it increasing control of the research of this division and, though you have consistently stated that such a policy was far from your objectives, the actual facts already visibly show that departmental control is fast losing ground."[92]

After the war, at the Yalta Conference, FDR brought along Alger Hiss, a member of the CFR who was later determined to be a Soviet spy. It was at Yalta that the Soviets were ceded three votes in the UN general assembly. All other countries, including the United States, have only one.

The CFR put its stamp on the UN as well. All of the men who made up the steering committee to plan the UN charter, with one exception, were CFR members. The three attorneys who ruled that the UN was constitutional were members of the CFR. At the UN founding conference in 1945 more than forty of the American delegates were CFR members. America was now for the first time, to the chagrin of our founding fathers, part of a world government. John D. Rockefeller Jr. gave a gift of $8.5 million to purchase land for the UN headquarters.

Interestingly enough, the Soviet embassy in New York City is across the street from CFR headquarters on East 68th Street. So, then, what do we have?

A. Of the eighteen secretaries of the treasury since 1921, twelve have been members of the CFR.

B. Of the sixteen secretaries of state, twelve have been CFR members (four have been presidents of Rockefeller Foundation).

C. The Defense Department, created in 1947, has had fifteen secretaries; nine have been CFR.

D. The CIA, also created in 1947, has had eleven directors; seven have been CFR.

E. Six of seven superintendents at West Point have been CFR.

F. Every supreme Allied commander in Europe has been CFR.

G. Every U.S. ambassador to NATO has been CFR.

H. The four key positions in every administration, Republican or Democratic, are routinely filled by CFR members:
    1. National Security Advisor
    2. Secretary of State
    3. Secretary of Defense
    4. Secretary of Treasury

I. There are increasing numbers of CFR members in the legislative branch of government. Pat Schroeder (D-CO), Christopher Dodd (D-CT), Newt Gingrich (R-GA), Warren Rudman (R-NH), Bob Graham (D-FL), Thomas Foley (D-WA), Charles Robb (D-VA), John D. Rockefeller, IV (D-WV) are all members.

J. George Bush had 387 members of the CFR in his administration. Ronald Reagan had 313.[93]

K. The team of Clinton and Gore is financed and supported by the CFR as well. Clinton is a member of the Council on Foreign Relations and the Trilateral Commission.

L. Perot, the outsider in the 1992 elections, picked CFR people to run his campaign.

M. Total CFR membership as of December 1992 was 2905.

When you pondered your vote in the 1992 election, you were likely unaware of the disturbing exposure of the truth regarding contemporary politics; that is: "...the business interests...intended to contribute to both and allow an alternation of the two parties in public office in order to conceal their own influence, inhibit any exhibition of independence by politicians, and allow the electorate to believe that they were exercising their own free choice."[94]

The founding of the CFR has been for the specific purpose of conditioning the people to accept and desire world government. Everywhere today we are being sold the global, one-planet, one-world concept. It is pure propaganda promoting that America move away from the one thing proclaiming it free—the U.S. Constitution! When the Rockefellers and Rothschilds, behind the veil of politics, have eliminated America's Constitution and America's guns, every freedom this country has ever known will be gone.

Two proofs of the CFR secret program are:

1. From its own documents: In Study No. 7 they detailed the exact purpose of the CFR as the "building (of) a new international order (which) may be responsible to world aspirations for peace (and) for social and economic change....An international order ...including states labeling themselves as Socialist (Communist)."[95]

2. Former member of the CFR, Rear Admiral Chester Ward (USN, ret.), has told the American people the truth:

"The most powerful clique in these elitist groups have one objective in common—they want to bring about the surrender of the sovereignty and the national independence of the U.S. A second clique of international bankers in the CFR...comprises the Wall Street international bankers and their key agents. Primarily, they want the world banking monopoly from whatever power ends up in the control of global government. They would probably prefer that this be an all-powerful United Nations organization; but they are also prepared to deal with and for a one-world government controlled by the Soviet Communists if U.S. sovereignty is ever surrendered to them."[96]

Ward persisted: the CFR (Round Table) influence is being used for the purpose of "promoting disarmament and submergence of U.S. sovereignty and national independence into an all-powerful one-world government."[97]

In the CFR's journal, *Foreign Affairs,* as early as September 1922, the CFR condemned "the dubious doctrines expressed in the phrases 'safety first' and 'America first.'"[98] When Pat Buchanan seeks to "put America first," he preaches the exact antithesis of the CFR. In 1959, CFR publication Study No. 7, *Basic Aim of the U.S. Foreign Policy,* proposed that the United States "build a new international order." The steps cited as necessary were to:

1. Search for an international order in which the freedom of nations is recognized as interdependent. *(Resulted in the United Nations)*

2. Safeguard U.S. security through preserving a system of

bilateral agreements and <u>regional</u> arrangements. *(Resulted in the Trilateral Commission, International Monetary Fund, World Bank)*

3. Maintain and gradually increase the authority of the UN. *(Resulted in Desert Storm)*

4. Make more effective use of the International Court of Justice, jurisdiction of which should be <u>increased</u> by withdrawal of reservations by member nations on matters judged to be <u>domestic</u>. *(Promoted vigorously today by our own American Bar Association)*

Edith Kermit Roosevelt summed it up in 1961: The result of the Establishment viewpoint "...has been policies which favor the growth of the super-state, gradual surrender of the United States sovereignty to the United Nations, and a steady retreat in the face of Communist aggression."[99]

Let's take a look at some facts:

United Nations Charter, Chapter VII, Article 43 states: "All members of the United Nations, in order to contribute to the maintenance of international peace and security, undertake to <u>make available to the Security Council,</u> or <u>its call</u> and in accordance with a special agreement, or agreements, armed forces assistance and facilities, including rights of passage, necessary for the purpose of maintaining international peace and security."[100]

On September 1, 1961, the United States Government filed with the U.N. Secretary General a plan for the <u>transfer</u> of our entire military establishment to the United Nations!

This policy document for surrender is *State Department Publication Number 7277*, titled *Freedom from War: The United States' Program for General and Complete Disarmament in a Peaceful World.*[101]

Note that at the present time, even after proof positive of our need for a U.S. military which fought so precisely in Iraq, President Bush soon thereafter dutifully dismantled the defense industry, true to his allegiance to the CFR and their UN, not to the USA. The result? Thousands of jobs lost, another dip in the economy, and another dent in the Constitution he was sworn to uphold.

The goal, to reiterate, is to place the defense of American citizens in the hands of the Communist-dominated (I believe they call themselves capitalists now) UN Security Council.

The <u>U.S. State Department</u> (CFR controlled), acting in the name of the American people, has set forth the objectives of its program of <u>general</u> and <u>complete</u> disarmament in a world where adjustment to change takes place in accordance with the principles of the United Nations. "The Nations of the world," says <u>our</u> State Department, "declare their goal to be the disbanding of all material national armed forces and the <u>prohibition of their reestablishment</u> in any form whatsoever, other than those required to preserve internal order and for contributions to a United Nations Peace Force."[102]

This was accomplished in February 1992, as George Bush lobbied for an end to building an entire list of armaments and also the factories which produce them. "The Nations of the world," says <u>our</u> State Department, will establish an effective International Disarmament Organization within the framework of the United Nations "to ensure compliance at all times within all disarmament obligations."[103]

"The Nations of the world," says <u>our</u> State Department, will institute effective means for the enforcement of international agreements for the settlements of disputes, and for the maintenance of peace "<u>in accordance with the principles of the United Nations.</u>"[104]

In his stunning book *The Most Secret Science,* retired Air Force Colonel Archibald Roberts states: "Under this plan, the United States will finance and man a <u>totalitarian</u> UN military complex."[105]

The State Department planned three stages in the disarmament of the United States. In stage three, progressively controlled disarmament and continuously developing principles and procedures of international law (not national) would proceed to a point where no state would have the military power to challenge the progressively strengthened UN Peace Force. This means <u>not even the United States would have the power to challenge the UN Peace Force</u>!

Congressman James B. Utt stated: "The so-called Disarmament Act sets up a super-agency with power greater than the power of Congress, which delegated it....There is every intention," said Utt, "on the part of the Disarmament Agency to destroy the Sovereignty of this nation and put us under the control of international tyranny, and they are moving rapidly in this direction."[106]

Colonel Roberts continues: "The enormity of this subversion is nearly incomprehensible—as is the failure of the American people to protest the criminal abrogation of the United States Constitution. As one American soldier, I bitterly resent being turned over to an organization whose every precept and very existence contravenes the Constitution I have sworn to uphold."[107]

Colonel Roberts suggests: "A major objective of the take-over crowd is, of course, the silencing of articulate anti-Communists within the military services...the success of the planners in imposing one-world government on the nations of the world is dependent upon eradication of resistance or possible resistance, by the U.S. military establishment."[108] Would homosexuals in the military complete the job?

A witch hunt was conducted in 1961 to locate and silence "radical" right-wing generals and admirals who were for putting America and the Constitution first. These directives were given under the heading of the Fulbright Memorandum by then Secretary of Defense Robert S. McNamara. You guessed it, another member of the CFR.

The articles for disarmament were written in 1961. In February 1992 President Bush implored Congress to do away with a large percentage of the present military establishment. The world is "safe" now, so the CFR-controlled media tell us. We no longer have a need for weapons. Yet, where was this philosophy when we needed weapons to outfit the freedom fighters in Afghanistan? (Most of which I understand they never received.) And most recently in our nationally televised Desert Storm?

Suffice it to say that Bush adhered to the documentation written in 1961. Not only did he desire to reduce our weaponry and our military personnel, but he wanted to phase out of commission the very factories wherein these defense capabilities are made. That means, then, just what the State Department CFR desired in 1961; i.e., to do away with any nation's attempt to thwart the directives of the super-state United Nations.

The Council on Foreign Relations, ever since its original plans were drawn up at the Paris Peace Conference at the end of World War I, has intended to destroy the freedom and independence of the United States. Since the League of Nations did not work, today the UN is more than acceptable.

Prior even to the formation of the League of Nations, however, the graduated income tax and private Federal Reserve Bank were established. Both became law in 1913. Both are two planks of the *Communist Manifesto*. Both allowed the financing of World War I. J.P. Morgan associates literally ran the show.

J.P. Morgan has been the American front for the silent Rothschild family to literally rape America. The CFR is an extension of the old-world imperialistic British oligarchy. The CFR is little known today because the media wants to control what you know. Do not expect the media to tell you the truth because they are sworn to secrecy. The infiltration is virtually complete. We can only imagine the immensity of the cover-up when from the council's own 1987 report we read that 262 of its members are "journalists, correspondents, and communications executives."[109]

As the size of the secret beast grows, it is necessary even for the conspiratorial to expand to maintain its web. In 1987 CFR president Peter Tarnoff indicated that: "...we have decided to increase the size of our operations in the nation's capital....Over the next three years, we also intend to allow the stated membership in Washington to rise from the present level of 464 to 600...."[110]

In October 1992 Bill Clinton stated: "There is just one thing I cannot do. I cannot take us back to the way it was before." That statement has significant meaning. Even though "back" is exactly where we need to go—to a righteous and moral nation under God and to a godly heritage and an untainted Constitution, Clinton knows as a CFR/TC member his destiny is with the money lenders pushing America deceitfully into a "New Age".

On October 11, 1992, we heard Ross Perot suggest that we alter the Constitution if that is what would make America successful. In the first place, Ross Perot, although a successful businessman, has an incredible loss of memory. If he could remember any history at all, he would recall that it was exactly that unique document, the Constitution, which made America the envy of every country in the world. It is only the adulteries of its many amendments, typically germinated at the Pratt House (New York City, home of the CFR), which have weakened that document over these many years.

The Committee on the Constitutional System (CCS), the bicentennial group which desires to revoke our Constitution because it prevents the CFR from placing the "capstone" on their plan of one-world government, is made up of forty-eight board directors, more than a third of which are members of the CFR! CCS Co-chairman Douglas Dillon believes "...needed changes can be made only after a period of great crisis."[111] Project '87 co-chairman, James MacGregor Burns, stated in *Reforming American Government:*

> "I doubt that Americans under normal conditions could agree on the package of radical and 'alien' constitutional changes that would be required. They would do so, I think, only during and following a stupendous national crisis and political failure."[112] In the October 1987 issue of *Atlantic*, CFR Chairman Peter G. Peterson forecast a debilitating economic crunch in the future.[113]

When the next great crash hits this country, as has been predicted by author Larry Burkett and others, remember that the hit was directed from London and through the Council on Foreign Relations; i.e., the Pratt House—58 East 68th Street in New York City. This is the same place from which the crash of 1929 took place, and the government can do nothing about it, unless it takes back its constitutional right to print money. In an instant, that would satisfy the annihilating debt problem and the money tyranny over the people.

Do you suppose we will be allowed to vote on whether the chief Machiavellian power of the New World Order is a Democrat or a Republican? Or are you beginning to understand that the reason things never change in U.S. Government is because of the subterfuge behind the conspirators we are constrained to vote for?

Thomas Jefferson explained it this way: "Single acts of tyranny may be ascribed to the accidental opinion of a day; but a series of oppressions, begun at a distinguished period, and pursued unalterably through every change of ministers (presidents), too plainly prove a deliberate systematical plan of reducing us to slavery."

Following are the charts proving twenty years of CFR oppression.

The Planned Destruction of America

"The CFR is the American Branch of a society which originated in England. . .(and). . .believes national boundaries should be obliterated and one-world rule established." *With No Apologies,* Senator Barry Goldwater.

". . .the Royal Institute of International Affairs (in England) agreed to regard the Council on Foreign Relations as its American Branch." *Tragedy and Hope,* Professor Carroll Quigley, Ph.D.

The TRILAT...

DAVID

MEDIA
Past & Present CFR/TC Members (partial listing)
(Brought up to date — 1982)

". . . federal reserve banks are not federal instrumentalities . . . but are independent, privately owned and locally controlled corporations." Lewis v United States. U.S. Court of Appeals, 9th Circuit, April 19, 1982.

CBS

William Paley	CFR
William Burden	CFR
Roswell Gilpatric	CFR
James Houghton	CFR
Henry Schacht	CFR TC
Marietta Tree	CFR
C.C. Collingwood	CFR
Lawrence LeSueur	CFR
Dan Rather	CFR
Harry Reasoner	CFR
Richard Hottelet	CFR
Frank Stanton	CFR
Bill Moyers	CFR

NBC/RCA

Jane Pfeiffer	CFR
Lester Crystal	CFR
R.W. Sonnenfeldt	CFR
T.F. Bradshaw	CFR
John Petty	CFR
David Brinkley	CFR
John Chancellor	CFR
Marvin Kalb	CFR
Irvine Levine	CFR
H. Schlosser	CFR
P.G. Peterson	CFR TC
John Sawhill	CFR TC

ABC

Ray Adam	CFR
Frank Cary	CFR
John Connor	CFR
T.M. Macioce	CFR
Ted Koppel	CFR
John Scali	CFR
Barbara Walters	CFR

CABLE NEWS NETWORK

Daniel Schorr	CFR

PUBLIC BROADCAST SERVICE

Hartford Gunn	CFR
Robert McNeil	CFR
Jim Lehrer	CFR
C. Hunter-Gault	CFR
Hodding Carter III	CFR

ASSOCIATED PRESS

Keith Fuller	CFR
Stanley Swinton	CFR
Louis Boccardi	CFR
Harold Anderson	CFR
Katharine Graham	CFR

U.P.I.

H.L. Stevenson	CFR

REUTERS

Michael Posner	CFR

BOSTON GLOBE

David Rogers	CFR

L.A. TIMES SYNDICATE

Joseph Kraft	CFR TC

BALTIMORE SUN

Henry Trewhitt	CFR

NEW YORK TIMES CO.

Richard Gelb	CFR
James Reston	CFR
William Scranton	CFR TC
A.M. Rosenthal	CFR
Seymour Topping	CFR
James Greenfield	CFR
Max Frankel	CFR
Jack Rosenthal	CFR
Harding Bancroft	CFR
Amory Bradford	CFR
Orvil Dryfoos	CFR
David Halberstram	CFR
Walter Lippmann	CFR
L.E. Markel	CFR
H.L. Matthews	CFR
John Oakes	CFR
Adolph Ochs	CFR
Harrison Salisbury	CFR
A. Hays Sulzberger	CFR
A. Ochs Sulzberger	CFR
C.L. Sulzberger	CFR
H.L. Smith	CFR
Steven Rattner	CFR
Richard Burt	CFR

TIME INC.

Ralph Davidson	CFR
Donald M. Wilson	CFR
Louis Banks	CFR
Henry Grunwald	CFR
Alexander Heard	CFR
Sol Linowitz	CFR TC
Rawleigh Warner, Jr.	CFR
Thomas Watson, Jr.	CFR

NEWSWEEK/WASH. POST

Katharine Graham	CFR
Philip Graham	CFR
Arjay Miller	TC
N. deB. Katzenbach	CFR
Frederick Beebe	CFR
Robert Christopher	CFR
A. De Borchgrave	CFR
Osborne Elliot	CFR
Phillip Geyelin	CFR
Kermit Lausner	CFR
Murry Marder	CFR
Eugene Meyer	CFR
Malcolm Muir	CFR
Maynard Parker	CFR
George Will	CFR
Robert Kaiser	CFR
Meg Greenfield	CFR
Walter Pincus	CFR
Murray Gart	CFR
Peter Osnos	CFR
Don Oberdorfer	CFR

DOW JONES & CO.
(Wall St. Journal)

William Agee	CFR
J. Paul Austin	TC
Charles Meyer	CFR
Robert Potter	CFR
Richard Wood	CFR
Robert Bartley	CFR
Karen House	CFR

NATIONAL REVIEW

Wm. F. Buckley, Jr.	CFR
Richard Brookhiser	CFR

INTERNATIONAL BANK FOR RECONSTRUCTION AND DEVELOPMENT

Robert McNamara	CFR TC
Hollis Chenery	CFR
Edward Fried	CFR
Ernest Stern	CFR

INTERNATIONAL FINANCE CORPORATION

Robert McNamara	CFR TC
Richard Richardson	CFR

FEDERAL COMMUNICATIONS COMMISSION

Abbott Washburn	CFR

INTERNATIONAL BROADCASTING AND COMMUNICATIONS

Olin Robison	CFR
John Reinhardt	CFR
Charles Bray	CFR
R. Peter Straus	CFR
Rita Hauser	CFR
Alice Ilchman	CFR

RED CROSS

Wm. Boeschenstein	CFR
Wm. McChesty Martin	CFR
Jerome H. Holland	CFR
Frank Stanton	CFR

CFR MEMBERSHIP BREAKDOWN (1978-1979)

Journalists, correspondents and communications executives 190 (10%)

Scholars & Educators 370 (19%)

Business 555 (28%)

Lawyers 190 (10%)

Government 292 (15%)

Non-Profit Organizations 272 (14%)

(These tax exempt foundations fund America's enemies at home and abroad, yet appear to be immune from congressional investigation.)

FEDERAL RESERVE

G. William Miller	CFR
Paul Volcker	CFR TC
Anthony Solomon	CFR TC
Henry Wallich	CFR
Emmet Rice	CFR
Henry Woodbridge, Jr.	CFR
Donald Platten	CFR
Robert Knight, Esq.	CFR
Steven Muller	CFR
Gerald Hines	CFR
Geo. H. Weyerhaeuser	CFR TC
Harold Anderson	CFR
Arthur F. Burns	CFR TC

ROBERT McNAMARA

CFR   TC

WORLD BANK

ANNE WEXLER

CFR

ASSISTANT TO THE PRESIDENT

HENRY KISSINGER

CFR   TC

ADVISOR

BRZEZINSKI

CFR   TC

NATIONAL SECURITY ADVISOR

MONDALE

CFR   TC

VICE PRESIDENT

VANC...

CFR

SECRETARY O...
Replaced...
Edmund Musk...

T. TANNENWALD, Jr.

CFR

U.S. TAX COURT

JOHN SAWHILL

CFR   TC

DEPT. OF ENERGY
John Deutch CFR

EMERGENCY COURT OF APPEALS

Dudley Bonsal CFR

DOMESTIC POLICY

Richard Neustadt CFR

INTERNATIONAL COURT OF JUSTICE

Richard R. Baxter CFR

OFFICE OF MANAGEMENT AND BUDGET

Peter Szanton CFR

PLEASE NOTE

The "NEW WORLD ORDER" views of Rockefeller, Kiss... are not shared by all members. Some join for prestige ... dow dressing". All Americans should closely examine ... mulated and implemented by the CFR through the yea...

COUNCIL
58 E. 68...
NORTH

TRILAT...
345 E. 4...
(Write...

(Charter me...
Trained fo...

NATIONA...

DEPARTMEN...

Cyrus Vance (Sec.)	CFR TC
Edmund Muskie (Sec.)	CFR
Warren Christopher	CFR TC
Harry G. Barnes, Jr.	CFR
(Director, Foreign Service)	
Douglas J. Bennet	CFR
(Congressional Relations)	
Lucy Wilson Benson	CFR TC
Priscilla A. Clapp	CFR
Stepher F. Cohen	CFR
(Human Rights)	
Richard N. Cooper	CFR TC
(Economic Affairs)	
Mark B. Feldman (Legal)	CFR
Leslie H. Gelb	CFR
(Politico-Military)	
David Gompert	CFR
Robert D. Hormats	CFR
(Economic-Business)	
Jerome H. Kahan	CFR
(Deputy Director)	
Paul H. Kreisberg	CFR
(Policy Planning)	
W. Anthony Lake	CFR
(Policy Planning)	
Karin Lissakers	CFR
(Policy Planning)	
David E. Mark	CFR
(Intelligence-Research)	
Edward Morse	CFR
David D. Newsom	CFR
(Board of Foreign Service)	
Matthew Nimetz (Legal)	CFR
Robert H. Nooter	CFR
(International development)	
Stephen A. Oxman	CFR
E. Raymond Platig	CFR
(Intelligence-Research)	
Ben H. Read (Management)	CFR
Stephen M. Schwebel (Legal)	CFR
Marshall D. shulman	CFR
(Soviet Affairs)	
Paul Warnke (Salt)	CFR
R.E. Earl, II (Salt)	CFR

AMBASSADORS...

Andrew Young (UN)	CFR
Donald F. McHenry (UN)	CFR
James F. Leonard (UN)	CFR
Richard R. Baxter (UN)	CFR
Roger J. Cochetti (UN)	CFR
W. Tapley Bennett, Jr. (NAT...	CFR
Morton I. Abramowitz	
(Thailand)	
Richard Bloomfield (Portuga...	
Kingman Brewster, Jr.	
(Britain/Northern Ireland)	
Walter L. Cutler (Zaire)	
Arthur R. Day (Jerusalem)	
Lawrence Eagleburger	
(Yugoslavia)	
Donald B. Easum (Nigeria)	
Hermann F. Ellts (Egypt)	
Thomas O. Enders (Canada...	
Richard N. Gardner (Italy)	
Raymond L. Garthoff	
(Bulgaria)	
Robert F. Goheen (India)	
Arthur A. Hartman (France)	
Ulric St. Clair Haynes, Jr.	
(Algeria)	
Philip M. Kaiser (Hungary)	
Samuel W. Lewis (Israel)	
Stephen Low (Zambia)	
James G. Lowenstein	
(Luxembourg)	
William H. Luers (Venezuela...	
Warren O. Manshel (Denmar...	
Rozanne L. Ridgway (Finlan...	
William E. Schaufele, Jr.	
(Poland)	
James W. Spain (Tanzania)	
Ronald I. Spiers (Turkey)	
Walter J. Stoessel, Jr.	
(Germany)	
William H. Sullivan (Iran)	
Terence A. Todman (Spain)	
Milton A. Wolf (Austria)	
W. Howard Wriggins	
(Maldives and Sri Lanka)	

CONGRESSIONAL RESEARCH LIBRARY

Ann L. Hollick CFR

CONGRESSIONAL COMMITTEES

William B. Bader	CFR
William J. Barnds	CFR
Pauline R. Baker	CFR
William G. Miller	CFR

1980 PRESIDENTIAL CANDIDATES

(It is standard practice for members to resign before running for public office.)

John Anderson	CFR
Howard Baker	CFR
George Bush	CFR TC
Jimmy Carter	TC
Ted Kennedy	CFR

(Boston Affiliate)

(Running CFR candidates from each party often provides Rockefeller continuing control of the Chief Executive.)

DO NOT DESTROY

RETAIN FOR FUTURE REFERENCE.

HOUSE & SENATE CFR/TC MEMBERS
(Past & Present)

SENATE

● Howard Baker, Jr. (Tenn.)	CFR	
● Birch Bayh (Ind.)	CFR	
● Lloyd Bentsen (Tex.)	CFR	
William Brock, Jr. (Tenn.)	CFR TC*	
● Edward Brooke (Mass.)	CFR	
● Clifford Case (N.J.)	CFR	
● Frank Church (Idaho)	CFR	
● Dick Clark (Iowa)	CFR	
William S. Cohen (Maine)	CFR TC	
● Alan Cranston (Calif.)	TC	
John Cooper (Ken.)	CFR	
● John Culver (Iowa)	CFR	
● John Danforth (Mo.)	CFR TC	
● John Glenn (Ohio)	TC	
Hubert Humphrey (Minn.)	CFR	
● Jacob Javits (N.Y.)	CFR	
● Ted Kennedy (Mass.)	CFR	
(Belongs to Boston Affiliate)		
Gale McGee (Wyo.)	CFR	
● George McGovern (S.D.)	CFR	
● Charles Mathias (Md.)	CFR	

HOUSE

Walter Mondale (Minn.)	CFR TC	
● Daniel Moynihan (N.Y.)	CFR	
● Edmund Muskie (Ma.)	CFR	
● Claiborne Pell (R.I.)	CFR	
● Abraham Riblcoff (Conn.)	CFR	
William Roth (Del.)	CFR TC	
● Paul Sarbanes (Md.)	CFR	
● Adlai Stevenson (Ill.)	CFR	
Stuart Symington (Mo.)	CFR	
Robert Taft, Jr. (Ohio)	TC	

John Anderson (Ill.)	CFR TC	
● Les Aspin (Wisc.)	CFR	
● J.B. Bingham (N.Y.)	CFR	
● John Brademas (Ind.)	CFR TC	
● Barber Conable, Jr. (N.Y.)	TC	
● William R. Cotter (Conn.)	CFR	
● Dante Fascell (Fla.)	CFR	
● Thomas Foley (Wash.)	TC	
● Donald Fraser	CFR	
● Stephen Solarz (N.Y.)	CFR TC	

* William Brock, Jr., Chrmn., Republican National Committee
● Voted to transfer ownership of the American canal in Panama to a Marxist dictatorship.

10-84   REVISED CARTER ADMINISTRATION CHART #102

72

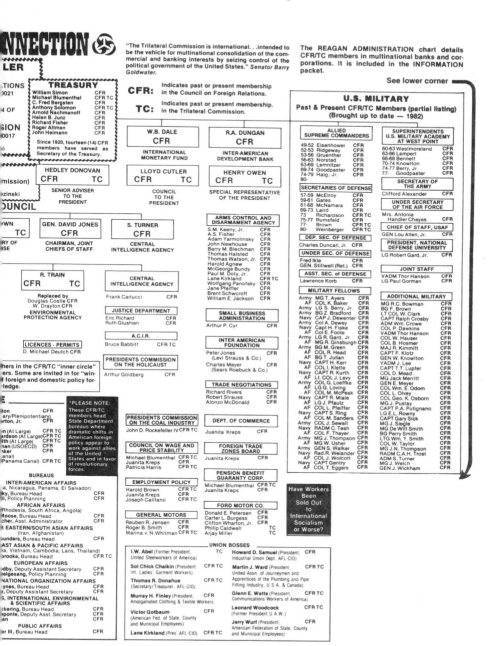

NNECTION ⊛

LER

TREASURY

William Simon	CFR
Michael Blumenthal	CFR TC
C. Fred Bergsten	CFR
Anthony Solomon	CFR TC
Arnold Nachmanoff	CFR
Helen B. Junz	CFR
Richard Fisher	CFR
Roger Altman	CFR
John Heimann	CFR

.TIONS 0021

N OF

SION 0017

Since 1920, fourteen (14) CFR members have served as Secretary of the Treasury.

CFR: Indicates past or present membership in the Council on Foreign Relations.

TC: Indicates past or present membership in the Trilateral Commission.

"The Trilateral Commission is international...intended to be the vehicle for multinational consolidation of the commercial and banking interests by seizing control of the political government of the United States." *Senator Barry Goldwater.*

The REAGAN ADMINISTRATION chart details CFR/TC members in multinational banks and corporations. It is included in the INFORMATION packet.

See lower corner ◾

HEDLEY DONOVAN
CFR TC
SENIOR ADVISER TO THE PRESIDENT

mission)

ezinski

JUNCIL

W.B. DALE
CFR
INTERNATIONAL MONETARY FUND

R.A. DUNGAN
CFR
INTER-AMERICAN DEVELOPMENT BANK

LLOYD CUTLER
CFR TC
COUNCIL TO THE PRESIDENT

HENRY OWEN
CFR TC
SPECIAL REPRESENTATIVE OF THE PRESIDENT

GEN. DAVID JONES
CFR
CHAIRMAN, JOINT CHIEFS OF STAFF

S. TURNER
CFR
CENTRAL INTELLIGENCE AGENCY

WN

TC

RY OF
ISE

R. TRAIN
CFR TC

Replaced by Douglas Costle CFR
W. Drayton CFR
ENVIRONMENTAL PROTECTION AGENCY

CENTRAL INTELLIGENCE AGENCY
Frank Carlucci CFR

JUSTICE DEPARTMENT
Eric Richard CFR
Ruth Glushien CFR

A.C.I.R.
Bruce Babbitt CFR TC

LICENCES · PERMITS
D. Michael Deutch CFR

hers in the CFR/TC "inner circle" ers. Some are invited in for "winf foreign and domestic policy for- ledge.

PRESIDENTS COMMISSION ON THE HOLICAUST
Arthur Goldberg CFR

U.S. MILITARY
Past & Present CFR/TC Members (partial listing)
(Brought up to date — 1982)

ALLIED SUPREME COMMANDERS

49-52	Eisenhower	CFR
52-53	Ridgeway	CFR
53-56	Gruenther	CFR
56-63	Norstad	CFR
63-69	Lemnitzer	CFR
69-74	Goodpaster	CFR
74-79	Haig, Jr.	CFR
80-		

SECRETARIES OF DEFENSE

57-59	McElroy	CFR
59-61	Gates	CFR
61-68	McNamara	CFR
69-73	Laird	CFR
73	Richardson	CFR TC
75-77	Rumsfeld	CFR
80-	Weinberger	CFR TC

DEP. SEC. OF DEFENSE
Charles Duncan, Jr. CFR

UNDER SEC. OF DEFENSE
Fred Ikle CFR
GEN. Stillwell (Ret.) CFR

ASST. SEC. of DEFENSE
Lawrence Korb CFR

MILITARY FELLOWS

Army	MG T. Ayers	CFR
AF	COL K. Baker	CFR
Army	LG S. Berry, Jr.	CFR
Army	BG Z. Bradford	CFR
Navy	CAP J. Dewenter	CFR
Army	Col A. Dewey	CFR
Navy	Capt H. Fiske	CFR
AF	Col E. Foote	CFR
Army	LG R. Gard, Jr.	CFR
AF	MG R. Ginsburgh	CFR
Army	BG M. Green	CFR
AF	BG R. Head	CFR
AF	BG T. Julian	CFR
Navy	CAPT H. Kerr	CFR
AF	COL I. Klette	CFR
Navy	CAPT R. Kurth	CFR
AF	Lt. COL J. Levy	CFR
Army	COL G. Loeffke	CFR
AF	LG G. Loving	CFR
AF	COL M. McPeak	CFR
Navy	CAPT R. Miale	CFR
AF	LG J. Pfautz	CFR
AF	COL L. Pfeiffer	CFR
Navy	CAPT S. Ring	CFR
AF	COL M. Sanders	CFR
Army	COL J. Sewall	CFR
Navy	RADM C. Tesh	CFR
AF	COL F. Thayer	CFR
Army	MG J. Thompson	CFR
AF	MG W. Usher	CFR
Army	GEN S. Walker	CFR
Navy	Rad.R. Welander	CFR
AF	COL J. Wolcott	CFR
Navy	CAPT Gentry	CFR
AF	COL T. Eggers	CFR

SUPERINTENDENTS U.S. MILITARY ACADEMY AT WEST POINT

60-63	Westmoreland	CFR
63-66	Lampert	CFR
66-68	Bennett	CFR
70-74	Knowlton	CFR
74-77	Berry, Jr.	CFR
77-	Goodpaster	CFR

SECRETARY OF THE ARMY
Clifford Alexander CFR

UNDER SECRETARY OF THE AIR FORCE
Mrs. Antonia Handler Chayes CFR

CHIEF OF STAFF, USAF
GEN Lou Allen, Jr. CFR

PRESIDENT, NATIONAL DEFENSE UNIVERSITY
LG Robert Gard, Jr. CFR

JOINT STAFF
VADM Thor Hanson CFR
LG Paul Gorman CFR

ADDITIONAL MILITARY

	MG R.C. Bowman	CFR
	BG F. Brown	CFR
	LT COL W. Clark	CFR
	CAPT Ralph Crosby	CFR
	ADM Wm. Crowe	CFR
	COL P. Dawkins	CFR
	VADM Thor Hanson	CFR
	COL W. Hauser	CFR
	COL B. Hosmer	CFR
	MAJ R. Kimmitt	CFR
	CAPT F. Klotz	CFR
	GEN W. Knowlton	CFR
	VADM J. Lee	CFR
	CAPT T.T. Lupfer	CFR
	COL D. Mead	CFR
	MG Jack Merritt	CFR
	GEN E. Meyer	CFR
	COL Wm. E. Odom	CFR
	COL L. Olvey	CFR
	COL Geo. K. Osborn	CFR
	MG J. Pustay	CFR
	CAPT P.A. Putignano	CFR
	LG E.L. Rowny	CFR
	CAPT Gary Sick	CFR
	MG J. Siegle	CFR
	MG De Witt Smith	CFR
	BG Perry Smith	CFR
	LTG Wm. Y. Smith	CFR
	COL W. Taylor	CFR
	MG J.N. Thompson	CFR
	RADM C.A.H. Trost	CFR
	ADM S. Turner	CFR
	MG J. Welch	CFR
	GEN J. Wickham	CFR

ARMS CONTROL AND DISARMAMENT AGENCY

S.M. Keeny, Jr.	CFR
A.S. Fisher	CFR
Adam Yarmolinsky	CFR
John Newhouse	CFR
Barry M. Blechman	CFR
Thomas Halsted	CFR
Thomas Watson, Jr.	CFR
Harold Agnew	CFR
McGeorge Bundy	CFR
Paul M. Doty, Jr.	CFR
Lane Kirkland	CFR TC
Wolfgang Panofsky	CFR
Jane Pfeiffer	CFR
Brent Schwcrott	CFR
William E. Jackson	CFR

SMALL BUSINESS ADMINISTRATION
Arthur P. Cyr CFR

INTER AMERICAN FOUNDATION
Peter Jones CFR
(Levi Strauss & Co.)
Charles Meyer CFR
(Sears Roebuck & Co.)

TRADE NEGOTIATIONS
Richard Rivers CFR
Robert Strauss CFR
Alonzo McDonald CFR

PLEASE NOTE: These CFR/TC members head bureaus where dramatic shifts in American foreign policy appear to work against allies of the United States and in favor of revolutionary forces.

ton CFR
ary/Plenipotentiary)
rton, Jr.

n (At Large) CFR TC
rdson (At Large) CFR TC
ith (At Large) CFR TC
nan (USOECD) CFR
nker CFR
anal)
Panama Canal) CFR TC

BUREAUS

INTER-AMERICAN AFFAIRS
a, Nicaragua, Panama, El Salvador)
ky, Bureau Head CFR
l, Policy Planning CFR

AFRICAN AFFAIRS
Rhodesia, South Africa, Angola)
Moose, Bureau Head CFR
cher, Asst. Administrator CFR

EASTERN/SOUTH ASIAN AFFAIRS
(Iran, Afghanistan)
aunders, Bureau Head CFR

AST ASIAN & PACIFIC AFFAIRS
ea, Vietnam, Cambodia, Laos, Thailand)
prooke, Bureau Head CFR TC

EUROPEAN AFFAIRS
dby, Deputy Assistant Secretary CFR
eigesang, Policy Planning CFR

NATIONAL ORGANIZATION AFFAIRS
ynes, Bureau Head CFR
r, Deputy Assistant Secretary CFR

S, INTERNATIONAL ENVIRONMENTAL & SCIENTIFIC AFFAIRS
ckering, Bureau Head CFR
sponte, Deputy Asst. Secretary CFR
an CFR

PUBLIC AFFAIRS
ar III, Bureau Head CFR

PRESIDENTS COMMISSION ON THE COAL INDUSTRY
John D. Rockefeller IV CFR TC

COUNCIL ON WAGE AND PRICE STABILITY
Michael Blumenthal CFR TC
Juanita Kreps CFR
Patricia Harris CFR TC

EMPLOYMENT POLICY
Harold Brown CFR TC
Juanita Kreps CFR
Joseph Califano CFR TC

GENERAL MOTORS
Reuben R. Jensen CFR
Roger B. Smith CFR
Marina v. N.Whitman CFR

DEPT. OF COMMERCE
Juanita Kreps CFR

FOREIGN TRADE ZONES BOARD
Juanita Kreps CFR

PENSION BENEFIT GUARANTY CORP.
Michael Blumenthal CFR TC
Juanita Kreps CFR

FORD MOTOR CO.

Donald E. Petersen	CFR
Carter L. Burgess	CFR
Clifton Wharton, Jr.	CFR
Philip Caldwell	TC
Arjay Miller	TC

UNION BOSSES

I.W. Abel (Former President, TC
United Steelworkers of America)

Sol Chick Chaikin (President CFR TC
Int. Ladies' Garment Workers)

Thomas R. Donahue CFR TC
(Secretary/Treasurer, AFL-CIO)

Murray H. Finley (President, CFR
Amalgamated Clothing & Textile Workers)

Victor Gotbaum CFR
(American Fed. of State, County
and Municipal Employees)

Lane Kirkland (Pres. AFL-CIO) CFR TC

Howard D. Samuel (President, CFR
Industrial Union Dept. AFL-CIO)

Martin J. Ward (President, CFR TC
United Assn. of Journeymen and
Apprentices of the Plumbing and Pipe
Fitting Industry, U.S.A. & Canada)

Glenn E. Watts (President, CFR TC
Communications Workers of America)

Leonard Woodcock CFR TC
(Former President U.A.W.)

Jerry Wurf (President, CFR
American Federation of State, County
and Municipal Employees)

Have Workers Been Sold Out to International Socialism or Worse?

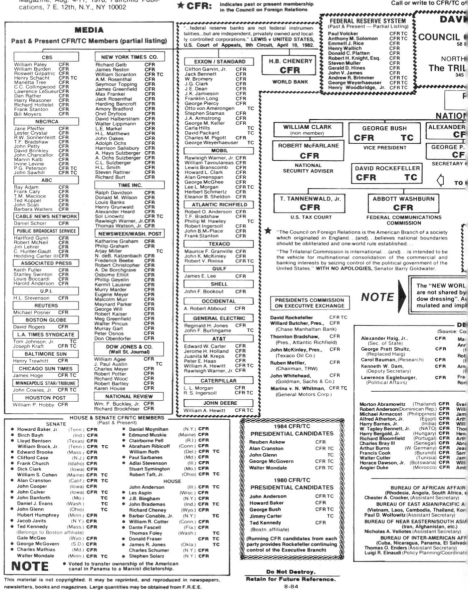

The C.F.R./TRIL...

"The Trilateral Commission doesn't secretly run the world. The Council on Foreign Relations does that."
Winston Lord, President, C.F.R., "W" Magazine, Aug. 4-11, 1978, Fairchild Publications, 7 E. 12th, N.Y., NY 10002

★ CFR: Indicates past or present membership in the Council on Foreign Relations

Call or write to CFR/TC o...

MEDIA
Past & Present CFR/TC Members (partial listing)

CBS
William Paley — CFR
William Burden — CFR
Roswell Gilpatric — CFR
Henry Schacht — CFR TC
Marietta Tree — CFR
C.C. Collingwood — CFR
Lawrence LeSueur — CFR
Dan Rather — CFR
Harry Reasoner — CFR
Richard Hottelet — CFR
Frank Stanton — CFR
Bill Moyers — CFR

NBC/RCA
Jane Pfeiffer — CFR
Lester Crystal — CFR
R.W. Sonnenfeldt — CFR
T.F. Bradshaw — CFR
John Petty — CFR
David Brinkley — CFR
John Chancellor — CFR
Marvin Kalb — CFR
Irvine Levine — CFR
P.G. Peterson — CFR TC
John Sawhill — CFR TC

ABC
Ray Adam — CFR
Frank Cary — CFR
T.M. Macioce — CFR
Ted Koppel — CFR
John Scali — CFR
Barbara Walters — CFR

CABLE NEWS NETWORK
Daniel Schorr — CFR

PUBLIC BROADCAST SERVICE
Hartford Gunn — CFR
Robert McNeil — CFR
Jim Lehrer — CFR
C. Hunter-Gault — CFR
Hodding Carter III — CFR

ASSOCIATED PRESS
Keith Fuller — CFR
Stanley Swinton — CFR
Louis Boccardi — CFR
Harold Anderson — CFR

U.P.I.
H.L. Stevenson — CFR

REUTERS
Michael Posner — CFR

BOSTON GLOBE
David Rogers — CFR

L.A. TIMES SYNDICATE
Tom Johnson, Jr. — TC
Joseph Kraft — CFR TC

BALTIMORE SUN
Henry Trewhitt — CFR

CHICAGO SUN TIMES
James Hoge — CFR TC

MINNEAPOLIS STAR/TRIBUNE
John Cowles, Jr. — CFR

HOUSTON POST
William P. Hobby — CFR

NEW YORK TIMES CO.
Richard Gelb — CFR
James Reston — CFR
William Scranton — CFR TC
A.M. Rosenthal — CFR
Seymour Topping — CFR
James Greenfield — CFR
Max Frankel — CFR
Jack Rosenthal — CFR
Harding Bancroft — CFR
Amory Bradford — CFR
Orvil Dryfoos — CFR
David Halberstram — CFR
Walter Lippmann — CFR
L.E. Markel — CFR
H.L. Matthews — CFR
John Oakes — CFR
Adolph Ochs — CFR
Harrison Salisbury — CFR
A. Hays Sulzberger — CFR
A. Ochs Sulzberger — CFR
C.L. Sulzberger — CFR
H.L. Smith — CFR
Steven Rattner — CFR
Richard Burt — CFR

TIME INC.
Ralph Davidson — CFR
Donald M. Wilson — CFR
Louis Banks — CFR
Henry Grunwald — CFR
Alexander Heard — CFR
Sol Linowitz — CFR TC
Rawleigh Warner, Jr. — CFR
Thomas Watson, Jr. — CFR

NEWSWEEK/WASH. POST
Katharine Graham — CFR
Philip Graham — CFR
Arjay Miller — TC
N. deB. Katzenbach — CFR
Frederick Beebe — CFR
Robert Christopher — CFR
A. De Borchgrave — CFR
Osborne Elliot — CFR
Phillip Geyelin — CFR
Kermit Lausner — CFR
Murry Marder — CFR
Eugene Meyer — CFR
Malcolm Muir — CFR
Maynard Parker — CFR
George Will — CFR
Robert Kaiser — CFR
Meg Greenfield — CFR
Walter Pincus — CFR
Murray Gart — CFR
Peter Osnos — CFR
Don Oberdorfer — CFR

DOW JONES & CO. (Wall St. Journal)
William Agee — CFR
J. Paul Austin — TC
Charles Meyer — CFR
Robert Potter — CFR
Richard Wooc — CFR
Robert Bartley — CFR
Karen House — CFR

NATIONAL REVIEW
Wm. F. Buckley, Jr. — CFR
Richard Brookhiser — CFR

EXXON / STANDARD
Clifton Garvin, Jr. — CFR
Jack Bennett — CFR
W. Bromery — CFR
J.G. Clark — CFR
J.E. Dean — CFR
J.K. Jamieson — CFR
Franklin Long — CFR
George Piercy — CFR
Otto von Amerongen — TC
Stephen Stamas — CFR
J.A. Armstrong — CFR
George M. Keller — CFR
Carla Hills — TC
David Packard — CFR
Charles M. Pigott — CFR
George Weyerhaeuser — TC

MOBIL
Rawleigh Warner, Jr. — CFR
William Tavoulareas — CFR
Lewis Branscomb — CFR
Howard L. Clark — CFR
Alan Greenspan — CFR
George McGhee — CFR
Lee L. Morgan — CFR TC
Herbert Schmertz — CFR
Eleanor B. Sheldon — CFR

ATLANTIC RICHFIELD
Robert O. Anderson — CFR
T.F. Bradshaw — CFR
Phillip M. Hawley — TC
Robert Ingersoll — CFR
John B.M. Place — CFR
Frank Stanton — CFR

TEXACO
Maurice F. Granville — CFR
John K. McKinley — CFR
Robert V. Roosa — CFR TC

GULF
James E. Lee — CFR

SHELL
John F. Bookout — CFR

OCCIDENTAL
A. Robert Abboud — CFR

GENERAL ELECTRIC
Reginald H. Jones — CFR
John F. Burlingame — TC

AT&T
Edward W. Carter — CFR
Jerome H. Holland — CFR
Juanita M. Kreps — CFR
Peter E. Haas — CFR
William A. Hewitt — CFR TC
Rawleigh Warner, Jr. — CFR

CATERPILLAR
L. L. Morgan — CFR
R.S. Ingersoll — CFR TC

JOHN DEERE
William A. Hewitt — CFR TC

"...federal reserve banks are not federal instrumentalities...but are independent, privately owned and locally controlled corporations." LEWIS v UNITED STATES, U.S. Court of Appeals, 9th Circuit, April 19, 1982.

H.B. CHENERY
CFR
WORLD BANK

FEDERAL RESERVE SYSTEM (Past & Present — Partial Listing)
Paul Volcker — CFR TC
Anthony M. Solomon — CFR TC
Emmett J. Rice — CFR
Henry Wallich — CFR
Donald C. Platten — CFR
Robert H. Knight, Esq. — CFR
Steven Muller — CFR
Gerald D. Hines — CFR
John V. James — CFR
Andrew R. Brimmer — CFR TC
George Weyerhaeuser — CFR TC
Henry Woodbridge, Jr. — CFR TC

WILLIAM CLARK (non member)

GEORGE BUSH — CFR TC
VICE PRESIDENT

ALEXANDER ... — CFR

ROBERT McFARLANE — CFR
NATIONAL SECURITY ADVISER

GEORGE P. ... — CF
SECRETARY ...

DAVID ROCKEFELLER — CFR TC

T. TANNENWALD, Jr. — CFR
U.S. TAX COURT

ABBOTT WASHBURN — CFR
FEDERAL COMMUNICATIONS COMMISSION

PRESIDENTS COMMISSION ON EXECUTIVE EXCHANGE
David Rockefeller — CFR TC
Willard Butcher, Pres., — CFR (Chase Manhattan Bank)
Thornton Bradshaw, — CFR (Pres., Atlantic Richfield)
John McKinley, Pres., — CFR (Texaco Oil Co.)
Ruben Mettler, — CFR (Chairman, TRW)
John Whitehead, — CFR (Goldman, Sachs & Co.)
Marina v. N. Whitman, — CFR TC (General Motors Corp.)

★ "The Council on Foreign Relations is the American Branch of a society which originated in England . . (and). . .believes national boundaries should be obliterated and one-world rule established. . . .

"The Trilateral Commission is international. . . (and). . . is intended to be the vehicle for multinational consolidation of the commercial and banking interests by gaining control of the political government of the United States." WITH NO APOLOGIES, Senator Barry Goldwater.

NOTE The "NEW WORL... are not shared by... dow dressing". A... mulated and impl...

Alexander Haig, Jr., — CFR (Sec. of State)
George Pratt Shultz, — CFR (Replaced Haig)
Carol Bauman, (Research) — CFR
Kenneth W. Dam, — CFR (Deputy Secretary)
Lawrence Eagleburger, — CFR (Political Affairs)

Morton Abramowitz (Thailand) CFR
Robert Anderson (Dominican Rep.) CFR
Michael Armacost (Philippines) CFR
Alfred Atherton, Jr. (Egypt) CFR
Harry Barnes, Jr. (India) CFR
W. Tapley Bennett, Jr. (NATO) CFR
Harry Bergold, Jr. (Hungary) CFR
Richard Bloomfield (Portugal) CFR
Charles Bray III (Senegal) CFR
Arthur Burns (W. Germany) CFR
Francis Cook (Burundi) CFR
Walter Cutler (Tunisia) CFR
Horace Dawson, Jr. (Botswana) CFR
Angier Duke (Morocco) CFR

BUREAU OF AFRICAN AFFAIR... (Rhodesia, Angola, South Africa, ...)
Chester A. Crocker, (Assistant Secretary)
BUREAU OF EAST ASIAN/PACIFIC A... (Vietnam, Laos, Cambodia, Thailand, Kor...)
Paul D. Wolfowitz (Assistant Secretary)
BUREAU OF NEAR EASTERN/SOUTH ASIA (Iran, Afghanistan, etc.)
Nicholas A. Veliotes (Assistant Secretary)
BUREAU OF INTER-AMERICAN AFF... (Cuba, Nicaragua, Panama, El Salvad...)
Thomas O. Enders (Assistant Secretary)
Luigi R. Einaudi (Policy Planning/Coordinati...)

HOUSE & SENATE CFR/TC MEMBERS (Past & Present)

SENATE
● Howard Baker, Jr. (Tenn.) CFR
● Birch Bayh (Ind.) CFR
● Lloyd Bentsen (Texas) CFR
● William Brock, Jr. (Tenn.) CFR TC
● Edward Brooke (Mass.) CFR
● Clifford Case (N.J.) CFR
● Frank Church (Idaho) CFR
● Dick Clark (Iowa) CFR
● William S. Cohen (Maine) CFR TC
● Alan Cranston (Calif.) CFR TC
John Cooper (Iowa) CFR
● John Culver (Iowa) CFR TC
● John Danforth (Mo.) TC
● Daniel J. Evans (Wash.) TC
● John Glenn (Ohio) TC
Hubert Humphrey (Minn.) CFR
● Jacob Javits (N.Y.) CFR
● Ted Kennedy (Mass.) CFR
(Belongs to Boston affiliate)
Gale McGee (Wyo.) CFR
● George McGovern (S.D.) CFR
● Charles Mathias (Md.) CFR
Walter Mondale (Minn.) CFR TC

● Daniel Moynihan (N.Y.) CFR
● Edmund Muskie (Maine) CFR
● Clairborne Pell (R.I.) CFR
● Abraham Ribicoff (Conn.) CFR
William Roth (Del.) CFR TC
● Paul Sarbanes (Md.) CFR
● Adlai Stevenson (Ill.) CFR
Stuart Symington (Mo.) CFR
Robert Taft, Jr. (Ohio) CFR TC

HOUSE
John Anderson (Ill.) CFR TC
● Les Aspin (Wisc.) CFR
● J.B. Bingham (N.Y.) CFR
● John Brademas (Ind.) CFR TC
● Richard Cheney (Wyo.) CFR
● Barber Conable, Jr. (N.Y.) CFR TC
● William R. Cotter (Conn.) CFR
● Dante Fascell (Fla.) CFR
Thomas Foley (Wash.) TC
● Donald Fraser (Minn.) CFR TC
● James R. Jones (Okla.) TC
Charles Schumer (N.Y.) CFR
● Stephen Solarz (N.Y.) CFR

1984 CFR/TC PRESIDENTIAL CANDIDATES
Reuben Askew — CFR
Alan Cranston — CFR TC
John Glenn — TC
George McGovern — CFR TC
Walter Mondale — CFR TC

1980 CFR/TC PRESIDENTIAL CANDIDATES
John Anderson — CFR TC
Howard Baker — CFR
George Bush — CFR TC
Jimmy Carter — TC
Ted Kennedy — CFR
(Bostn. affiliate)

(Running CFR candidates from each party provides Rockefeller continuing control of the Executive Branch)

NOTE ● Voted to transfer ownership of the American canal in Panama to a Marxist dictatorship.

This material is not copyrighted. It may be reprinted, and reproduced in newspapers, newsletters, books and magazines. Large quantities may be obtained from F.R.E.E.

Do Not Destroy.
Retain for Future Reference.
8-84

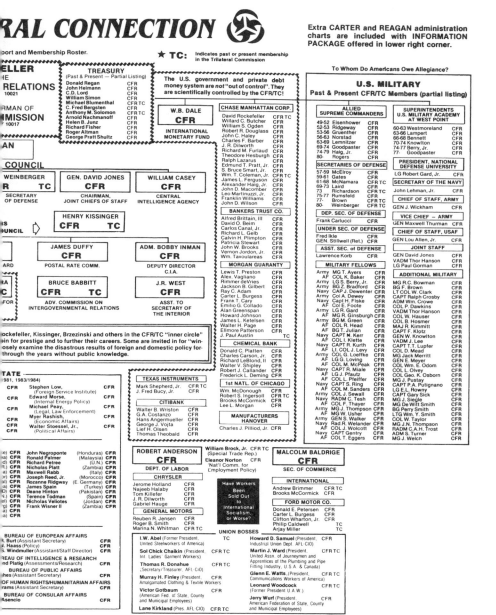

RAL CONNECTION 🔄

Extra CARTER and REAGAN administration charts are included with INFORMATION PACKAGE offered in lower right corner.

...port and Membership Roster.

★ TC: Indicates past or present membership in the Trilateral Commission

...ELLER
...E RELATIONS 10021

...RMAN OF
...MISSION 10017

TREASURY
(Past & Present — Partial Listing)

Donald Regan	CFR
John Heimann	CFR
C.D. Lord	CFR
William Simon	CFR
Michael Blumenthal	CFR TC
C. Fred Bergsten	CFR
Anthony M. Solomon	CFR TC
Arnold Nachmanoff	CFR
Helen B. Junz	CFR
Richard Fisher	CFR
Roger Altman	CFR
George Pratt Shultz	CFR

The U.S. government and private debt money system are *not* "out of control". They are scientifically controlled by the CFR/TC!

W.B. DALE
CFR
INTERNATIONAL MONETARY FUND

To Whom Do Americans Owe Allegiance?

U.S. MILITARY
Past & Present CFR/TC Members (partial listing)

CHASE MANHATTAN CORP.

David Rockefeller	CFR TC
Willard C. Butcher	CFR
William S. Ogden	CFR
Robert R. Douglass	CFR
John C. Haley	CFR
Charles F. Barber	CFR
J. R. Dilworth	CFR
Richard M. Furlaud	CFR
Theodore Hesburgh	CFR
Ralph Lazarus	CFR
Edmund T. Pratt, Jr.	CFR
S. Bruce Smart, Jr.	CFR
Wm. T. Coleman, Jr.	CFR TC
James L. Ferguson	CFR
Alexander Haig, Jr.	CFR TC
John D. Macomber	CFR
Leo Martinuzz, Jr.	CFR
Franklin Williams	CFR
John D. Wilson	CFR

...AN

...COUNCIL

WEINBERGER	GEN. DAVID JONES	WILLIAM CASEY
...R TC	**CFR**	**CFR**
SECRETARY OF DEFENSE	CHAIRMAN, JOINT CHIEFS OF STAFF	CENTRAL INTELLIGENCE AGENCY

...S
...UNCIL ▷

HENRY KISSINGER
CFR   TC

JAMES DUFFY	ADM. BOBBY INMAN
CFR	**CFR**
POSTAL RATE COMM.	DEPUTY DIRECTOR C.I.A.

...ARD

BRUCE BABBITT	J.R. WEST
CFR TC	**CFR**
ADV. COMMISSION ON INTERGOVERNMENTAL RELATIONS	ASST. TO SECRETARY OF THE INTERIOR

...ockefeller, Kissinger, Brzezinski and others in the CFR/TC "inner circle" ...ein for prestige and to further their careers. Some are invited in for "win- ...osely examine the disastrous results of foreign and domestic policy for- ...through the years without public knowledge.

BANKERS TRUST CO.

Alfred Brittain, III	CFR
David O. Beim	CFR
Carlos Canal, Jr.	CFR
Richard L. Gelb	CFR
Calvin H. Plimpton	CFR
Patricia Stewart	CFR
John W. Brooks	CFR
Vernon Jordon, Jr.	CFR
Wm. Tavoulareas	CFR

MORGAN GUARANTY

Lewis T. Preston	CFR
Alex. Vagliano	CFR
Rimmer deVries	CFR
Jackson B. Gilbert	CFR
Ray C. Adam	CFR
Carter L. Burgess	CFR
Frank T. Cary	CFR
Emilio G. Collado	CFR
Alan Greenspan	CFR
Howard Johnson	CFR
James L. Ketelsen	CFR
Walter H. Page	CFR
Ellmore Patterson	CFR
J. Paul Austin	TC

CHEMICAL BANK

Donald C. Platten	CFR
Charles Carson, Jr.	CFR
Richard LeBlond, II	CFR
Walter V. Shipley	CFR
Robert J. Callander	CFR
Frederick L. Deming	CFR

TEXAS INSTRUMENTS

Mark Shepherd, Jr.	CFR TC
J. Fred Bucy, Jr.	CFR

CITIBANK

Walter B. Wriston	CFR
G.A. Costanzo	CFR
Hans Angermueller	CFR
George J. Vojta	CFR
Lief H. Olsen	CFR
Thomas Theobald	CFR

1st NATL. OF CHICAGO

Wm. McDonough	CFR
Robert S. Ingersoll	CFR TC
Brooks McCormick	CFR
Lee L. Morgan	CFR

MANUFACTURERS HANOVER

Charles J. Pilliod, Jr.	CFR

ALLIED SUPREME COMMANDERS

49-52	Eisenhower	CFR
52-53	Ridgeway	CFR
53-56	Gruenther	CFR
56-63	Norstad	CFR
63-69	Lemnitzer	CFR
69-74	Goodpaster	CFR
74-79	Haig, Jr.	CFR
80-	Rogers	CFR

SECRETARIES OF DEFENSE

57-59	McElroy	CFR
59-61	Gates	CFR
61-68	McNamara	CFR TC
69-73	Laird	CFR
73	Richardson	CFR TC
75-77	Rumsfeld	CFR
77-	Brown	CFR TC
80-	Weinberger	CFR TC

DEP. SEC. OF DEFENSE
Frank Carlucci   CFR

UNDER SEC. OF DEFENSE

Fred Ikle	CFR
GEN. Stillwell (Ret.)	CFR

ASST. SEC. of DEFENSE
Lawrence Korb   CFR

MILITARY FELLOWS

Army	MG T. Ayers	CFR
AF	COL K. Baker	CFR
Army	LG S. Berry, Jr.	CFR
Army	BG Z. Bradford	CFR
Navy	CAP J. Dewenter	CFR
Army	Col A. Dewey	CFR
Navy	Capt H. Fiske	CFR
AF	Col E. Foote	CFR
Army	LG R. Gard	CFR
AF	MG R. Ginsburgh	CFR
Army	BG M. Green	CFR
AF	COL R. Head	CFR
AF	BG T. Julian	CFR
Navy	CAPT N. Kerr	CFR
AF	COL I. Klette	CFR
Navy	CAPT R. Kurth	CFR
AF	LT. COL J. Levy	CFR
Army	COL G. Loeffke	CFR
AF	LG G. Loving	CFR
AF	COL M. McPeak	CFR
Navy	CAPT R. Miale	CFR
AF	LG J. Pfautz	CFR
AF	COL L. Pfeiffer	CFR
Navy	CAPT S. Ring	CFR
AF	COL M. Sanders	CFR
Army	COL J. Sewall	CFR
Navy	RADM C. Tesh	CFR
AF	COL F. Thayer	CFR
Army	MG J. Thompson	CFR
AF	MG W. Usher	CFR
Army	GEN S. Walker	CFR
Navy	Rad.R. Welander	CFR
AF	COL J. Wolcott	CFR
Navy	CAPT Gentry	CFR
AF	COL T. Eggers	CFR

SUPERINTENDENTS U.S. MILITARY ACADEMY AT WEST POINT

60-63	Westmoreland	CFR
63-66	Lampert	CFR
66-68	Bennett	CFR
70-74	Knowlton	CFR
74-77	Berry, Jr.	CFR
77-	Goodpaster	CFR

PRESIDENT, NATIONAL DEFENSE UNIVERSITY
LG Robert Gard, Jr.   CFR

SECRETARY OF THE NAVY
John Lehman, Jr.   CFR

CHIEF OF STAFF, ARMY
GEN J. Wickham   CFR

VICE CHIEF — ARMY
GEN Maxwell Thurman   CFR

CHIEF OF STAFF, USAF
GEN Lou Allen, Jr.   CFR

JOINT STAFF

GEN David Jones	CFR
VADM Thor Hanson	CFR
LG Paul Gorman	CFR

ADDITIONAL MILITARY

MG R.C. Bowman	CFR
BG F. Brown	CFR
LT COL W. Clark	CFR
CAPT Ralph Crosby	CFR
ADM Wm. Crowe	CFR
COL P. Dawkins	CFR
VADM Thor Hanson	CFR
COL W. Hauser	CFR
COL B. Hosmer	CFR
MAJ R. Kimmitt	CFR
CAPT F. Klotz	CFR
GEN W. Knowlton	CFR
VADM J. Lee	CFR
CAPT T.T. Lupfer	CFR
COL D. Mead	CFR
MG Jack Merritt	CFR
GEN E. Meyer	CFR
COL Wm. E. Odom	CFR
COL L. Olvey	CFR
COL Geo. K. Osborn	CFR
MG J. Pustay	CFR
CAPT P.A. Putignano	CFR
LG E.L. Rowny	CFR
CAPT Gary Sick	CFR
MG J. Siegle	CFR
MG De Witt Smith	CFR
BG Perry Smith	CFR
LTG Wm. Y. Smith	CFR
COL W. Taylor	CFR
MG J.N. Thompson	CFR
RADM C.A.H. Trost	CFR
ADM S. Turner	CFR
MG J. Welch	CFR

...TATE ...981; 1983/1984)

CFR	Stephen Low, (Foreign Service Institute)	CFR
CFR	Edward Morse, (Internal Energy Policy)	CFR
CFR	Michael Peay, (Legal, Law Enforcement)	CFR
CFR	Myer Rashish, (Economic Affairs)	CFR
CFR	Walter Stoessel, Jr., (Political Affairs)	CFR

...e)	CFR	John Negroponte (Honduras)	CFR
...a)	CFR	Ronald Palmer (Malaysia)	CFR
...d)	CFR	Richard Petree (U.N.)	CFR
...R)	CFR	Nicholas Platt (Zambia)	CFR
a)	CFR	Maxwell Rabb (Italy)	CFR
...r)	CFR	Joseph Reed, Jr. (Morocco)	CFR
...a)	CFR	Rozanne Ridgway (E. Germany)	CFR
a)	CFR	James Spain (Turkey)	CFR
O)	CFR	Deane Hinton (Pakistan)	CFR
...\)	CFR	Terence Todman (Spain)	CFR
...e)	CFR	Nicholas Veliotes (Jordan)	CFR
...g)	CFR	Frank Wisner II (Zambia)	CFR
...a)	CFR		
...a)	CFR		

BUREAU OF EUROPEAN AFFAIRS

...R. Burt (Assistant Secretary)	CFR
...J. Haass (Policy)	CFR
...5. Windmuller (Assistant/Staff Director)	CFR

...REAU OF INTELLIGENCE & RESEARCH
...nd Platig (Assessments/Research)   CFR

BUREAU OF PUBLIC AFFAIRS
...hes (Assistant Secretary)   CFR

OF HUMAN RIGHTS/HUMANITARIAN AFFAIRS
...rams (Assistant Secretary)   CFR

BUREAU OF CONSULAR AFFAIRS
...Asencio   CFR

ROBERT ANDERSON
CFR
DEPT. OF LABOR

CHRYSLER

Jerome Holland	CFR
Najeeb Halaby	CFR
Tom Killefer	CFR
J. R. Dilworth	CFR
Gabriel Hauge	CFR

GENERAL MOTORS

Reuben R. Jensen	CFR
Roger B. Smith	CFR
Marina N. Whitman	CFR TC

William Brock, Jr. CFR TC
(Special Trade Rep.)

Eleanor Norton CFR
'Nat'l Comm. for Employment Policy)

Have Workers Been Sold Out to International Socialism, or Worse?

UNION BOSSES

I.W. Abel (Former President, United Steelworkers of America)	TC
Sol Chick Chaikin (President, Int. Ladies' Garment Workers)	CFR TC
Thomas R. Donahue (Secretary/Treasurer, AFL-CIO)	CFR TC
Murray H. Finley (President, Amalgamated Clothing & Textile Workers)	CFR
Victor Gotbaum (American Fed. of State, County and Municipal Employees)	CFR
Lane Kirkland (Pres. AFL-CIO)	CFR TC

MALCOLM BALDRIGE
CFR
SEC. OF COMMERCE

INTERNATIONAL

Andrew Brimmer	CFR TC
Brooks McCormick	CFR

FORD MOTOR CO.

Donald E. Petersen	CFR
Carter L. Burgess	CFR
Clifton Wharton, Jr.	CFR
Philip Caldwell	TC
Arjay Miller	TC

Howard D. Samuel (President, Industrial Union Dept. AFL-CIO)	CFR
Martin J. Ward (President, United Assn. of Journeymen and Apprentices of the Plumbing and Pipe Fitting Industry, U.S.A. & Canada)	CFR TC
Glenn E. Watts (President, Communications Workers of America)	CFR TC
Leonard Woodcock (Former President U.A.W.)	CFR TC
Jerry Wurf (President, American Federation of State, County and Municipal Employees)	CFR

Good Times - Bad Times
Recession - Depression

Influence or control of money, mail, media, military, IRS/tax courts, commerce, energy, unions, domestic and foreign policy, etc. provides an apparent opportunity for massive fraud, robbery, and control of the American people!

THE CFR / TRILATERAL /

MEDIA

CBS
Laurence A. Tisch,CEO CFR
Roswell Gilpatric CFR
James Houghton CFR/TC
Henry Schacht CFR/TC
Dan Rather CFR
Richard Hottelet CFR
Frank Stanton CFR

NBC/RCA
John F. Welch,Jr.,CEO CFR
Jane Pfeiffer CFR
Lester Crystal CFR/TC
R. W. Sonnenfeldt CFR/TC
John Petty CFR
Tom Brokaw CFR
David Brinkley CFR
John Chancellor CFR
Marvin Kalb CFR
Irving R. Levine CFR
Herbert Schlosser CFR
Peter G. Peterson CFR
John Sawhill CFR

ABC
Thomas S. Murphy, CEO CFR
John Connor CFR
Diane Sawyer CFR
John Scali CFR

CABLE NEWS NETWORK
Daniel Schorr CFR

PUBLIC BROADCAST SERVICE
Robert McNeil CFR
Jim Lehrer CFR
C. Hunter-Gault CFR
Hodding Carter III CFR
Daniel Schorr CFR
David Gergen CFR

ASSOCIATED PRESS
Keith Fuller CFR
Stanley Swinton CFR
Louis Boccardi CFR
Harold Anderson CFR
Katharine Graham CFR/TC

REUTERS
Micheal Posner CFR

BALTIMORE SUN
Henry Trewhitt CFR

WASHINGTON TIMES
Arnaud de Borchgrave CFR

CHILDREN'S TV WORKSHOP (Sesame Street)
Joan Ganz Cooney, Pres. CFR

NEW YORK TIME CO.
Richard Gelb CFR
William Scranton CFR/TC
John F. Akers Dir. CFR
Louis V. Gerstner, Jr. " CFR
George B. Munroe " CFR
Donald M. Stewart " CFR
Cyrus R. Vance " CFR
A.M. Rosenthal CFR
Seymour Topping CFR
James Greenfield CFR
Max Frankel CFR
Jack Rosenthal CFR
John Oakes CFR
Harrison Salisbury CFR
H.L. Smith CFR
Steven Rattner CFR
Richard Burt CFR

TIME, INC.
Ralph Davidson CFR
Donald M. Wilson CFR
Henry Grunwald CFR
Alexander Heard CFR
Sol Linowitz CFR/TC
Thomas Watson, Jr. CFR

NEWSWEEK/WASH. POST
Katharine Graham CFR
N. deB. Katzenbach CFR
Frederick Beebe CFR
Robert Christopher CFR
Osborne Elliot CFR
Phillip Geyelin CFR
Murry Marder CFR
Maynard Parker CFR
George Will CFR/TC
Robert Kaiser CFR
Meg Greenfield CFR
Walter Pincus CFR
Murray Gart CFR
Peter Osnos CFR
Don Oberdorfer CFR

DOW JONES & CO. (Wall St. Journal)
Richard Wood CFR
Robert Bartley CFR/TC
Karen House CFR

NATIONAL REVIEW
Wm. F. Buckley, Jr. CFR

READERS DIGEST
George V. Grune, CEO CFR
William G. Bowen, Dir. CFR

SYNDICATED COLUMNISTS
Georgie Anne Geyer CFR
Ben J. Wattenberg CFR

BUSINESS & INDUSTRY LEADERS

Richard D. Wood	CEO, Eli Lily & Co.	CFR
Richard M. Furlaud	CEO, Bristol-Myers Squibb Co.	CFR
Frank Peter Popoff	CEO, Dow Chemical Co.	CFR
Charles Peter McColough	Chmn Ex. Comm, Xerox	CFR
Rozanne L. Ridgeway	Dir., 3M, RJR Nabisco, Union Carbide	CFR
Ruben F. Mettler	former CEO, TRW, Inc.	CFR
Henry B. Schacht	CEO, Cummins Engines	CFR
Edmund T. Pratt, Jr.	CEO, Pfizer, Inc.	CFR
Rand V. Araskog	CEO, ITT Corp.	CFR
W. Michael Blumenthal	Chmn, UNISYS Corp.	CFR
Joseph John Sisco	Dir., GEICO, Raytheon, Gilette	CFR
J. Fred Bucy	former Pres, CEO, Texas Instruments	CFR

Sources:
1. *The United States Government Manual 1991/92*, Office of the Federal Register - National Archives and Records Administration
2. *Standard & Poor's Register of Corporations, Directors and Executives 1991*
3. *Annual Report 1991/92*, The Council on Foreign Relations, Pratt House, New York City

★ ★ ★ ★ ★ ★ ★ ★ ★ ★ ★ ★

100 Copies shipped postpaid for contribution of $25.00 or more. State quantity wanted when larger contribtutions are made.

★ ★ ★ ★ ★ ★ ★ ★ ★ ★ ★ ★

Non-copyrighted educational material: Order or re-print for distribution to local/state/federal officials, law enforcement officers, ministers,friends, relatives, students, teachers, and citizens from every walk of life. It may be reprinted, and reproduced in newspapers, newsletters, books and magazines. Large quantities may be obtained from F.R.E.E.
PLEASE GIVE CREDIT TO F.R.E.E.

★ ★ ★ ★ ★ ★ ★ ★ ★ ★ ★ ★

Fund to Restore an Educated Electorate
★ ★ ★ ★ P.O. BOX 33339 KERRVILLE, TX 78029 ★ ★ ★ ★

ENERGY COMPANIES

EXXON CORPORATION
Lawrence G. Rawl, Chmn, CFR
Lee R. Raymond, Pres. CFR
Jack F. Bennett, Sr. VP CFR
Jack G. Clarke, Sr. VP CFR

TEXACO
Alfred C. DeCrane, Jr. Chmn. CFR
John Brademas Dir. CFR
Willard C. Butcher " CFR
William J. Crowe, Jr. " CFR
John K. McKinley " CFR
Thomas S. Murphy " CFR

ATLANTIC RICHFIELD-ARCO
Hannah H. Gray CFR
Donald M. Kendall CFR/TC

SHELL OIL CO.
Frank H. Richardson, CEO CFR
Rand V. Araskog, Dir. CFR

MOBIL CORP.
Allan E. Murray, Chmn. & Pres. CFR
Lewis M. Branscomb, Dir. CFR
Helene L. Kaplan, " CFR
Charles S. Sanford, Jr. " CFR

TENNECO, INC.
James L. Ketelsen, Chmn. CFR
W. Michael Blumenthal, Dir. CFR
Joseph J. Sisco, " CFR

INDUSTRY

DEERE & CO.
Hans W. Becherer,Chmn & CEO CFR

IBM
John F. Akers, Chmn. CFR
C. Michael Armstrong, Sr. VP CFR
Richard W. Lyman, Dir. CFR

AMTRAK (National RR Passenger Corp.)
William S. Norman, Exec. VP CFR

AMERICAN TELEPHONE & TELEGRAPH CO. (AT&T)
Robert E. Allen, Chmn, & CEO CFR
Juanita M. Krepo, Dir. CFR
Donald F. McHenry " CFR
Henry B. Schacht " CFR
Michael I. Sovern " CFR
Franklin A. Thomas " CFR
Rawleigh Warner, Jr. " CFR
Thomas H. Wyman " CFR

CHRYSLER CORPORATION
Joseph A. Califano, Jr. Dir. CFR
Peter A. Magowan " CFR

GENERAL MOTORS CORP.
Anne L. Armstrong Dir. CFR
Marvin L. Goldberger " CFR
Edmund T. Pratt, Jr. " CFR
Dennis Weatherstone " CFR
Leon H. Sullivan " CFR
Thomas H. Wyman " CFR

FORD MOTOR COMPANY
Clifton R. Wharton Dir. CFR
Roberto C. Goizueta " CFR/TC
Drew Lewis " CFR

GE / NBC
John F. Welch, Jr. Chmn. CFR
David C. Jones CFR
Lewis T. Preston CFR
Frank H.T. Rhodes CFR
Walter B. Wriston TC

AMERICAN EXPRESS CO.
James D. Robinson, CEO CFR
Anne L. Armstrong CFR
William g. Bowen CFR
Charles W. Duncan, Jr. CFR
Richard M. Furland CFR
Vernon E. Jordan, Jr. CFR
Henry A. Kissinger CFR
Frank P. Popoff CFR
Robert V. Roosa CFR
Joseph H. Williams CFR

"The Council on Foreign Relations is the American Branch of a society which originated in England...(and)...believes national boundaries should be obliterated and one-world rule established...

"The Trilateral Commission is international ...(and)... is intended to be the vehicle for multinational consolidation of the commercial and banking interests by siezing control of the political government of the United States."
WITH NO APOLOGIES.
Senator Barry Goldwater

Da
C
COUNCIL
58 E. 68th St. New York, NY
NORTH A
The TRIL
345 E. 46th St. New

1992 PRESIDENTIAL CANDIDATES
Bill Clinton CFR/TC
Mario M. Cuomo CFR
Jesse L. Jackson, Sr. CFR

(Forme
NATION

Brent Scowcroft CFR/TC — NATIONAL SECURITY ADVISOR
Dan Quayle (Non-Member) — VICE PRESIDENT
James Ba (Non-Memb — SECRETARY OF
Dick Thornburgh CFR — ATTORNEY GENERAL
Nicholas F. Brady CFR — TREASURY SECRETARY
Ri

JUDICIARY
Sandra Day O'Connor, Asso. Justice, U. S. Supreme Court CFR
Steven G. Breyer, Chief Judge US Court of Appeals, First Circuit, Boston CFR
Ruth B. Ginsburg, US Court of Appeals, Wash., DC Circuit CFR
Laurence H. Silberman, US Court of Appeals, Wash., DC Circuit CFR

U.S. INSTITUTE FOR PEACE
John Norton Moore, Chairman CFR
Elspeth Davies Rostow, Vice Chmn CFR
Samuel W. Lewis, President CFR
John Richardson, Counselor CFR
David Little, Senior. Scholar CFR
William R. Kintner, Dir. CFR
W. Scott Thompson, Dir. CFR

DEPARTMENT OF TRANSPORTATION
Elaine L. Chao, Deputy Secretary CFR

FEDERAL JUDICIAL CENTER
William W. Schwarzer, Director CFR

AGENCY FOR INTERNATIONAL DEVELOPEMENT (AID)
Donald W. Roskens, Actg. Dir., Adm of AID CFR
Richard E. Bissell, Asst.Adm. For Science CFR

OFFICE OF U. S. TRADE REP.
Gary R. Edson, Ch. of Staff & Counselor CFR
Joshua Bolten, Gen. Counsel CFR
Daniel M. Price, Dep. Gen. Counsel CFR

OFFICE OF TECHNOLOGY ASSESSMENT
Joshua Lederberg, V. Chmn Adv. Counc. CFR
John H. Gibbons, Director CFR
Lewis M. Branscomb, Adv. Council CFR

ENVIRONMENTAL PROTECTION AGENCY
James M. Strock, Asst. Adm., Enforcement & Compliance CFR

AFRICAN DEVELOPMENT FOUNDATION
Leonard H. Robinson, Jr., President CFR

"The People are entitled to know who controls their government."

Johnny Stewart
Founder of F.R.E.E.

TREASURY DEPARTM (Past & Present)
John Heimann
William E. Simon
Michael Blumenthal
C. Fred Bergsten
Anthony M. Solomon
Arnold Nachmanoff
Helen B. Junz
Richard W. Fisher
Roger C. Altman
Robert R. Glauber, Under Sec., Finance
David C. Mulford, Under Sec., Intntl Affairs
Robert M. Bestani, Dep. Asst. Sec., Intntl. Monetary Affairs
J. French Hill, Dep. Asst. Sec., Corp. Finance
John M. Niehuss, Dep. Asst. Sec., Intntl. Monetary Affairs

Reginald Bartholome
International Security
Lawrence S. Eagleba
Brandon H. Grove, Di
Service Institute
H. Allen Holmes, Asst
Military Affairs
John H. Kelly, Asst. S
South Asian Affairs
Robert M. Kimmitt, Un
Ivan Selin, Under Sec.
Richard H. Solomon,
& Pacific Affairs
Alexander F. Watson,
Thomas R. Pickering,
Jonathan Moore, UN
Joseph Verner Reed,
Dennis B. Ross, Dir. P
Herman J. Cohen, Ass
Edward Perkins, Dir. o
Abraham David Sofae
Robert B. Zoellick, Co

UNITE

SENATORS
David L. Boren (D), OK CFR
Rudy Boshwitz (R), MN CFR
William Bradley (D), NJ CFR
John H. Chafee (R), RI CFR
William S. Cohen (R), ME CFR
Christopher J. Dodd (D), CT CFR
Bob Graham (D), FL CFR
Joseph I. Lieberman (D), CT CFR
George J. Mitchell (D), ME CFR
Claiborne Pell (D), RI CFR
Larry Pressler (R), SD CFR
Charles S. Robb (D), VA CFR
John D. Rockefeller, IV (D), WV CFR

NOTE: The "New World Order" views of Rockefeller, Kissinger, Brzezinski and others in the CFR/TC "inner circle" may not be shared by all members. Some join for prestige and to further their careers. Some are invited in for "window dressing".However, all members have had ample opportunity to observe the disastrous results of foreign and domestic policy formulated and implemented by the CFR without public knowledge and should be held accountable.

ME-2

WORLD ORDER CONNECTION

★ CFR	Indicates membership in the Council on Foreign Relations.
★ TC	Indicates membership in the Trilateral Commision:

FEDERAL RESERVE SYSTEM
(Past & Present) - Partial Listing

Alan Greenspan, Chairman	CFR/TC
E. Gerald Corrigan, V. Chmn.	
Pres., NY Fed. Res. Bank	CFR
Richard N. Cooper,Chmn. Boston	CFR
Sam Y. Cross, Mgr. Foreign Open Market Acct.	CFR
Robert F. Erburu, Chmn., San Fran	CFR
Robert P. Forrestal, Pres. Atlanta	CFR
Bobby R. Inman, Chmn., Dallas	CFR/TC
Robert H. Knight, Esq.	CFR
Steven Muller	CFR
John R. Opel	CFR
Anthony M. Solomon	CFR/TC
Edwin M. Truman, Staff Dir. International Finance	CFR
Cyrus R. Vance	CFR
Paul Volcker	CFR/TC

The Federal Reserve System and Bank is a privately owned corporation. By its control of the money supply and the interest rate, it effectively controls the economy of the United States.

U.S. MILITARY

DEPARTMENT OF DEFENSE		JOINT CHIEFS OF STAFF	
Richard B. Cheney, Secretary of Defense	CFR	Gen. Colin L. Powell, Chmn.	CFR
Henry S. Rowen, Asst. Sec.	CFR	Gen. Carl E. Vuono, Army	CFR
Judy Ann Miller, Dep. Asst. Sec. for Manpower	CFR	Gen. Michael J. Dugan, AF	CFR
Franklin C. Miller, Dep. Asst. Sec. Nuclear Fcs & Arms Control	CFR	Gen. John T. Chain, CO SACC Gen. Merrill A. McPeak, CO	CFR CFR
W. Bruce Weinrod, Dep. Asst.Sec. Europe & NATO	CFR	Pac AF Lt. Gen. George L. Butler, Dir. Strat Plans & Policy	CFR
Adm. Seymour Weiss, Chmn, Defense Policy Bd.	CFR	Lt. Gen. Charles T. Boyd, Com. Air Univ.	CFR
Charles M. Herzfeld, Dir. Def. Research & Eng.	CFR	Lt. Gen. Bradley C. Hosmer AF Inspector General	CFR
Andrew W. Marshall, Dir. Net Assessment	CFR	SECRETARIES OF DEFENSE	
Michael P. W. Stone, Secretary of the Army	CFR	57-59 McElroy	CFR
Donald B. Rice, Secretary of the Air Force	CFR	59-61 Gates	CFR
		61-68 McNamara	CFR/TC
		69-73 Laird	CFR
ALLIED SUPREME COMMANDERS		73-75 Richardson	CFR/TC
49-52 Eisenhower	CFR	75-77 Rumsfeld	CFR
52-53 Ridgeway	CFR	77-80 Brown	CFR/TC
53-56 Gruenther	CFR	80-88 Weinberger	CFR/TC
56-63 Norstad	CFR	88- Carlucci	CFR
63-69 Lemnitzer	CFR	88- Cheney	CFR
69-74 Goodpaster	CFR	ADDITIONAL MILITARY	
74-79 Haig	CFR	MG R.C. Bowman	CFR
		BG F. Brown	CFR
SUPERINTENDENTS U.S. MILITARY ACADEMY AT WEST POINT		LT COL. W. Clark	CFR
		ADM Wm. Crowe	CFR
60-63 Westmoreland	CFR	COL P. M. Dewkins	CFR
63-66 Lampert	CFR	V.ADM Thor Hanson	CFR
66-68 Bennett	CFR	COL W. Hauser	CFR
70-74 Knowlton	CFR	MAJ R. Kimmitt	CFR
74-77 Berry	CFR	GEN W. Knowlton	CFR
		V. ADM J. Lee	CFR
CFR MILITARY FELLOWS, 1991		COL D. Mead	CFR
Col. William M. Drennan, Jr. USAF		M G Jack Merritt	CFR
Col. Wallace C. Gregson, USMC		GEN E. Meyer	CFR
Col. Jack B. Wood, USA		COL Wm. E. Odom	CFR
		COL L. Olvey	CFR
CFR MILITARY FELLOWS, 1992		COL Geo. K. Osborn	CFR
Col. David M. Mize, USMC		MG J. Pustay	CFR
Col. John P. Rose USA		LG E.L. Rowny	CFR
		CAPT Gary Sick	CFR
		MG De Witt Smith	CFR
		BG Perry Smith	CFR
		LTG Wm. Y. Smith	CFR
		COL W. Taylor	CFR
		ADM S. Turner	CFR
		MG J. Welch	CFR
		GEN J. Wickham	CFR

CHASE MANHATTAN CORP.

Thomas G. Labrecque, Chmn. & CEO	CFR/TC
Robert R. Douglass, V. Chmn.	CFR
Willard C. Butcher, Dir.	CFR
Richard W. Lyman	* CFR
Joan Ganz Cooney	* CFR
David T. McLaughlin	* CFR
Edmund T. Pratt, Jr.	* CFR
Henry B. Schacht	* CFR

CHEMICAL BANK

Walter V. Shipley, Chmn.	CFR
Robert J. Callander, Pres.	CFR
William C. Pierce, Exec. Off.	CFR
Randolph W. Bromery Dir.	CFR
Charles W. Duncan, Jr.	* CFR
George V. Grune	* CFR
Helen L. Kaplan	* CFR
Lawrence G. Rawl	* CFR
Michael I. Sovern	* CFR
Richard D. Wood	* CFR

CITICORP

John S. Reed, Chmn.	CFR
William R. Rhodes, V. Chmn.	CFR
Richard S. Braddock, Pres.	CFR
John M. Deutch Dir.	CFR
Clifton C. Garvin, Jr.	* CFR
C. Peter McColough	* CFR
Rozenne L. Ridgeway *	CFR
Franklin A. Thomas	CFR

FIRST CITY BANCORP, TEXAS
A. Robert Abboud, CEO.	CFR

MORGAN GUARANTY
Lewis T. Preston, Chmn.	CFR

BANKERS TRUST NEW YORK CORPORATION

Charles S. Stanford, Jr. , Chmn.	CFR
Alfred Brittain III, Dir.	CFR
Vernon E. Jordan, Jr., *	CFR
Richard L. Gelb,	* CFR
Patricia Carry Stewart, *	CFR

FIRST NATIONAL BANK OF CHICAGO
Barry F. Sullivan	TC

MANUFACTURERS HANOVER DIRECTORS

Cyrus Vance	CFR
G. Robert Durham	CFR
George B. Munroe	CFR
Marina V. N. Whitman	CFR/TC
Charles J. Pilliod, Jr.	CFR

BANK AMERICA

Andrew F. Brimmer Dir.	CFR
Ignazio E. Lozano, Jr.	* CFR
Ruben F. Mettler	* CFR

SECURITIES & EXCHANGE COMM.
Michael D. Mann, Dir. Intntl. Aff.	CFR

RELATIONS
(..)4-0400, FAX (212) 861-1789

N OF
SSION
(212) 661-1180

Dir.)
OUNCIL

Richard B. Cheney		Colin L. Powell		Robert M. Gates	
CFR		CFR		CFR	
SECRETARY OF DEFENSE		CHAIRMAN JOINT CHIEFS OF STAFF		DIRECTOR CENTRAL INTELLIGENCE AGENCY	

Lynn Martin		Michael Calhoun	
CFR		CFR	
SECRETARY OF LABOR		DEPT. HEALTH & HUM. SER. CHIEF OF STAFF	

WHITE HOUSE STAFF

...en Bromley, Asst. to Pres.. Nat'l Affairs; Chmn, Nat'l Critical Mat'l ...ncil.	CFR
...d D. Blackwill, Spec. Asst., NSA	CFR
...d Kanter, " "	* CFR
...la A. Lampley, " "	* CFR
...C. Miller, Jr. " "	* CFR
...W. Rodman, " "	* CFR
...las Rostow, " "	* CFR

LIBRARY OF CONGRESS

James H. Billington, Librarian, Chmn. Trust Fund Board	CFR
Ruth Ann Stewart, Asst.Librarian National Programs	CFR

NATIONAL SCIENCE FOUNDATION

Frank H. T. Rhodes, Bd. of Directors	CFR
James B. Holderman, Bd. of Directors	CFR
D. Allen Bromley, Bd. of Directors	CFR

U.S. ARMS CONTROL & DISARMAMENT AGENCY

Thomas Graham, Jr., General Council	CFR
William Schneider, Chmn.. General Advisory Council	CFR
Richard Burt, Negotiator on Strategic Defense Arms	CFR
David Smith, Negotiator, Defense & Space	CFR
R. James Woolsey, Negotiator, European Arms	CFR

EXPORT-IMPORT BANK

... Macomber, Pres. & Chmn	CFR
...s K. Lawson, 1st VP & Vice Chmn	
...Rodriguez, Director	CFR
...ssenden, General Council	CFR

OFFICE OF SCIENCE & TECHNOLOGY POLICY
...n R. Graham, Jr., ...ce Advisor To President & Director	CFR

PARTMENT OF STATE
CFR

CFR/TC
...co - CFR
CFR
...ffairs CFR
CFR
...ions CFR
CFR
CFR
CFR
CFR
CFR
CFR
CFR

AMBASSADORS

Morton I. Abramowitz,	(Turkey)	CFR
Michael H. Armacost,	(Japan)	CFR
Shirley Temple Black	(Czechoslovakia)	CFR
Julia Chang Bloch	(Nepal)	CFR
Henry E. Catto, Jr.,	(Great Britain)	CFR
Frances Cook	(Camaroon)	CFR
Edward P. Djerejian	(Syria)	CFR
George E. Moose	(Senegal)	CFR
John D. Negroponte,	(Mexico)	CFR
Edward N. Ney,	(Canada)	CFR
Robert B. Oakley	(Pakistan)	CFR
Robert H. Pelletreau, Jr.	(Tunisia)	CFR
Christopher H. Phillips	(Brunei)	CFR
Nicholas Platt,	(Philippines)	CFR
James W. Spain,	(Maldives & Sri Lanka)	CFR
Robert S. Strauss	(Russia)	CFR
Terence A. Todman,	(Argentina)	CFR
Frank G. Wisner II,	(Egypt)	CFR
Warren Zimmerman,	(Yugoslavia)	CFR

CFR INFLUENCE IN THE SMITHSONIAN INSTITUTE

Robert McCormick Adams, Secretary	CFR
Anne L. Armetrong, Bd. of Regents	CFR
William J. Baroody, Jr. Chmn. Bd. of Trustees, Woodrow Wilson International Center For Scholars	CFR
William G. Bowen, Bd. of Regents	CFR
James D. Wolfensohn, Chmn, John F. Kennedy Center For Performing Arts	CFR
Murray Gell-Mann, Bd. of Regents	CFR
R. James Woolsey, Bd. of Regents	CFR

No one escapes when freedom fails.
The best men rot in filthy jails, and those who cried,
'Appease, Appease!'
Are hanged by those they tried to please.

NGRESS CFR/TC MEMBERS

... (R), DE	CFR/TC	
...nan (R), NH	CFR	
...), NC	CFR	
...h (D), CO	CFR	
ESENTATIVES		
...n	CFR	
...an (D), CA	CFR	
...l (D), FL	CFR	
...(D), WA	CFR	
...(D), CT	CFR	
...hardt (D), MO	CFR	
...rich (R), GA	CFR	
...ry	CFR	
..., III (R), NY	CFR	

Amory Houghton, Jr. (R), NY	CFR
Nancy Lee Johnson (R), CT	CFR
John Lewis (D) GA	CFR
Robert T. Matsui (D), CA	CFR
Dave K. McCurdy (D), OK	CFR
Jim Moody (D), WI	CFR
Thomas E. Petri (R), WI	CFR
Patricia Schroeder (D), CO	CFR
Peter Smith (R) VT	CFR
Olympia J. Snow (R) ME	CFR
Stephen J. Solarz (D), NY	CFR
John M. Spratt (D), SC	CFR
Louis Stokes (D), OH	CFR
Howard Wolpe (D), MI	CFR

COLLEGE & UNIVERSITY PRESIDENTS

Ellen V. Futter, Barnard College	CFR	Hanna Holborn Gray, University Of Chicago	CFR
Morris B. Abram, Brandeis University	CFR	Steven Muller, Johns Hopkins University	CFR
Michael I. Sovern, Columbia University	CFR	Joseph Duffey, Chans., Univ. of Massachusetts	CFR
Frank H.T. Rhodes, Cornell University	CFR	John M Deutch, Provost, MIT	CFR
John Brademus, New York University	CFR	Bernard Harleston, City College of New York	CFR
Joshua Lederberg, Rockefeller University	CFR	Nannerl O. Keohane, Wellesley University	CFR
Alice S. Ilchman, Sarah Lawrence College	CFR	William H. Danforth, Washington University St. Louis	CFR
Donald Kennedy, Stanford University	CFR	William G. Bowen, Princeton University	CFR
Richard Wall Lyman, Pres. Em., Stanford	CFR	Chang-Lin Tien, Jr., Chmn, Rice University	CFR
Benno C. Schmidt, Jr. Yale University	CFR	Donna E. Shalala, University Of Wisconsin	CFR/TC
Edward T. Foote, II, University Of Miami	CFR	Wesley W. Posvar, University Of Pittsburg	CFR
James T. Laney, Emory University	CFR	Vartan Gregorian, Brown University	CFR
Thomas Ehrlich, Indiana University	CFR	Randolph W. Bromery, Westfield, Mass. State Coll.	CFR
S. Frederick Starr, Oberlin College	CFR	John D. Wilson, Washington & Lee University	CFR

Chapter 6

THE TRILATERAL COMMISSION

In July 1972 the organizational meetings of the Trilateral Commission were held at the estate of David Rockefeller, chairman of the Council on Foreign Relations. The eight American representatives at this meeting were all members of the CFR. David Rockefeller, chairman of the Chase Manhattan Bank, along with Jimmy Carter's national security advisor, Zbigniew Brzezinski, officially established the Trilateral Commission in 1973.

In the July 1973 issue of *Foreign Affairs*, Brzezinski set the direction for America: "Without closer American - European - Japanese cooperation the major problems of today cannot be effectively tackled...the active promotion of such trilateral cooperation must now become the central priority of U.S. policy."[114]

Members are drawn from international business, banking, government, academia, and mass media. The purpose of the Trilateral Commission is to engineer an enduring partnership among the ruling classes of North America, Western Europe, and Japan— thus trilateral. These trilateral "regions" have the largest shares of world trade and finance and produce two-thirds of the world's output. The desire of the Trilateral Commission is that these regions remain the vital centers of management, finance, and technology; that is, power and control for the world economy.

The Trilateralists have kindly "volunteered" to take the lead in "coping with pressing problems and shaping emerging conditions."[115]

They seek an age of post-nationalism when, devoid of ethnic culture and history, the social, economic, and political values esteemed by the Trilateral "volunteers" will be transformed into universal values. That is, a universal economy, a universal government (appointed, not elected), and a universal faith. Like-minded government officials and business leaders are to carry out national and international policy formation. There must be "more technical focus, and lesser public awareness."[116] This lessens the chance for people to grasp the overall scheme of the world managers and organize serious resistance.

The Trilateralists assert that "the public and leaders of most countries continue to live in a mental universe which no longer exists—a world of separate nations—and have great difficulty thinking in terms of global perspectives and interdependence."[117] One of the most pressing issues the Trilateralists face is the citizens' love for their country. Brzezinski has nixed that concept in pointing out that "national sovereignty is no longer a viable concept."[118]

In his book *With No Apologies*, Senator Barry Goldwater says, "What the Trilaterals truly intend is the creation of a worldwide economic power superior to the political government of the nation-states involved. As managers and creators of the system they will rule the world."[119]

The commission's aim is to "nurture habits and practices of working together," and to "renovate" the international political economy in the interest of global business and finance. The recent signing of the free-trade pact with Canada and Mexico is a perfect example of Trilateral legislation at work. Close Trilateral cooperation in keeping the peace (UN vs. Iraq, UN vs. Libya), in managing the world economy (IMF and World Bank), in fostering economic redevelopment (dependence), and alleviating world poverty (through population control) will improve the chances of a smooth and peaceful evolution of the "global" system.

Trilateral commissioners claim that every effective international system requires a custodian. This particular self-appointed custodian is an onerous one. In 1972 (Trilateralists plan twenty to thirty years ahead) the Trilateral Commission released a report titled "The Crisis of Democracy."

In this report the Trilateralists discussed the governability of democracies. The Harvard professor who authored the section on the

United States proposed a "reassertion of elite rule and decades of public apathy."[120] This was to be achieved by:

1. Reducing the expectations of the poor and middle class.
2. Increasing presidential authority.
3. Strengthening business-government cooperation in economic planning.
4. Stricter regulation and government oversight of the press.
5. Pacification of rank-and-file labor.

Hasn't this agenda begun to look familiar in the 1990s? Every time I hear the government bantering about "rights," I am certain it is my rights as an American citizen that are being stripped away. At its 1980 national convention, the American Legion passed a resolution which demanded "in the best interests of our country that the Congress of the United States launch a comprehensive investigation into the Trilateral Commission and its parent organization the Council on Foreign Relations, to determine what influence has been and is being exerted over the foreign and domestic policies of the United States."[121] Now you are beginning to understand why, in his chapter called "The Non-Elected Rulers," Goldwater wrote:

> "In my view, the Trilateral Commission represents a skillful, coordinated effort to seize control and consolidate the four centers of power: political, monetary, intellectual, and ecclesiastical."[122]

Some say that the Trilateral Commission has little, if any, influence on American politics. Or, as one Congressman's aide told me: "The Trilateral Commission has no more effect on Congress than the AARP." If that were the general belief in Washington (which it isn't), then that in itself would explain the decline and fall of the American republic.

In fact, the Trilateral Commission publishes task force reports which provide clear emphasis on policy recommendations. They also hold "impact" meetings in order to affect the decision-makers. These generate favorable press coverage for their global ideas. Meetings take place not only with the monopolized press but with congresspersons, senators, executive and congressional staffers, embassy officials, leaders of international organizations, and political bodies, e.g., the Commission of European Communities.

Proposals found in Trilateral pamphlets become embodied in summit decisions which cause implementation of policy at the highest levels. "The effect of the technique is to present to Congress, IMF amendments, World Bank commitments, trade agreements, and commodity agreements....Congress can either pass or refuse to act on these issues, but cannot substantially reformulate them."[123]

Trilateral policies do not reflect the needs of the people in the United States or even the people of the other Trilateral countries. While the politicians stress work, the family, God, and patriotism, the commission works behind the scenes to gain governmental influence "to foster understanding and support of commission recommendations both in governmental and private sectors in the three regions."[124]

Holly Sklar, in her book *Trilateralism*, says, "These men make the most important foreign, economic, and domestic policy decisions of the U. S. government today; they set the goals and direction for the administration."[125] The shape of their plan deals with an ever increasing appetite for authority, power, and control. The transnational ruling elite works to preserve the special interests of the godless capitalist upper class. Note one of the ultimate insiders, Henry Kissinger. After leaving government in 1977, he immediately became a director of the CFR and a member of the executive committee of the Trilateral Commission. To complete the picture, he was made chairman of the International Advisory Board of the Chase Manhattan Bank, owned by Mr. Trilateral himself—David Rockefeller.

Those who could benefit most from the commission's "policy-making" funded the organization from its inception. From commission financial statements these founders are listed:

David Rockefeller	$109,328
David Packard (Hewlett Packard)	88,438
George Franklin*	41,920
Ford Foundation	500,000
Lilly Endowment	300,000
Rockefeller Brothers Fund	150,000
Kettering Foundation	40,000
Thyssen Foundation	94,978
General Motors	30,000
Sears	30,000
Caterpillar	30,000
Deere	30,000
Exxon	30,000
Texas Instruments	20,000
Coca-Cola	3,500-7,500
Time	3,500-7,500
CBS	3,500-7,500

| Wells Fargo Bank | 3,500-7,500 |
| Total receipts for 1974–1976: | $1,577,133 |

*Franklin was a Rockefeller-in-law. He was executive director of the CFR 1953-1971, as well as North American secretary of the Trilateral Commission.

Senator Barry Goldwater termed the Trilateral Commission "David Rockefeller's newest international cabal." He said, "It is intended to be the vehicle for multinational consolidation of the commercial and banking interests by seizing control of the political government of the United States."[126]

Corporations and banks who now have or have had chairmen of the board, presidents, vice presidents, and directors serve on the Trilateral Commission are:

Exxon	General Electric
Texaco	ITT
Mobil	Westinghouse
Standard Oil	Union Carbide
Royal Dutch Shell	RCA
British Petroleum	NBC
Philips	CBS
General Motors	ABC
Ford	CNN
Toyota	Associated Press
Nissan	Hitachi
Mitsubishi	Sony
IBM	Proctor & Gamble
Dow Chemical	Goodyear
International Harvester	Bethlehem Steel
Bank America	Chase Manhattan
Mitsubishi Bank (Japan)	Barclays Bank (UK)
J.P. Morgan	Dresdner Bank (Germany)

Swiss Bank Corporation
Amsterdam Rotterdam Bank (Netherlands)
Bank of Montreal (Canada)
Caisse Nationale de Credit Agricole (France)

George Bush's call for a Trilateral "New World Order" is a call for a world order responsive to corporate management and corporate aspirations. Worst of all, it is in <u>direct</u> <u>violation</u> of the U.S. Constitution, the very document the President swears to uphold. The philosophical essence of the "New World Order" is in complete opposition to the U.S. Constitution and its proclamation of God-given (not man-given) dignity and American sovereignty. It is all part of the Trilateralist scheme to convert the once great USA to USA, Inc.

To promote the internationalist agenda and keep governments in line is one David Rockefeller. His opening statement to the secret Bilderberger meeting in Germany 1991 included the acknowledgment: "We are grateful to the *Washington Post, The New York Times, Time* magazine, and other great publications whose directors have attended our meetings and respected their promises of discretion [silence] for almost forty years....It would have been impossible for us to develop our plan for the world if we had been subject to the bright lights of publicity during these years."[127] This means that the machinations of the Trilateral Commission and its predecessor, the Council on Foreign Relations, have been completely blacked out by the media for forty years!

David Rockefeller is the same Trilateral founder who in 1973 met with twenty-seven heads of state including the rulers of the Soviet Union and Red China. In January 1974 Rockefeller had an audience with Pope Paul VI. Shortly thereafter the pope wrote an encyclical urging the nations of the world to form a world government. In July 1964 David Rockefeller met with Soviet Premier Nikita Khruschev. Less than four months later Premier Khruschev was out of a job. Coincidence? In August 1976 Australian Prime Minister Malcolm Fraser came to the United States to meet with President Jimmy Carter. However, before he met with the president, he met with David Rockefeller. Yet David Rockefeller, in humblest form, explains that "the Trilateral Commission is in reality a group of concerned citizens interested in fostering greater understanding and cooperation among international allies."[128]

Most recently, Rockefeller led a Trilateral delegation to Moscow (January 1989) and had a lengthy meeting with Gorbachev. He urged the Soviets to become "full partners in the global economy" and offered IMF and World Bank membership. In February of the same year, Rockefeller led a similar delegation from the Council on Foreign Relations to Warsaw, Poland, where the same kind of promises were made.

Zbigniew Brzezinski has indicated that "movement toward such a community [of developed nations] will, in all probability, require two broad and overlapping phases. The first of these would involve the forging of community links among the United States, Western Europe, and Japan. The second phase would include the extension of these links to the communist countries."[129]

Since Jimmy Carter, as governor of Georgia, had opened up trade offices for the State of Georgia in Brussels and Tokyo, Brzezinski and Rockefeller selected him as a prospective member for the Trilateral Commission. In fact, he became a founding member of the commission, and thereafter his destiny became calculable; he was a rising star.

Even though on December 13, 1973, not one panel member on "What's My Line?" could identify Carter and his occupation as governor of Georgia, Carter was already known to be dining with David Rockefeller both at his estate in New York and in London, England. Now you understand why a virtual unknown could zoom to the presidency in 1976. Carter was labeled the ultimate outsider, but he was an insider—a Trilateralist and a traitor.

In the book *I'll Never Lie to You*, Carter blatantly lied: "The people of this country know from bitter experience that we are not going to get these changes merely by shifting around the same group of insiders. The insiders have had their chance and they have not delivered. And their time has run out. The time has come for the great majority of Americans...to have a President who will turn the government of this country inside out."[130]

Carter even went so far as to denounce those "unholy alliances that have formed between money and politics,"[131] yet he didn't find them unholy enough to exclude them from his coterie.

Early on in Carter's appointee process, the *Washington Post* remarked, "If you like conspiracy theories about secret plots to take over the world, you are going to love the administration of President-elect Jimmy Carter...."[132] In his White House memoirs, Brzezinski acknowledged, "Moreover, all the key foreign policy decision-makers of the Carter Administration had previously served in the Trilateral Commission...."[133] From *U.S. News and World Report*, February 21, 1977, came this appraisal: "The 'Trilateralists' have taken charge of foreign policy making in the Carter Administration, and already the immense power they wield is sparking some controversy. Active or former members of the Trilateral Commission now head every key agency involved in mapping U.S. strategy for dealing with the rest of the world ... some see this concentration of power as a conspiracy at work."[134]

In 1979 Senator Goldwater explained: "David Rockefeller and Zbigniew Brzezinski found Jimmy Carter to be their ideal candidate. They helped him win the nomination and the presidency. To accomplish this purpose, they mobilized the money power of the

Wall Street bankers, the intellectual influence of the academic community—which is subservient to the wealth of the great tax-free foundations—and the media controllers represented in the membership of the CFR and the Trilateral."[135]

Two of the typical appointees of Carter's administration were his vice president, Walter Mondale, and Federal Reserve chairman, Paul Volcker. Mondale is a humanist. His preacher father was a humanist, and his brother Lester was a Unitarian minister and chairman of the Fellowship of Religious Humanists. Lester is a signer of the *Humanist Manifesto I* (1933) and *Humanist Manifesto II* (1973). The *Humanist Manifesto II* called for "the building of a world community" based upon "the development of a system of world law and a world order based upon transnational federal government."[136]

Volcker had the typical ruling elite background and served under both Democratic and Republican administrations. His resumé reads:

Princeton
Harvard - M.A.
London School of Economics, 1951–1952
Federal Reserve Bank of New York - Economist, 1952–1957
Chase Manhattan Bank - Economist, 1957–1961
Treasury Department, 1961–1965
Deputy Secretary for Monetary Affairs, 1963–1965
Under Secretary for Monetary Affairs, 1969–1974
President, Federal Reserve Bank, 1975–1979
Chairman, Federal Reserve Board, 1979

Frustrated with Democrat Carter, the American people voted overwhelmingly for Republican Reagan. Reagan's new choice for Federal Reserve chairman? Paul Volcker, Trilateral Commission, USA.

Zbigniew Brzezinski was Carter's head of national security. Since it was he and Rockefeller who groomed Carter, it was customary to return the favor. The Trilateral Commission by this time had already planned the deliberate demise of the American dollar and the deliberate decline of our heretofore improving standard of living.

In the planning stages, prior to his appointment as executive director of the Trilateral Commission, Brzezinski had formulated the plan that would carry America into the next century. His book *Between Two Ages* told America that there should be:

1. A new monetary system replacing the American dollar.
2. A reduced standard of living in order to achieve it.

He forecast that, "In the economic-technological field some international cooperation has already been achieved, but further progress will require greater American sacrifices. More intensive efforts to shape a new world monetary structure will have to be undertaken, with some consequent risk to the present relatively favorable American position."[137]

To get a view of where the Trilateral Commission is pointing the ship of American government, let's review its executive director's own words:

> 1. Marxism is simultaneously a victory of the external man over the inner, passive man and a victory of reason over belief.
>
> 2. In the absence of social consensus society's emotional and rational needs may be fused—mass media makes this easier to achieve—in the person of an individual who is seen as...making the necessary innovations in the social order.
>
> 3. Such a society would be dominated by an elite whose claim to political power would rest on allegedly superior scientific know-how. Unhindered by the restraints of traditional liberal values, this elite would not hesitate to achieve its political ends by the latest modern techniques for influencing public behavior and keeping society under close surveillance and control. (In New Jersey and Florida, expensive video monitoring equipment has been placed in the major cities and on highways. This has been alluded to as "traffic control," yet the states found money for these surveillance systems even when the states' budgets were screaming and four thousand Florida teachers were informed they were being laid off.)
>
> 4. Movement toward such a community (of developed nations)...would involve the forging of community links among the United States, Western Europe, and Japan (a Trilateral Commission stated objective).
>
> 5. Though the objective of shaping a community of the developed nations is less ambitious than the goal of world government, it is more attainable.[138]

Jimmy Carter's secretary of state, Cyrus Vance (CFR/TC), was a nephew of John W. Davis, the founding president of the Council on Foreign Relations. He had served in both the Kennedy and Johnson administrations. He was a product of Yale and Wall Street.

Carter never did keep his promise to "turn the government of this country inside out," but he did manage to turn the country and its foreign policy upside down. The country under Trilateralist Carter had the highest inflation it has ever known. The United States under Carter gave support to communism and lied to Americans about who it was supporting and why. Some examples:

1. Carter gave his official blessing to the Communist government in Hungary in 1977 by returning the venerated crown of Saint Stephen to the Communist dictator, Janos Kadar.

2. Carter used his office to depose the Shah of Iran, who wrote, "The Americans wanted me out. Certainly this is what the human rights champions in the State Department wanted."[139] The Shah argued repeatedly in his memoirs that the great multinational oil companies subverted his rule because of his insistence that Iran get a greater share of oil revenues.

3. Carter lied to the American people and to President Somoza about Nicaragua (see chapter 7).

Today President Carter promotes homosexual and lesbian political planks and supports abortion.

Larry Abraham, in *Call It Conspiracy*, says the question being asked around Washington in the late 1970s was:

Q. Why won't Jimmy Carter's image ever be carved on Mount Rushmore?

A. Because there isn't room for two more faces.[140]

After four years of Jimmy Carter, the American people had had enough—runaway inflation and high unemployment. They had become a hostile public. What almost all Americans missed was that they needed not loathe Jimmy Carter, deceiver though he was, but the group that used him as a stooge of their plan.

Larry Abraham, a watchdog on the "insiders," wrote, "We have already said it would be unfair to claim that the Trilateral Commission dominated the Carter Administration. In fact, the Trilateral Commission was the Carter Administration. (Some 40 percent of the Trilateral Commission's American members became members of the Administration!)"[141]

Generally, it is those who scream the loudest against the Establishment who are most likely subverted to it. Bill Clinton is a Trilateralist. So is George Bush. Each preaches his own different philosophy, but both are slaves to mammon masters. They are liars for their own personal gain. Through pride and intellectual arrogance they deceive themselves and undermine the nation.

Since the Trilateralists have taken control of government, we have noticed a metamorphosis from Republican and Democrat to "Republicrat." On national television in 1980, Senator Barry Goldwater warned our nation, "This might be the last Republican convention and in two weeks the last Democratic convention. There are forces working against our country. There are selfish forces working for their own interest in our country."[142] When interviewing Senator Goldwater after his speech, Dan Rather conveniently forgot to ask Mr. Goldwater what he meant by his charges.

Americans are a good and fair people. They like competition, but they also like rules. It is hard for American citizens to imagine that the leaders of their own government are covertly managing their secular destiny and destruction. Why is it that so few realize there is a ruling elite which controls this country? The reason is that the American people are not meant to know! Ex-CIA agent Victor Marchetti explained, "In the covert world of the CIA, everyone knows—the KGB knows, the Mossad knows, only the American people are lied to over and over again."[143]

The day before he selected his running mate, Ronald Reagan was approached by a group of conservative activists who promoted him to select a conservative not connected to the elitist groups. Not only did Reagan appoint Trilateralist and CFR member George Bush, but he shot down a proposed Republican party platform plank to denounce the Trilateral Commission and the Council on Foreign Relations.

Syndicated columnist, Kevin Phillips, on August 4, 1980, noted the Ronald Reagan ticket had been taken over by the Trilateralist - CFR - Round Table group: "... for a man who only this April gave an interview to the *Christian Science Monitor* saying he'd shun the directions (and presumably the membership) of David Rockefeller's controversial Trilateral Commission, Reagan has eaten rather fully of the Trilateralite fruit...."[144]

Reagan's conservative supporters were surprised when he too became a pawn of the Socialist, Communist-supporting Establishment. Even the typically controlled media shouted surprise: "Reagan's first moves after the November 4 election generally pleased moderate Republicans and Democrats, some of whom feared he would follow the dictates of his most conservative supporters. 'Hell with them,' Vice President Bush declared on November 10 in Houston, referring to right-wing groups that supported the President-elect."[145] "We've all been had," said one typical conservative aide on Capitol Hill. "We boys on the right have gotten snookered."[146] The chairman of the National Conservative Political Action Committee, John "Terry" Dolan, echoed this after the first days of the new administration: "It's mind boggling that conservative, pro-Reagan activists are being bumped off job lists, while people who have no commitment to Ronald Reagan are being given jobs."[147]

Prior to 1970, James Baker, then a Democrat, managed George Bush's unsuccessful Senate race in Texas. In the 1976 Republican primary, Baker worked for Gerald Ford against Ronald Reagan. Nonetheless, as president, Reagan appointed James Baker as his Chief of Staff. No one in his right mind would select a former opponent's principal strategist as the man responsible for his implementation of policy. The Trilateralists were at it again!

A survey of top Reagan appointees revealed that "almost half had worked in previous administrations (37 percent under Ford or Nixon, 12 percent under Democrat Carter); and only 14 percent of the appointees worked in the Reagan campaign, in a sort of reverse spoils system."[148]

U.S. News & World Report reported, "The new administration includes so many former Nixon-Ford people that some Reaganites have been asking: 'who won the election?'"[149]

"I'm not sure what the explanation is for this pattern of picking up left-wing retreads," claimed David S. Broder of the *Washington Post*. "Some of my conservative friends see it as evidence of the 'conspiracy' by White House Chief of Staff Jim Baker and 'the Bush network' to infiltrate their moderate allies into Reagan's government."[150]

....

George Bush's duplicity toward the freedom-seeking citizens of China is a long story of Trilateral control through many administrations. In 1964, in his campaign for the U.S. Senate, George Bush told the people of Texas, "If Red China should be admitted to the UN, then the UN is hopeless and we should withdraw."[151]

As ambassador to the UN in 1970, Bush urged the seating of Red China in the general assembly. While ambassador Bush was urging the admittance of the Communists to the UN, the Senate Internal Security Subcommittee was releasing a report, *The Human Cost of Communism* in China, which had documented that possibly as many as 64 million persons have been killed by the Chinese Communists.

Given this kind of record, it should be no surprise that on July 15, 1971, Radio Peking, China's official radio station, issued the statement: "People of the World, unite and defeat the U.S. aggressors and all their running dogs."[152] That message didn't phase our foreign relations department CFR. On the very same day, President Nixon accepted an invitation by Premier Chou En Lai to visit China. Apparently it had slipped Nixon's mind that in his book *Six Crises* he had written: "Admitting Red China to the United Nations would be a mockery of the provision of the Charter which limits its membership to 'peace-loving nations'...."[153] Dr. Chiu-Yuan Hu later told a congressional committee: "To recognize the Chinese Red Regime is to discourage the people in the whole world....It will make the world know that the great nation of the United States is unworthy to be a friend, that it sometimes betrays its most loyal allies."[154]

Henry Kissinger had made secret trips to Red China earlier in 1971 as part of President Nixon's plan to confer legitimacy on the illegitimate Mao Communist regime. Politics, I am learning, is a charade for that which has already happened. According to a *Time* article of 1973, trade had already been firmly established:

"Sino-American trade has already taken a great leap forward. It will probably exceed $800 million, up from $92 million in 1972. In only three years, the U.S. has become China's second most important international trading partner after Japan.

"...The Chinese are also anxious to do business with giant American oil companies such as Exxon, Mobil, and Caltex, and makers of petroleum and drilling equipment...

"...In January (1973), the government disclosed that the Chinese were willing to seek 'deferred payment arrangements'—a euphemism for foreign credits—to pay for still more technology...."[155]

After a visit to China in 1973, Trilateralist David Rockefeller said: "The social experiment of China under Chairman Mao's leadership is one of the most important and successful in human history."[156] It was successful for Rockefeller, since he was reaping millions from his investments in Communist China.

Let me elucidate what the Chinese experiment is. Since 1947, when the Communists captured the mainland, forced labor has been the crux of the Chinese economy. An estimated 20 million slave laborers turn out textiles, chemicals, iron, coal, tools, machinery, and other consumer goods. In 1989 Red China exported $13 billion worth of goods to the United States alone. Americans who buy these items support the regime's slave-labor system. Norman Girvan in his article *Economic Nationalism vs. Global Corporation* suggests that "many MNCs (multinational corporations) may well prefer to deal with socialist countries than with many of those in the capitalist world—particularly the underdeveloped part of it. Socialist countries are seen to be safer and more stable: there is virtually no risk of expropriation, practically no strikes or labor unrest, little exchange risk since payment is made in cash or in kind, and they offer greater political stability than either the developed capitalist countries or the Third World. In short, the investment climate in socialist countries is superior."[157]

In 1977 the Trilateral Commission published a report titled "Collaboration With Communist Countries in Managing Global Problems: An Examination of the Options." The Trilateral report read: "Both the USSR and China are exporters of energy and apparently possess substantial oil reserves. The Trilateral countries import energy....There are immediate advantages for the Trilateral countries in diversifying their sources of supply. Trilateral-Communist cooperation in energy may thus be feasible and desirable. This cooperation might take the form of investment by Trilateral countries in Soviet or Chinese energy production to secure energy exports from these countries."[158] Is it any wonder that we have given both the former Soviet Union and China favored-nation status?

After President Jimmy Carter severed diplomatic relations with the elected government of Taiwan, Senator Barry Goldwater responded at a news conference, "I have no idea what motivated him other than [that] the Trilateral Commission, composed of bankers in this country and others, want to expand big business. This is a dangerous thing because it puts fear in our allies, especially our small allies, as to how the U.S. will keep its word."[159] Goldwater charged that President Carter's motives were economic, saying, "He did it for the big banks of the world—Chase Manhattan and the French bankers (Rothschild)—and for companies like Coca-Cola."[160]

Lest you think the Trilateralists are unfair and selfish, it is appropriate to note that they do share the wealth that they parasitize from their "host" country. Now that Henry Kissinger is no longer an official member of government, as a member of the Trilateral Commission executive committee he is surely due some of the spoils.

Kissinger Associates is a consulting firm which has lined up lucrative business deals for U.S. companies and bank heads with Communist China. Kissinger's two associates are George Bush's head of national security, Brent Scowcroft, and deputy secretary of state behind James Baker, Lawrence S. Eagleburger. Both are members of the CFR/TC. Former ambassador to Romania, David Funderburk, says, "Eagleburger and Scowcroft made from $500,000 to $1 million annually in the Kissinger firm positions, dispensing advice and counsel to other governments—often Communist—and wiring business deals."[161]

Funderburk continues, "For Eagleburger to be cutting deals with Communist clients which benefited him financially and politically was no surprise to me. I watched him over three and one half years offer U.S. Government support and assistance to one of the world's most monstrous tyrants, Nicolae Ceausescu of Romania...."[162]

Overlooking what was morally right and ignoring human-rights concerns, Eagleburger focused on Kissinger's global geopolitical concerns. This focus emphasized a policy of "...making the worldwide climate safe for the major multinational corporations' acquisition of wealth and power."[163] Funderburk discloses further: "At Kissinger Associates, Scowcroft made in excess of $500,000 annually as a consultant for some two dozen multinational corporations and Communist governments in Beijing, Moscow, and Belgrade. Scowcroft apparently has blind faith in the one-world idea associated with the United Nations....

"For Bush to rely on Kissinger aides and protégés Scowcroft and Eagleburger for assessments of Soviet, Romanian, and Chinese Communist mind-sets is to play right into the hands of the Communists."[164]

Kissinger clients include:
    Chase Manhattan Bank (Rockefellers)
    American Express
    General Electric
    L.M. Ericsson
    Global Motors Corporation & Yugo

Kissinger sits on the boards of American Express, Union Pacific, R.M. Macy, Continental Grain, CBS, Revlon, Freeport-McMoRan, and the private grain exporting giant—Cargill. He is the chairman of the board and sole stockholder of a corporation called China Ventures, Inc. Larry Abraham in his newsletter *Insider Report* indicates that the "...chairman has been paid $991,667 from just one company in one year, not counting all reasonable out-of-pocket expenses."[165] From one small venture alone, Kissinger made close to $1 million.

In 1961 Michael Goloniewski, a Polish army intelligence officer, defected to the United States. Former FBI agent John Norpel testified before the Senate Internal Security Subcommittee that "...no information [the defector] gave our government ever turned out to be wrong."[166]

Nevertheless, there was one Soviet spy named by Goloniewski who was never brought to trial. The colonel contended that "...Secretary of State Henry Kissinger has been a Soviet agent and that his involvement with Soviet Intelligence was made to agencies of our government even before his rise to prominence."[167]

Now, perhaps, it becomes clear why, before the blood of thousands of students and Chinese patriots had dried on Tiananmen Square, George Bush gave most favored nation status to China. The Trilateral club desired business as usual.

Let's review the sequence of events as they occurred:

1. May 20, 1989, Communist China declares martial law.
2. May 31, 1989, Bush grants Beijing most favored nation (MFN) status.
3. June 4, 1989, Thousands massacred at Tiananmen Square.
4. June 5, 1989, Bush refuses to revoke MFN benefits.
5. July 7, 1989, Secretary of State Baker approves the sale of four Boeing commercial jet liners to Red China.
6. July 1989, Bush secretly sends Scowcroft and Eagleburger to Red China.
7. September 26, 1989, Communist party boss Jiang Zemin said he did not believe "there was any tragedy in Tiananmen Square...." (His son was studying in the U.S. at that time.)
8. October 2, 1989, at CFR headquarters, NYC, Red Chinese foreign minister rules out U.S. criticism of the massacre, warning it would be "interference in China's internal affairs."
9. December 1989, Scowcroft and Eagleburger return to Beijing.
10. December 19, 1989, President Bush allows the export of three communications satellites to Red China, and permits the taxpayer subsidized Export-Import bank to issue loans and guarantees for U.S. exports to the Communist mainland.[168]

When Scowcroft and Eagleburger secretly returned to China in July, the post-massacre crackdown was already underway. Merle Goldman, professor of Chinese history at Boston University, deplored the move. "You've really got to question the president's judgment when he would send Scowcroft back, even though there was nothing to show the Chinese were interested in reforming themselves."[169]

Moreover, when Scowcroft and Eagleburger were in Beijing in December, Chinese police were arresting dozens of Roman Catholic priests. John Davies, president of Free the Fathers, an organization to free jailed clergymen in Communist countries, sadly stated the irony: "It is a gross insult...[that] the Chinese turn around and jail priests while they're wining and dining Scowcroft."[170]

Li Lee, deputy commander of the student demonstrations, pleaded: "Last April, May, and June...army tanks and guns killed and wounded thousands. Hundreds of thousands were arrested; many were tortured....Yet in July, before the blood was dry in Tiananmen Square, President Bush's national security advisor, Brent Scowcroft, secretly went to Beijing to confer with the killers of Chinese students. And this month (December 1989), he and Deputy Secretary of State Lawrence Eagleburger went back...publicly toasting China's regime. Our hopes in Tiananmen Square were built on the principles that frame the U.S. Constitution and Bill of Rights....Why has the Bush administration left us in the cold?"[171]

Perhaps Li Lee and his freedom-fighting cohorts have not heard of the Trilateral Commission. The Trilateralists do not beieve in the Constitution nor in the Bill of Rights unless it applies to themselves. When the Communist regime had killed or jailed most of its unarmed opposition, it announced the lifting of martial law in January 1990. President Bush called it "a very sound step." It was only a minor pause in an otherwise good economic year—a few months' delay in secret deals, hush money, bribes, greed, and idolatry.

In February 1990 the Beijing regime received 299,150 metric tons of taxpayer-subsidized U.S. wheat, a $9.75 million loan from the taxpayer-subsidized Export-Import Bank, a $30 million loan from the World Bank, and another $23.1 million from the Export-Import Bank. In May, Bush granted China a renewal of most favored nation trade status, which means it will cost 40 percent less to send its slave-labor products to the United States.

Coincidentally, this is the same China that has stolen American secrets from the Livermore National Laboratory in California and successfully produced and tested a nuclear neutron bomb using those secrets.[172] Also, in June 1990, the State Department confirmed that Red China was continuing to sell poison gas, cruise and ballistic missiles, and other weapons to Iran, Iraq, Syria, and Libya.[173]

On November 30, 1990, President Bush hosted the Red Chinese foreign minister, Qian Quichen, in Washington and assured him that "we have many things in common."[174]

It scares me to imagine what those things in common might mean to America.

The Trilateralists continue to consolidate power through their control of the International Monetary Fund (IMF). They succeeded in their parasitic advance even during the years of "the great conservative," Ronald Reagan.

"Probably the most damning indication that the President may be in the pocket of the megabankers is his unrelenting personal support for the bill (which was passed) authorizing an increase of $8.4 billion in America's 'contribution' to the International Monetary Fund. This money would in turn be 'loaned' by the IMF to deadbeat Third World governments to help them make interest payments on the gargantuan debts they owe to the Big Banks. Sadly, the Reagan administration even opposed and defeated an amendment to the bill which would have banned the use of such funds to bail out Communist regimes."[175]

The IMF has become an important tool for the implementation of Trilateralist policy in Third World countries. The U.S-dominated IMF supports and strengthens economic expansionism for the power brokers in a style of "world economic management." The two fundamental purposes of the fund were to promote free and unrestricted world trade and to stabilize world currencies. Essentially, this gives the IMF a tight form of foreign control over the economic and financial policies of needy recipient nations.

The policies and operation of the IMF affect the daily lives of millions of people in the Third World and in the Trilateral world itself. The chief objective of economic imperialism is to destroy the liberation movement of a given country. The Trilateralists intend to destroy any form of organization which enables the people to liberate themselves.

The example of IMF use in Jamaica during the period 1972–1979 elucidates the means by which Trilateralists have used the fund as a potent vehicle to implement U.S. foreign policy and corporate interest in the Third World.

In March 1972, the Caribbean nation of Jamaica democratically elected Prime Minister Michael Manley and the People's National Party (PNP). During his first two years in office, Manley instituted an economic program with two major goals:
1. To gain greater control over its own resources and wealth, especially bauxite (mineral processed into aluminum).
2. To use some of this wealth to finance social programs for the poor and unemployed.

Legislation passed in 1974 altered the basis on which the government obtained revenue from bauxite mining. This led to a fivefold increase in income to Jamaica and much revenue for social programs and land reform.

The significance of aluminum to the Trilateral nations is critical. Jamaica has consistently remained the largest or second-largest exporter of bauxite. Aluminum is one of the thirteen most critical strategic materials in defense and a common element in consumer and industrial goods. Jamaica alone supplies 50 to 60 percent of all the bauxite ore used in the United States. At the inception of Manley's administration, Kaiser, Reynolds, Alcoa, Revere (all U.S. companies), and Alcan of Canada controlled 100 percent of the bauxite industry in Jamaica.

Under Manley, the government began to negotiate for 51 percent controlling interest. The companies resisted.

Suddenly, in 1975, a destabilization campaign, similar to that which toppled Allende in Chile, began to undermine the Jamaican government. A concerted plan, later exposed as "Operation Werewolf", was put into effect by the CIA and other U.S. agencies which always represent international business. People by the dozens were burned out of their homes; paid gunmen shot or threatened those trying to escape; food supplies were poisoned; and the Jamaican police and defense force uncovered guns, explosives, and hundreds of rounds of ammunition never before seen on the island. Along with the violence, U.S. assistance dropped from $13.2 million in 1974 to $2.2 million in 1976. Jamaica's credit rating with the U.S. Export-Import Bank dropped from a top to a bottom category. They were cut off from acquiring a single loan from either the public or private lending market.

Although the campaign of fear and violence slowed production, frightened away foreign investors, and had a devastating effect on the tourist industry, Manley was reelected in a landslide victory. After an increase in oil prices (100 percent imported) and a huge drop in the sugar market (Jamaica's prime agricultural export), Jamaica's foreign exchange reserves quickly dwindled and the nation suffered a significant deficit in its balance of payments.

To the rescue came Jimmy Carter and the Trilateral Commission's bevy of bankers. Out of necessity, Manley reopened negotiations with the IMF, which granted a $74 million standby loan. The conditions of the loan were:

    1. A 40 percent devaluation of the Jamaican dollar

    2. A wage freeze

    3. Cutbacks of subsidies on basic commodities

    4. Cutbacks in government spending for social programs

This meant additional profits for the aluminum companies since they bought bauxite in U.S. dollars.

Obviously this became aggravated hardship for the Jamaican poor. Their living standard eroded as prices escalated and wages were frozen. Without funds to support social programs, Manley lost support among the poor.

This was not enough for the Trilateralists. The original standing loan was granted in mid-July of 1977. In December 1977 the IMF canceled the arrangement. Why? Because the amount of money in circulation in the national economy was higher than stipulated by the IMF. Yes! They even control the volume of money in the economy of a sovereign nation!

Rothschild's quote comes back to us: "Let me issue and control a nation's money, and I care not who writes the laws."

This maneuver by the IMF forced Manley to replace his own finance minister with one better trusted by the international bankers. He had previously agreed to the resignation of several of his closest advisors. Manley renegotiated with the Trilateral IMF and received far more stringent conditions from his taskmasters. The new arrangements: a further 30 percent devaluation for a total of 70 percent devaluation of the Jamaican dollar and price controls were lifted allowing basic food staples to rise dramatically. In one month, May to June 1978, the overall cost of living leaped 13 percent. That's over 150 percent per year! Then the IMF demanded a balanced budget. This led to further cuts in social programs and even cuts in essential services, including cutbacks in government operating budgets. All the advances made in health care, nutrition, education, and social welfare were undone.

To achieve needed revenue, the IMF demanded added taxation measures from the Jamaican government. The People's National Party tried to tax corporations—those which could afford it best. This was disallowed in the interest of "business expansion" by the IMF. As a result, new taxes were placed on consumer items which included basic necessities. With a wage freeze, one can only imagine the frustration of the enslaved Jamaican worker. Naturally, the economic position of Jamaica was worse after the IMF "helped" than before. Jamaica's foreign debt more than doubled, and the country must continue borrowing to service its exponential debt.

Proverbs 22:7 declares: "The borrower is servant to the lender." So it is for Jamaica and every Third World country which uses the International Monetary Fund.

This is only one example of how the Trilateral Commission

deploys its executive advisory committee to manage transnational finance capital. The commission "seeks to subordinate territorial politics to non-territorial economic goals."[176]

A U.S. Senate Report of August 1977 suggests how the IMF would be calibrated to undermine Third World countries' efforts for self-determination and implant in its place Trilateral hegemony over the Third World. "Once the public and private lenders join forces, deficit countries will be left with no alternative sources of financial assistance; there will be no escaping IMF conditionality, little choice but to accept whatever terms the IMF and private banks choose to lay down."[177] (Remember, America is now a deficit country according to plan.)

The Senate report explains further that the debtor countries will experience a reduced standard of living under IMF austerity imposed with political repression. An early proponent of Trilateralism, U.S. Secretary of the Treasury Blumenthal, proposed that there be a merger between the IMF and private bank lending (since instituted) and that lending programs be subject to tighter measures of accountability and control by the IMF over the monetary and economic policies of the recipient nation. Certainly, says Trilateral founder David Rockefeller, the IMF and multinational enterprises have been endowed with the responsibility "...to get on with the unfinished business of developing the world economy."[178]

The IMF has been so successful, first controlling and then destroying the financial independence of the Third World countries, that now the front men for banking are determined to push it on the United States. That, of course, would be the final straw, and a one-world bank would be firmly at the helm of an already sinking USA, Inc.

Sir Harold Lever of the giant European conglomerate Unilever has stated, "The United States will soon have to realize that it will be no better than any Third World country when the IMF takes control."[179] Felix Rohatyn of the Council on Foreign Relations has spoken of the great need to change U.S. banking laws so that the IMF could play a greater role in this country. Other members of the Round Table have spoken enthusiastically in support of surrendering U.S. fiscal sovereignty to the IMF. One group of banking delegates said, "The United States must be forced to surrender to the higher authority of the World Bank to allow further progress toward the New World Order...."[180]

The increasing control over emerging Third World economies along with the deepening world economic crisis is being used as the condition for ever-greater integration of national economies into a larger system. In 1973 Trilateral Policy Program Director Zbigniew Brzezinski recommended the study *Control Over Man's Development and Behavior.* Such a task-force undertaking was to study "the social-educational implications of the availability of new means of social control."[181]

Social Darwinism means a "controlled recession" imposed by money lenders to *houseclean* the economy by streamlining industry and labor for more efficient competition in the international arena. This is the plan behind the massive job eliminations that America is presently experiencing.

The Trilateral Commission's recipe for a New World Order is nothing other than the exploitation of people throughout the world in a pervasive atmosphere of mind-bending control.

Wake up, America!

Chapter 7

MULTINATIONAL CORPORATIONS

The working unit of the CFR-Trilateral-media combine is the multinational corporation. When George Bush informed America it was time to forget nationalism, disarm, and get ready for the New World Order, he was not speaking idly. That is because, except for our acceptance of such, it is already virtually locked in place. Axel Madsen wrote an anti-American book called *Private Power, Multi-national Corporations for the Survival of Our Planet.* He suggests that the MNCs are revolutionary new powers unto themselves. "They are world citizens and as such a counterforce to the extremes of nationalism."[182] Allegiance to the company is now of higher order than allegiance to one's country.

I always thought my country was important. I was proud of America. Every citizen of every other nation in the world envied our freedom, our liberty, our private enterprise, and our good character. However, over the years an evil has crept into the country. Some might call it a necessary evil, but an evil is an evil nonetheless. As we enter the decade of the antiquity of nationalism, we also accept the slavery of America. America has always sought freedom for others even at the expense of life. Yet, can it or will it be able to fight for its own existence? Or will we become USA, Inc.?

Trilateralist George Ball, investment banker and former under secretary of state, explains that global corporations are "the best means yet devised for utilizing world-resources according to the criterion of profit...."[183] Since the locomotive of profit is consumption, the global corporations depend upon the political, economic, and repressive power commanded by the ruling class of a nation-state (USA, Inc.) to maintain a "favorable investment climate." Because the Trilateralists know that issues related to economics are at the heart of politics, they are determined to develop and consolidate a world economy. This will give them a stable supply of raw materials, cheap labor, and an ever-expanding marketplace. Michael Corleone, in *The Godfather Part III,* says "Finance is a gun. Politics is knowing when to pull the trigger. All my life I've been trying to go up in society. The higher I go, the crookeder it gets."

For those who would listen, many have come from behind the scenes to describe how Western governments (particularly the USA-CIA) train and supply the military and police of other countries to keep "sympathetic political leaders" in power and suppress working-class movements. This has been accomplished repeatedly through assassination and CIA-led overthrow of foreign governments; and, less conspicuously, but even more effectively, through the choker-chain of the International Monetary Fund (IMF). In Chile, Salvador Allende had a democratically elected government. Since he was not behaving in the globalists' best interest, CFR Secretary of State Henry Kissinger let out the word to "make the economy scream."[184] U.S. Ambassador Korry had communicated the ruling elite's sinister promise: "Not a nut or bolt shall reach Chile under Allende. Once Allende comes to power, we shall do all within our power to condemn Chile and all Chileans to utmost deprivation and poverty...."[185]

More than 30,000 people were killed, including President Allende, resisting the military coup of September 11, 1973. Since then, over 2,000 people "disappeared" and are presumed dead. More than 100,000 people have been jailed for political reasons. Torture became commonplace. Thousands were forced to flee into exile. Chile was one other calamity of Trilateral philosophy.

Trilateralism is the creed of the international ruling class whose locus of power is fixed in the global corporation. The owners and directors of multinational corporations view the entire world as their factory, farm, supermarket, and playground. These corporations (MNCs) control vast amounts of natural resources and monopolize the production of commodities vital to daily life.

MNCs have transformed international trade into transnational capitalism. There is power in the MNC. Companies like GM and Exxon have gross national products (sales) greater than the majority of countries in the United Nations, greater than countries such as Denmark and Switzerland. If you list GNPs of countries and nations together, of the largest ninety-nine economies of the world, forty are MNCs!

The power in the MNC is concentrated in a small group of senior executives at the corporate head. As in governments, so in corporations. The key instrument to service this power is financial control. A specific consequence of this power is that large areas of global economic life—such as the distribution of production and employment among countries, the volume, value and direction of exports and imports, and the value and stability of currencies—are falling increasingly under the control of a small number of committees of corporate managers.

In any one industry, production is dominated at this time in history by a small number of giant corporations which operate throughout the world and affect the world economy. The consequence is an enormous oligopolistic market power on a world scale. Since the corporations in any industry fix their prices in sympathy with one another (notice any gas wars lately?), what is oligopoly in form becomes monopoly in fact.

The growth of the power of the MNC executives over the international distribution of jobs and income growth, over the direction and value of trade and monetary flows, and over advanced technology has considerably strengthened their bargaining power over even the most powerful countries. The question has been asked, can the traditional loyalty of multinationals to their home country and its government still be counted on? The answer is no! U.S.-based MNCs have already exported over 1.5 million U.S. jobs to cheaper labor abroad! These American jobs have been forever eliminated.

Higher oligarchal prices, e.g., oil, mean declining real wages for the working class. Recession and unemployment are used to beat wages back to a minimum, to make the workers thankful and more complacent, less demanding on capital.

Since corporations have adopted a truly global view, we are witnessing a denationalization of capital. Consider that in the Soviet Union a few years ago, the people tore down the statue of Lenin, and the West gloated over "victory"; Pyrrhic victory it was, since as long ago as 1916 Lenin wrote: "Imperialism, the Highest Stage of

Capitalism." He would certainly be chuckling at America's naive understanding of contemporary global finance.

The power of transnational capital today is the power to withhold or relocate investments from a country, thereby threatening it with the specter of economic stagnation and technological retrogression. According to the proponents of the MNC, the nation-state is a technologically obsolete institution. As we wave good-bye to patriotism, we should remember it was the liftoff pad of the MNC. Professor Raymond Vernon, director of Harvard's Multinational Enterprise Project, stated, "It may be that, in the end, sovereign states (countries) will learn to live with a decline in their perceived economic power. But one marvels at the tenacity with which man seeks to maintain a sense of differentiation and identity, a feeling of control even when the apparent cost of the identity and the control seems out of proportion to its value."[186]

Cultural and family tradition is now labeled as "quaint" but inimical to the ushering in of the New Age of global capitalism where there are no countries, only regions of earth. The Trilateralists have already divided the entire earth into ten regions. With this kind of view, the educated observer begins to understand why the "New World Order" is so eager to rid itself of our beloved Constitution.

Today, more worlds are conquered in the boardroom than on the battlefields. A company like Exxon is a country unto itself. Petroleum is the foundation material of most electrical generating plants, plastics, chemicals, and drugs. Exxon sells oil in more than one hundred countries, through three hundred subsidiaries and affiliates that make up a "United Nations" for oil. Exxon is one of the largest coal-reserve owners. Besides coal, Exxon owns lead, zinc, iron ore, and uranium in the United States and Canada; copper in Chile; and solar energy systems (Day Star) in the United States.

In 1976 Exxon had $35.8 billion in sales, leaping to $60.3 billion in 1980. As the biggest industrial company in the world, Exxon literally has power over nations. The Rockefeller family maintains control over Exxon and other offshoots of the Standard Oil Trust—Mobil, Chevron, Sohio, Phillips 66, and Marathon.

Banking, however, is the Rockefellers' biggest business. The Chase Manhattan Bank is the third largest banking enterprise in the world. As of 1976, it had twenty-eight foreign branches of its own. But even more incredible, it had fifty thousand correspondent banks around the world! Today, that number is estimated to be sixty thousand! This could give the Rockefeller family upwards of <u>$500 billion</u>! Chase Manhattan even has a full-time envoy to the United

Nations!

The Rockefeller banks interlock with the board of directors of three of the four largest life insurance companies: Metropolitan Life, Equitable Life, and New York Life. The Rockefeller group of banks accounts for over 25 percent of all the assets of the fifty largest commercial banks in the country and 30 percent of all the assets of the fifty largest life insurance companies.

The Rockefellers can and do leverage direct control over the economy of the United States. Through major stockholder control, the following companies fall within the Rockefeller orbit:

Exxon	Inland Steel
Mobil	Marathon Oil
Standard of California	Quaker Oats
Standard of Indiana	International Harvester
Wheeling Pittsburgh Steel	Freeport Sulphur

International Basic Economy Corporation

Chase's trust department controls the single largest block of stock in twenty-one major American corporations. Other corporations can be controlled through interlocking directorates. Listed are some of the MNCs which fall under Rockefeller-CFR domain:

United Air Lines	IBM
Northwest Airlines	Xerox
Eastern Airlines	Westinghouse
TWA	IT&T
Delta	Bendix
National Airlines	DuPont
Boeing	Union Carbide
Braniff	Stauffer Chemical
Gulf	Allied Chemical
Atlantic Richfield Oil	American Cyanamid
Texaco	Dow
Continental Oil	Monsanto
Union Oil	Olin Mathison
Cities Service	Celanese
American Motors	Pittsburgh Plate Glass
Chrysler	Pfizer
Long Island Lighting	Merck
International Paper	Sperry Rand
Anaconda Copper	Penn Central
American Home Products	Borden
Consolidated Freightways	Avon
National Distillers	R.H. Macy

CIT Financial	S.S. Kresge
National Steel	National Cash Register
Minnesota Mining & Manufacturing (3M)	

The original Constitution says absolutely nothing about separation of church and state. However, it should say something about separation of business and government. Today it is impossible to know who is seducing whom. Whether you call the Rockefeller-CFR-MNC control system "Corporate Fascism" or "State Socialism," the answer is YES!

The Trilateral plan for America is for America's standard of living to decline. This has occurred and will continue to occur because to integrate the United States into the international co-op we must allow other countries to catch up as consumers. Remember the point:

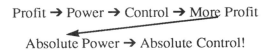

Profit → Power → Control → More Profit

Absolute Power → Absolute Control!

Many MNCs portrayed as American are in fact foreign owned:

Columbia Pictures	Sony	Japan
20th Century Fox	News Corporation	Australia
Doubleday	Bertelsman AG	Germany
Burger King	Grand Metropolitan PLC	Britain
Mentholatum Company, Inc.	Rohto Pharmaceutical	Japan
Arrow Shirts	Biderman Group	France
Tropicana	Seagram Company	Canada
Stroehmann Bread Bakeries	George Weston, Ltd.	Canada
Yale Locks	Valor PLC	Britain
Pebble Beach Golf Course	Minoru Isutani	Japan

The U.S. Government has offered generous tax breaks to foreign corporations. IRS statistics show that foreign-owned companies are more likely than American companies to file tax returns showing little or no profit. They, therefore, pay little or no income tax. Out of 100 foreign-owned companies doing business in the United States, 59 (for federal income tax purposes) supposedly lost money. A House Ways and Means subcommittee investigation of foreign-owned businesses showed that more than half "paid little or no federal income tax." The subcommittee discovered in one case an electronics company reported sales of $4 billion over seven years. According to Patrick G. Heck, assistant counsel for the committee, "the company always had net operating losses available to zero out any tax. In ten years, the company ultimately paid no federal income tax."[187]

From 1984 to 1987, revenues for foreign-controlled companies in the United States rose 50 percent, yet their taxes went up only 2 percent. Japanese-controlled companies (many people believe SONY stands for Standard Oil—New York, a Rockefeller conglomerate) have done even better. Their profits rose 64 percent from 1984 to 1987 soaring from $130 billion to $185 billion. Yet their federal income taxes paid went <u>down</u> 14 percent from $1.1 billion in 1984 to $951 million in 1987. If you as a <u>private</u> citizen enjoyed the same increase the foreigners received, your annual salary would have increased, for example, from $30,000 to $49,200 and your federal taxes would have been reduced from $2,729 to $2,347. Government of the people, by the people, and for the people?

During the 1950s, when the middle class expanded enormously, of the combined $478 billion in collected taxes, corporations paid 39 percent and individuals paid 61 percent. During the 1980s total collections were $4 trillion! But the corporate share had <u>shrunk</u> to only <u>17</u> percent and the private taxpayer share increased to <u>83</u> percent! It is the corporations themselves who have helped the government rewrite the rule book that permits a virtually unlimited deduction for interest on debt. Meanwhile, the U.S. Government has <u>taken away</u> a student's ability to deduct interest on his debt and has <u>taken away</u> the citizen's ability to deduct interest on all purchases. The taxes that corporations escaped paying due to interest deductions were <u>$92.2 billion</u> in the 1980s! This was, of course, made up by the working serfs of the United States. From 1950 to 1980 taxes paid by individual working-class members <u>increased 1,041</u> percent! Why isn't the playing field level? Where is the sleeping middle class of America?

Because of global MNC legislation as enacted by elitist government, the American standard of living continues to decline. This is just as Brzezinski stated it would be in his book *Between Two Ages*. Please don't consider for a minute that our declining way of life, our crime, and our immorality is not part of a plan. It is indeed a well-executed plan, as Colonel Peck has described (see chapter 6) at the "highest levels" of government.

Due to constant changes in the rules as decided upon by the ruling elite, the average individual and family has a constant shortage of money to spend on housing, food, clothing, and education. During the 1950s, median-income families paid a total of 1.7 percent of their income for Social Security taxes. In the 1980s it was 7 percent. Now it is over 7.5 percent and for the private small businessman it is close to 15 percent! The burden of this tax is heavily weighted against middle- and lower-income workers. From 1970 to 1989 individuals with incomes above $500,000 received a tax cut of 45 percent. Not only are superstar athletes overpaid, they are also a cost-effective distraction to prevent you from being angry over your declining lifestyle. The puppeteers believe if they give Americans a good escapade or competition on TV and a six-pack of beer, they will be unlikely to recognize the state of their demise. Sadly, they appear to be right.

Via the usual political monologue of "Let's get tough on the rich" came the 1986 Tax Reform Act. One of the principal authors was Dan Rostenkowski (D-Illinois). This bill was to transfer the tax burden from individual citizens to corporations. Senator Jay Rockefeller (D-West Virginia) exclaimed that "What the bill really does is broaden the tax base and shift the tax burden from individuals to corporations."[188] As if they didn't know, the new tax law actually resulted in $35 billion less being collected from corporations from 1987 to 1990. How much proof do you need before you finally accept the fact that the constitutional government of the United States has been usurped and is not and has not been pro-American in nearly a century?

One example of how a Socialist-CFR-controlled Congress and its inventory of incestuous bankers has written off America is our new government rule book regarding Puerto Rico. In fact, the new laws established by the Internal Revenue Code provide enormous tax credits for American companies to move to U.S. possessions.

The provision allows subsidiaries to transfer profits from Puerto Rico to parent companies in the United States *without paying taxes* on those profits! Thus, the U.S. Government will provide a generous tax break to a company which terminates jobs in America. The company saves millions of dollars in income taxes and millions of dollars in salaries. The taxpayers have the 1976 Tax Reform Act to thank for this. How about a moratorium on all congressional legislation? We would be better off if they enacted no law and went on a vacation for a year. Actually, for this they would deserve the raise they voted themselves despite the outcry of 80 percent of the American people.

Since passage of the 1976 Tax Reform Act, corporations have terminated the jobs of tens of thousands of factory workers in the United States who were replaced with lower-paid workers in Puerto Rico and escaped billions of dollars in taxes.

Many of the companies which have moved south are pharmaceutical, typically subsidiaries of Big Oil; again, CFR-Rockefeller controlled. According to Treasury Department data, companies claiming the "possessions" tax credit escaped payment of $14 billion in income taxes during the 1980s. Has anyone called his congressman yet?

It gets worse....

From the pharmaceutical industry alone, the lost tax revenue to the U.S. Government adds up to $60,000 for every $6 an hour job created. Therefore, it turns out that it would be cheaper both for the U.S. Government and the American taxpayer to send an annual subsistence check of $12,000 to the island residents who work for American drug companies, and keep the jobs here. More simply, Congress is spending $60,000 of taxpayers' money to eliminate one job in the United States that paid $28,000 and to create one job in Puerto Rico that pays $12,000.[189] UNBELIEVABLE!

Panama is the other main colonial enclave for MNCs in the Caribbean. Panama is the location of what is called the "Colon Free Port"—the second largest free port in the world, where 600 multinational corporations enjoy special conditions such as tax-free benefits and where over 50,000 paper or brass-plate offices are set up to carry out paper transactions (i.e., altering the destination, ownership, and prices of products moving through the canal), resulting in millions of dollars in added profits for the MNCs.

Panama City is also the home of a hemisphere banking center consisting of more than 80 banks representing Trilateral Commission nations and their personal interests throughout Latin America. Panama is a hemispheric bastion of free enterprise—at least for the MNCs.

Bo Gritz, in his elucidating book *Called to Serve*, states: "It wasn't until Manuel [Noriega] threatened to 'nationalize' U.S. assets—including Bush holdings—that the marines went in. Twenty-six U.S. soldiers died, 324 were wounded to preserve the President's personal holdings. Bush installed Gillermo Endara, former director of a bank known to launder Medellin drug money...."[190]

Gritz goes on to say, "The greatest threat to U.S. interests [MNCS] in the Third World is that the individual nations will stop being export slaves for big business and begin to look toward their own national interests and development. We must keep them oppressed so that big business and international banking can direct and exploit their resources."[191]

In his opinion, "Anyone who thinks that our pre-Christmas invasion of Panama with 24,000 paratroops and stealth fighters was to nab Noreiga for his drug dealings is wrong...the major reason the U.S. invaded Panama was to install our own people in government there....the Endara government we have inserted in Noriega's place [is] made up of heads of the banks...."[192]

Indeed, one of Endara's key Cabinet people was actually a lawyer for one of the Colombian drug lords.

To comfort the Panamanians, $250 million taxpayer dollars were promised to rebuild their city. Also $150 million was earmarked for interest payments to international banks.

The 1989 campaign to remove Noriega from office and "appoint" a friendly dictator to office was a move from the CIA file to "destabilize" an unfriendly foreign ruler. Most Third World countries have natural resources (assets) which the MNCs need; therefore, an open avenue of access is necessary.

Foreign investment and foreign oil are seen as the two principal solutions to the instability of Third World nations. In reality they are money-making ventures, but especially tools of control.

The rhetoric of the U.S. press, backed by the government for purposes of keeping the ruling class who own the MNCs in power, always speaks so kindly of "restoring the operation of the laws of supply and demand" or the need to "curb inflation" or "prevent the collapse of the world monetary system." However, power is what it is all about—that is their aim and preoccupation. George Bush has oil holdings in Kuwait and business (travel) in Panama. So what is going on? The new economic (world) order shows every sign of accentuating rather than reducing the contradiction of increasing wealth accompanied by growing poverty on a world scale. It is not well-known in America due to cover-up and media propaganda, but around the world, democratization is a political face-lift for undemocratic economic and political practices.

Another example of MNC planning is the history of the Dominican Republic. Since 1900, the United States and special interests have held control of the Dominican economy. If that doesn't seem possible, recognize that the U.S. dollar was imposed as the national currency in 1905. In 1912 the U.S. National Bank was established, and in 1917 the International Banking Company of New York was created.

In 1916 U.S. Marines settled a Dominican "internal" problem and set up a U.S. monopoly government for the next eight years. Within weeks of the U.S. Marine invasion, two private U.S. businesses were established—the Puerto Rico Sugar Company and the Grenada Fruit Company. There was immediate action taken to <u>disarm</u> the Dominican Armed Forces and civilian population. (Note how much the media and ruling powers desire to disarm Americans! The NRA says we have a "right" to keep and bear arms for hunting. Nothing could be further from the truth! The right we have is to bear arms to protect ourselves from the kind of tyranny our own government CFR has established around the world. In causing guns to be registered, the ruling elite, through the NRA, knows every person who owns a "licensed" gun.). There was a formal military withdrawal in 1924, but not before the United States left behind a thoroughly trained and armed Dominican National Guard to keep the population under control.

Although President Trujillo held office for thirty-one years from 1930 to 1961, he was left alone by the United States until he began to nationalize private industries. He acquired the National City Bank and all of its branches. Not only does National City have ties to Rothschild, but it is also tied to sugar interests. This was a serious no-no. In 1950 he established a sugar refinery to compete with the private companies on the island, another no-no. In 1961 he was assassinated.

When Juan Bosch succeeded Trujillo, everything was all right until he moved to reform the constitution and increase the rights of peasants and limit the power of foreign interests. Soon thereafter, Bosch was toppled by a military coup. The Pentagon, the CIA, and the MNC business (sugar) interests supported the military triumvirate which followed, led by Donald Reid Cabral, a known CIA agent!

In 1965 the puppet Cabral government was overthrown by Bosch supporters. That was unacceptable to the MNCs. Over 20,000 marines were called in. Soon, 2,500 civilians lay dead. In 1965 a truce was signed under the auspices of the Organization of American States (OAS). Since the United States dominates the OAS, this meant business as usual for MNC business interests—not freedom for the Dominican Republic. After fraudulent elections, Joaquin Balaguer became president and immediately changed the constitution to eliminate the clause that prohibited presidential reelections.

In the next twelve years, the U.S. Government sought to create *its* kind of stability in the Dominican Republic through massive development of programs, land seizures, control of sugar production, mining, tourism, military aid, and repressive and disruptive labor practices. To protect the new investment of capital by foreign investment ($800 million), the United States supplied the highest amount of aid per capita in Latin America for police training in 1966.

Even after a massive influx of money into the Dominican Republic, unemployment was 30 percent and wages were thirty cents an hour in urban areas and twenty cents an hour in the countryside. Dominican external debt was $800 million, and the United States bought 66.6 percent of all exports. Children (as is common now in Brazil) found their meals in garbage cans.

Antonio Guzman, who followed Balaguer into power, continued the game. In his administration the vice president of Gulf and Western Corporation was appointed president of the Central Bank, and the president of Falconbridge Nickel was appointed director of the state sugar board. This placed the heads of corporation in a position to make the rules and laws for the Dominican government. This is a matter of fact in America today.

Central and South Africa are no different from Latin America in providing natural resource riches for the Trilateralist MNCs. The masters of finance fear any kind of liberation movements which might cut off their supplies of crucial minerals or even change the terms of trade, making them less favorable to international capital and reduced profits. Few Americans understand the importance of countries like Zambia, Zaire, Zimbabwe, Namibia, and South Africa, which produce critical minerals used in industrial production. Chromium, manganese, cobalt, and platinum are key materials in producing metal alloys like steel, as well as strategic defense-related imports like uranium.

The United States relies on Africa for:

    41 percent manganese
    32 percent ferromanganese
    77 percent cobalt
    33 percent platinum
    30 percent chromite
    58 percent ferrochromium
    56 percent vanadium

The Planned Destruction of America

South Africa supplies the Trilateralist countries with over half the world's gold and platinum and holds over half the world's known reserves of platinum, vanadium, chrome, and manganese ore; it is one of the top three producers of uranium, diamonds, and asbestos. Note: In the case of some strategic minerals, the only major producer outside of Africa is the Soviet Union. This must make anyone cringe who understands who Nelson Mandela and the ANC really are, since we are literally in the process of turning over vital minerals for national defense to the Communists.

What is occurring in South Africa today is a progressive evolution of late nineteenth-century colonialism. Rhodesia gets its very name from the Round Table colonialist—Cecil Rhodes. Mining companies set up legislation which robbed the African peasantry of its land, making it an impoverished working class. The Native Land Act was passed in 1913, giving 80 percent of the land to foreign mining companies and white farmers.

The mining sector is a monopoly. Seven large interlocking mining/finance houses dominate the production of minerals in South Africa and Namibia. Anglo-American Corporation (a Rockefeller-Rothschild MNC) mines gold, diamonds, coal, copper, platinum, and other minerals. Anglo's main international link is Charter Consolidated, which owns the Malaysia Tin Mining Corporation, tin and tungsten mining in Europe, and has diversified investments throughout Australia, North America, continental Europe, and Africa.

Anglo-American is cross-linked with U.S. capital through Englehard Minerals and Chemical Corporation, the world's largest refiner and fabricator of precious metals. Charles Englehard had close ties with both the Kennedy and Johnson administrations. Sigma, the nation's largest auto supplier, is also a subsidiary of Anglo-American.

British MNCs are involved in sectors such as motor vehicles, chemicals, metals, and computers. British investments are almost always interlocked with Anglo-American and Lonrho, the London Rhodesian Company, which is the largest industrial-financial holding company in South Africa. *The Guardian* (London) reported November 11, 1978, that Lonrho and another company, Liebigs, owned between them over two million acres of ranching land. South Africa's Imperial Chemicals has controlling equity in African Explosives and Chemical Industry (AECI), the second largest commercial explosive company in the world. Rio Tinto Zinc Corporation, a Rothschild firm, controls Palabora Mining Company

112

and Namibian Rossing mine (Rio Tinto Zinc Corporation has always been heavily represented in the Trilateral Commission).

South Africa is Japan's number-one trading partner. German Volkswagens are assembled in South Africa and reexported to other African nations. U.S. investment has expanded in high-tech industries like uranium processing, computers, and chemicals. IBM, ICI, Burroughs, Control Data, and Sperry-Rand control the computer market in South Africa.

What has all of this meant for black Africans? Transnational enterprise translates into economic exploitation. Computers have helped the MNCs compensate for the shortage of skilled workers and avoid having to upgrade blacks. Most gold is not conducive to mechanization, so black labor is exploited for its extraction. Miners often scrape ore with their bare hands from veins with threads one inch thick. The foreign MNC develops high rates of profit made possible by low costs of a non-unionized and primarily migrant labor force. For one example, the average annual income for the Bantustan tribe has been approximately $97 a year! That is low compared to the $120 a year in Tanzania, $180 in Nigeria, or $510 in Zambia. The infant mortality rate for Bantustan approaches 50 percent. Welcome to the wonderful world of Western industrialization!

Zaire is a major producer of copper, cobalt, and diamonds. Mineral-rich Kantanga province was assaulted in 1977 and 1978 by exiles who disrupted mineral production and threatened the Mobutu regime. Zaire fell $1 billion in arrears in repayment of its $3 billion in foreign loans. The altruistic IMF came to its assistance and set conditions for a "stabilization plan." They forced Mobutu to accept almost total administrative control over the economy by a group of IMF advisors from the Trilateralist states. The principal director of Zaire's central bank, La Banque de Zaire, was replaced by Erwin Blumenthal, former head of the West German Bundesbank. Foreign officials were placed in charge of the Finance Ministry, and the Belgian government reorganized the Customs Department! The IMF decreed, as usual, appropriate provisions to bring Zaire to its knees: wage freezes, currency devaluations, and the total impoverishment of the Zaire population.

Robert Mugabe of Zimbabwe, although faced with the same kind of dirty tricks from the West, has shown his understanding of how the Trilateral system works: "We try to work on a political level against the strategy worked out by Britain and the United States. Since the Kissinger Plan, Geneva Conference, and the Anglo-American proposals, we resisted the bid to create a neo-colonial state in the country. We have also had the same diplomatic drive on the Zimbabwe question. That is at the political level the joint [military] operations that we envisage are intended to balance the cooperation we have at the political level."[193]

Ex-CIA operative Philips Agee summed it up: "Everything that the CIA is doing, in the propaganda area and in the political warfare area, tends in one way or the other to help create the optimum operating conditions for multinational corporations in that particular country."[194]

There has been worldwide turmoil, leaders assassinated, nationalists killed, CIA-laundered money, government importation of drugs all in the name of business. Aside from the fact that, in the end, this hurts people and families from every nation including America, what is going on?

The Senate report of June 15, 1978, titled *Interlocking Directorates among the Major U.S. Corporations* shows that five banks hold a total of 470 interlocking directorates in the 130 major corporations of the United States. The five New York banks are:

Citicorp	97 directorates
J.P. Morgan Co.	99 directorates
Chase Manhattan	89 directorates
Manufacturers Hanover	89 directorates
Chemical Bank	96 directorates

This is essentially centralized control over American industry. But by whom? Eustace Mullins explains that "this centralized control over American industry by five New York banks <u>controlled from London</u> suggests that instead of 130 major U.S. Corporations we may have only one, which in itself is an outpost of the London Connection."[195] It turns out that these banks are the very owners of the majority stock in the private Federal Reserve Bank, to whom the American taxpayers pay $400 billion a year (interest only) for producing money out of thin air as debt money! So who owns these banks that control the government, the CFR, and the world? Mullins, in *World Order*, states: "Besides its controlling interest in the Federal Reserve Bank of New York, the Rothschilds had developed important financial interests in other parts of the United States."[196] He demonstrates with vivid documentation that American industry, many MNCs, and the New York banks are controlled from London. He goes so far as to say: "The entire Rockefeller empire was financed by the Rothschilds."[197] Today the Rothschilds own approximately 53 percent of the private Federal Reserve Bank of the United States![198]

The May 1976 Staff Report of the House Banking and Currency Committee noted that "The Rothschild banks are affiliated with Manufacturers Hanover of London in which they hold 20 percent interest, a merchant bank, and Manufacturers Hanover Trust of N.Y."[199] The same House Banking and Currency Committee Report concluded that a single banking conglomerate, Rothschild Intercontinental Bank, LTD., made up of Rothschild banks in London, France, Belgium, New York, and Amsterdam, had three American subsidiaries: National City Bank of Cleveland ($6.5 billion in assets), First City National Bank of Houston ($17 billion in assets), and Seattle First National Bank.

It was the National City Bank of Cleveland which financed John D. Rockefeller's exploitation of his oil competitors. It was also John D. who said "competition is a sin." National City Bank of Cleveland has been involved in politics for years. It dominates Midwestern industry and politics. Its primary law firm spent $5 million for office space to house a staff of 60 lawyers for lobbying purposes. Perhaps the greatest proof of all that the Rothschilds have controlled the American economy via the Federal Reserve Bank is that the very legislation used to promulgate this private central bank was modeled on their previous acquisitions: The Reichsbank, the Bank of England, and the Bank of France (among many others)![200]

Even before 1935, some were beginning to notice an odor to our foreign policy. There are many who think our foreign policy is inconsistent or that we have no foreign policy at all. Nothing could be further from the truth! In the November 1935 issue of *Common Sense,* General Smedley D. Butler wrote regarding his Marine career, "I helped make Mexico and especially Tampico safe for American oil interests in 1914. I helped make Haiti and Cuba a decent place for the National City Bank boys to collect revenues in....I helped purify Nicaragua for the international banking house of Brown Brothers in 1909–1912.

"In China in 1927, I helped see to it that Standard Oil went its way unmolested. In 1899 J.P. Morgan floated the first important foreign loan on behalf of the Mexican Government. In 1901, he lent $50 million to the British Government to fight the Boer War. It was mainly into the countries of Spanish America that American Capital found its way."[201]

Mullins ties J.P. Morgan into the Rothschild allowance as well, but the more interesting story is that of Brown Brothers, which later became Brown Brothers Harriman. In the December 1935 issue of *Common Sense,* Butler continued to reveal, "In 1910, six months after the Nicaraguan Revolution which ousted President Zelaya, his successor, Dr. Madris, grew cold towards the Nicaraguan investment of Brown Brothers and Seligman Co. Another revolution immediately 'occurred.'"[202]

Brown Brothers has two very interesting tie-ins for us since we are now beginning to discover who really is in charge of America. The first is that there is and has always been a historic link between Brown Brothers and the Bank of England. The governor of the Bank of England, Lord Montague Norman, was a director of Brown Brothers. Now, for the most part, I would encourage the reader not to get hung up in worrying about names. There are themes to follow and things to learn; the names only lead us to the melody. However, even if I told you to forget one upcoming name, you could not do it. In 1931 W. Averill Harriman, son of E.H. Harriman, merged his banking house with Brown Brothers. In the 1920s W.A. Harriman was a prime supporter of the Bolshevik (Communist) Revolution with both finance and diplomatic assistance, at a time when such aid was strictly forbidden by U.S. law. Nor did Harriman inform the State Department of his plans. Nonetheless, Averill Harriman was later to become the U.S. ambassador to Russia!

The State Department was not allowed to investigate. At a later date in history the Union Banking Corporation of New York played an incongruous role in history. This bank, of which E. Roland Harriman was a director, helped finance Hitler! Other directors on the board of Brown Brothers Harriman and the Union Banking Corporation included none other than Prescott Sheldon Bush, father of George Bush! As it turns out, these same groups helped to establish RCA and finance CBS.

Is it any wonder we can't get the truth in news?

To make matters worse, W. Averill Harriman, E. Roland Harriman, Prescott Sheldon Bush, and George Bush are all members of a secret Yale Society called the *Skull & Bones.* Although referred to as a harmless social organization by some, Antony C. Sutton in his book *America's Secret Establishment* proposes that the preponderance of evidence shows that this is an American branch of the Bavarian Illuminati which espoused the overthrow of the Bavarian government and sought world dictatorship![203] Other

116

famous members of the *Skull & Bones* include: Henry Luce (Time-Life) and Mr. Conservative, William Buckley Jr. (*National Review*).

Prescott Bush was also: chairman of the board, Pennsylvania Water & Power Co.; director, U.S. Rubber, Pan Am, CBS, Dresser Mtg. Co. Vanadium, U.S. Guaranty, Prudential Insurance; partner of Brown Brothers Harriman; chairman of National War Fund 1943–1944 USO.

George Herbert Walker Bush, grandfather of George Bush, was: president, W.A. Harriman Company, 1928; chairman, Habershaw Cable Corp., International Great Northern Railway; director, Belgian-American Coke Ovens Corp., Certain Tweed Products American Shipping & Commerce Corp., American International Corp., Cuba Railway Co., Pennsylvania Coal & Coke, Donor Walker Cup (Golf); president, U.S. Golf Association; financed Madison Square Garden.

W.A. Harriman et. al. are still financing the Soviets. Recently Harriman gave $15 million to the Russian Institute at Columbia. The recipients were so elated they changed the name to the Harriman Institute.

With the development of a New World Order of finance and commerce, the Anglo-American-CFR combine has one peg already in the ground. The second obviously is the many appointments to the State Department and other high-level offices through the CFR and Trilateral Commission. Throughout the Nelson Rockefeller years it was reported that Nelson Rockefeller demanded and received the privilege of naming his own men to top administrative posts. So much for the Rush Limbaugh charade of Republican versus Democrat.

The MNC has been on the road to global occupation since the turn of the century. Big business actually helps government write the laws and regulations which encourage a global economy. This is nothing new; the international bankers wrote the rule book on the Federal Reserve Bank which is 100 percent a private bank and which receives billions of back-breaking interest from honest, hard-working American people. The true owners and controllers of the major international MNCs are also the bankers who own the Federal Reserve Bank. Given the amount of funds which the U.S. taxpayers have paid in interest on our spiraling debt, these bankers have well afforded to purchase every major money-producing asset (i.e., mine, factory, forest, and corporation) in the world!

Chapter 8

THE MEDIA BLACKOUT

For some time now, even before CNN, Americans have been inundated with "the news." We have been made to feel as if every major happening anywhere in the world is being quickly relayed to our home screen for our analysis. If this is so:

1) Why is it that all of the major networks always agree? Since childhood I cannot remember ever turning the channel from ABC to NBC or to CBS and receiving a totally different view on any subject. The laundry gets aired, but no disparate views are presented. There may be an occasional disagreement on views between two people interviewed, but never between stations.

2) If there is true competition, why do the television networks all choose to present the same thing (news, weather, sports) at the same time? If I wanted you to receive my view, I wouldn't speak when someone else was speaking. In other words, I would air my news just after my competitor, so you, the viewer, could see my point of view.

3) Why are all the interviewees from a particular organization I know nothing about? What is the Hudson Institute, and the Brookings Institute? Whose views do they represent? Why is it none of the major networks ever seem to

represent my view, my beliefs, or those of my friends or relatives?

4) Why is it always negative news—news meant to depict all of us as being morally outrageous and out of control, faithless, and "in need" of discipline or, even worse— legislation and <u>control</u>?

Whenever the facts haven't been covered up, it is always helpful to use them as a resource for evidence. The Congressional Record often is purposeful for these kinds of interesting glimpses. In 1917 Congressman Oscar Callaway made the statement: "In March 1915, the J.P. Morgan interests...got together 12 men high up in the newspaper world and employed them to select the most influential newspapers in the U.S. and [a] sufficient number of them to control generally the policy of the daily press of the United States. These 12 men worked the problem out by selecting 179 newspapers, and then began, by an elimination process to retain only those necessary for the purpose of controlling. They found it was necessary to purchase control of 25 of the greatest papers. The 25 papers were agreed upon; emissaries were sent to purchase the policy, national and international of these papers; an agreement was reached; the policy of the papers was bought, to be paid for by the month, an editor was furnished for each paper to <u>properly</u> supervise and edit information regarding the questions of preparedness, militarism, financial policies, and other things of national and international nature considered vital to the interests of the purchasers....This policy also included the <u>suppression</u> of everything in opposition to the wishes of the interests served."[204] The mass media are subject to the same "power behind the throne" as Washington. We do not have honest or free information or news. We have what the movers and shakers of Socialism desire us to know. John Swinton, a *New York Times* editor, once said: "There is no such thing as an independent press in America...."[205] Herman Dinsmore, editor of the foreign edition of the *New York Times* from 1951 to 1960, charged that the: "*New York Times*...is deliberately pitched to the so-called liberal point of view." Moreover, "Positively and negatively, the weight off the *Times* has generally been on the side of the Communists since the end of World War II."[206] Is it possible that the J.P. Morgan CFR interests have been publishing biased views and biased news since 1916? Yes, it is! Over and over men who worked in the news media have tried to warn us that there is no truth in news. In fact, it is worse than that. It is not so much what is reported as what is <u>not</u> reported. It is not so much what is reported but <u>how</u> it is reported. We are being "seeded" day after day with repetitive information which we come to believe as truth, information which *seems* accurate, which is reported from high-sounding officials, educators and scientists and philosophers, and which *could* make sense. (What better example than the travesty in Waco, Texas, after which there was not one dissenting headline throughout the nation's major newspapers.)

One of the most glaring examples of news manipulation is the Vietnam POW-MIA issue. There have been numerous statements made by our government (through the supposed free press) indicating there are no POW-MIAs in Southeast Asia. However, there have been equally numerous reports of sightings of live POW-MIAs in Vietnam, Laos, and Cambodia. The media recently reported that John Kerry and his infidel colleagues were going to Southeast Asia to settle this matter "once and for all." That is exactly the way it was reported in the news.

The trouble is, the news forgot to tell us about the Senate Minority report that has traveled through government circles since May 1991. In this Senate Report, prepared by the U.S. Senate Committee on Foreign Relations, the cover-up on the POW-MIA issue is finally exposed. This document discusses that the U.S. Government has received in excess of 1400 eyewitness sightings of live American POWs. "In addition, the U.S. Government has received thousands and thousands of second-hand reports—accounts often full of vivid detail such as 'my brother told me he saw 11 American POWs being transported in a truck at such and such a place.'"[207]

The Senate report uncovers a predisposition by Department of Defense (DOD) evaluators to ignore corroborative evidence. (Both CIA director Robert M. Gates and Joint Chiefs of Staff head Colin Powell are CFR members.) Even though for the record the DOD has articulated a "they are all dead" policy, documents and witnesses available to the Senate Minority staff showed that the CIA and DIA (Defense Intelligence Agency) knew of Private Robert Garwood's location prior to his return in 1979.

An internationally recognized expert in forensic medicine, Dr. Michael Charney, conducted an extensive review of physical remains "identified" as missing Americans from Southeast Asia by the Army Central Identification Laboratory, Hawaii (CIL-HI). His findings proved that the misidentification of these individuals had to be intentional. Dr. Charney states: "This facility (CIL-HI), entrusted with the analysis of mostly skeletonized remains of our servicemen and women in the identification process, is guilty of unscientific, unprofessional work. The administrative and technical personnel have engaged knowingly in <u>deliberate</u> <u>distortion</u> of details deduced from the bones to give credibility to otherwise impossible identification."[208] Charney goes on to level that the Army Central Intelligence Laboratory "has blatantly and <u>deliberately</u> <u>lied</u> about a large number of the remains...."[209] He proposes that "the only conceivable reason for this demonstrable pattern of misidentification was a desire to clear the lists of MIA while <u>deceiving</u> the MIA families...."[210]

Where are the media investigative reporters when these findings come out? To what degree do media outlets represent the people of this country, or to what degree do they represent the planning and secrecy of the clandestine figures behind the government? Who wouldn't desire to know that there are still live fighting men stuck in labor camps after having fought valiantly for their country? If he were your husband, father, brother, son, uncle, or friend, would you care?

It gets worse. The report discusses a letter, hand-carried by Henry Kissinger CFR, not revealed even to the highest-ranking senators and members of Congress, which promised upwards of $5 billion to Hanoi. Apparently Kissinger, the State Department, and the executive branch had forgotten the constitutional caveat that these funds were supposed to be appropriated by the U.S. Congress. This "secret executive agreement" should not be a surprise to anyone by now. The CFR is no respecter of Congress. It owns Congress and the media. Were it not for free, analytical thinkers, it would own the American people.

The Foreign Relations Staff found: "In fact, the total number of U.S. POWs repatriated by the North Vietnamese during Operation Homecoming in April 1973 was 591. At that time, the U.S. Government listed 2,538 missing in action. However, sources interviewed by the Committee staff stated that this official number did not include MIAs assigned to covert or black operations. They estimated the number of covert MIAs at another 2,500, making a total of over 5,000 MIAs—over twice the official number!

"Thus, the 591 U.S. POWs, who were returned by North Vietnam represent about 12 percent of the total number missing. In actuality, the vast majority of the 591 returned POWs were known POWs, not listed as MIA; therefore, the percentage of MIAs who were returned is much, much less. For example, a former National Security Agency employee listening to enemy communications intercepts compiled a list of 305 names of U.S. personnel who were captured alive according to enemy field reports. Yet only 15 of these men known to have been taken alive were included in the 591 who were repatriated—only 2.5 percent!"[211]

This is a public document! Where are the media crying foul!

The Minority Staff reported "evidence that a number of non-repatriated Americans may have been turned over to Soviet control...[they] have been sent to the Soviet Union for interrogation and subsequent use of their special skills."[212] Now that the USSR is a so-called "democracy", we should have no problem getting our POW-MIAs back. However, it would be impolite to ask them, threatening to our government to receive them, and too late for many who have been there since 1919.

What? Yes! The Senate report establishes that, as far back as World War I, it was official American policy that "An administrative determination has been placed on each of their records that they were killed in action on the date they were reported as missing."[213] This means that all the men who were missing in action were determined automatically to be KIA-BNR (Killed In Action-Body Not Recovered) on the date of missing. This is a neat and tidy system which prevents any messy follow-up of having to search out, locate, or retrieve any POWs or MIAs. Where is the cry of the media? Oh, how treasonous!

After the Korean War a secret memorandum explained that "a further complicating factor in the situation is that to continue to carry this personnel in a missing status is costing over one million dollars annually. It may become necessary at some future date to drop them from our records as 'missing and presumed dead.'"[214] The problem was termed "philosophical" and the Defense Department did in fact "drop them" from DOD records.

The U.S. Government documents state that the government knew that nearly 1,000 U.S. POWs—and approximately 8,000 U.S. MIAs—were still held captive after operation BIG SWITCH (Korean War). Many of the unrepatriated servicemen were Negroes, as reported by a Greek refugee. The Establishment ruling class probably doesn't have much remorse over losing a few black patriots to Communists. The trouble is, it seems apparent they don't care about American patriots period!

The charade is appropriately depicted in 1980 by a memorandum written from Michael Oksenberg to CFR director Zbigniew Brzezinski: "a letter from you is important to indicate that you take recent reports of sighting of live Americans 'seriously'. This is simply good politics; DIA and State are playing this game, and you should not be the whistle-blower. The idea is to say that the President [Carter] is determined to pursue any lead concerning possible live MIAs."[215]

Consider fighting for America. You might reconsider, once you understand the U.S. position on your hopes of returning to the land of the free and the brave. The Senate report goes on to exclaim, "Despite the total victory in Europe by Allied Forces, thousands and thousands of U.S. Soldiers—perhaps as many as 20,000—were never repatriated from prisoner of war camps, prisons, and forced labor and concentration camps."[216] These were soldiers held in Nazi prison camps which were overrun by the Red Army. An OSS report subtitled *Treatment of American PWs* (World War II), revealed that the "Russian security was more stringent there [Odessa] than German security had been in the various Stalags and Oflags."[217] The Soviets weren't partial, however; the Senate document estimates 500,000 Japanese prisoners, tens of thousands of Dutch and Belgians, and hundreds of thousands of French prisoners.

Actually, the POW-MIAs were never meant to be discovered. If so, why would General Dwight D. Eisenhower CFR, the Supreme Allied Commander in Europe, decide to stop the U.S. and British drive eastward into Germany and allow the Soviet forces to drive westward into Berlin? That allowed the Soviets not only to keep the POWs and have a source of slave labor to rebuild their industrial base, but also to contain and control millions of people in what became the Warsaw Pact. The media says the Soviets are no more. But in fact Boris Yeltsin has more dictatorial power now than any of his predecessors. He is just not using it. Yet, how can we blame the Soviets, when again we discover the traitorous nature of our own "elected" government.

On May 19, 1945, a cable signed by General Eisenhower at the Allies Supreme Headquarters stated that: "Numbers of U.S. prisoners estimated in Russian control 25,000."[218] On May 30, 1945, Eisenhower's Surgeon General Kenner received a memorandum stating that 20,000 Americans remained under Red Army control. Yet, on June 1, 1945, an Eisenhower signed cable read: "It is now estimated that only small numbers of U.S. prisoners of war still remain in Russian hands. These no doubt are scattered singly and in small groups as no information is available of any large numbers in specific camps...."[219] Amazing how things can change in 48 hours! To echo the propaganda newsline was "all the news that's fit to print," *New York Times*. Without substantiation, they announced, "substantially all"[220] of the American soldiers taken prisoner in Europe are accounted for.

The charge of the Senate Report, dated May 23, 1991, is burdensome: "but as the investigation proceeded, the weight of evidence of failure—of the U.S. Government to meet its sacred trust—became overpowering."[221] The resignation of Colonel Millard A. Peck, chief of the Special Office for Prisoners of War and Missing in Action, is a sad eulogy to what was once a country of free men with a free press. He describes what he believes to be a government conspiracy manipulated by a "totally Machiavellian group of players outside of DIA" (Defense Intelligence Agency). He suggests that the POW-MIA issue has been abandoned and that the bureaucrats would sacrifice anyone who became troublesome as quickly as they have excised the POW-MIA problem. He describes how there is no "audit trail" to discern who these black figures are. Worse yet, he concludes that "any soldier left in Vietnam, even inadvertently, was in fact, abandoned years ago."[222] In his *Farewell to Arms*, Colonel Peck laments:

"So as to avoid the annoyance of being shipped off to some remote corner, out of sight and out of the way, in my own 'bamboo cage' of silence somewhere, I further request that the Defense Intelligence Agency, which I have attempted to serve loyally and with honor, assist me in being retired immediately from active military service."[223]

Millard A. Peck
Colonel, Infantry
USA

Suffice it to say that there has been a complete government cover-up on the POW-MIA issue.

What else is the government/media/one-world clique not telling us? Anyone who has not figured out by now that John F. Kennedy was killed by an operative of our own government working for the CFR/CIA network has been in suspended animation on planet Neptune and has just been revived. All of the government's reactions to this have been lies. What else? How about the fact that there were two other men in 1992 who were running for president on the Independent party ticket—Colonel "Bo" Gritz and Howard Phillips. Neither of them desired any allegiance to the "Republicrat" parties and each is a God-fearing, honest man representing constitutional and patriotic, American interests. That, in itself, was enough reason for the media propaganda artists not to notice their existence. Since they hold no union with the Round Table-CFR network, they are simply "avoided" for the global plan (meaning misery and poverty for America) to succeed.

Again, what the media tells us is as deceptive as what the media does not tell us. Just lately, it was reported that the altruistic International Monetary Fund (IMF) has accepted the suddenly democratic Soviet Union into its financial cluster of debtor nations. The one thing the media forgot to report is that like the Export-Import Bank of 1934, we, the American taxpayers, subsidize all unpaid monies to the bank. The bankers couldn't care less if they lend money to Old MacDonald's cow. They receive the control and domination of the debtor country, and Americans pay the bill.

Anyone who watches TV, listens to the radio, or reads the press and/or periodicals must observe that, without exception, there is a liberal, socialistic tone. Never will there be an honest sharing of viewpoints. If there is any question at all, it is weighted so heavily in favor of what they desire us to believe that it may as well go unmentioned. Or they will "set up" someone for an interview and nonchalantly make a fool out of him in front of the public audience. Anyone who has ever given a truly opposing view has been smeared or ridiculed by the press and media. Remember, however, that there are unseen powers behind the thrones visible in Washington and in the media.

We have all now witnessed the "fall" of the Soviet empire. You may say, "Who cares? Their system failed them. That's obvious." Every TV newscast, newspaper, and journal has shown us that. Yes, the door now has opened, but where did the leaders go? Did they just dry up? Have they all become Democrats? Have they given up their faith in socialism, which has been their only known god? Recently a troupe of missionaries spoke at our church. They stated that although the door to evangelism has been opened to the Communist countries—all the heads of state of every previous Communist country has remained the same! Then why has the door been opened? The media made a big to-do about the huge statue of Lenin being brought down. Ironically, no one reported one of Lenin's most famous works: *Imperialism, The Highest Stage of Capitalism.*

Any citizen who operates in contemporary society should have noticed by now that we are constantly bombarded by "mother earth," the environment, planetary awareness, and "global" concerns. What most people never stop to consider is why in every ad in every newspaper, every billboard, even at the Hard Rock Cafe and McDonald's do we encounter the planet and its desperate concerns.

The Planned Destruction of America

Why does *every* major corporation, news channel, periodical, and newspaper suddenly, all at once, start chirping for us to be ecologically-minded dwellers of mother earth? This is better known as media propaganda. In Russia they called it Pravda. In the United States it is called a "free press." Free means free to distill whatever message the news media chooses to send in order to coerce us into its hidden agenda.

Do all these major global corporations suddenly feel guilty about the environment they have done the most to pollute? Is there global warming? Many scientists say no! We don't hear from them! Was there a creation? Many scientists have much evidence to indicate there was. We don't hear from them.

Is abortion killing a baby? The media disregards even the thought of an opposing view. Once you watch Shari Richard's "A Window to the Womb," a video of ultrasound images, you will identify the certainty of another view as well. In her video, Shari explains that the fetal heartbeat begins at 4 weeks. Beyond a shadow of a doubt the viewer can see a 10-week-old baby literally propelling himself off the walls of the womb. At the subcommittee meeting where she was called to give her side of the story Senator Brenner stated, "This is an attempt at censorship of a pro-life witness's testimony that is not in keeping with a subcommittee that is supposed to be concerned about 'civil rights'..." Senator Brenner then stormed out of the meeting. (Refer to Appendix, number 15)

No, we are not given the truth. We are not even given alternative choices. As a matter of fact, I have wondered if the average American isn't so brainwashed by now, that given viable alternatives, he has any reasoning and analytical powers left. If the media and its behind-the-scene puppeteers really believed that their plan for us is the best plan, then we should be presented all the views concerning the issues and judge for ourselves. Rather than be forthright, however, their plan is best kept behind the secret corridors of the CFR. The masters believe our understanding is too shallow to decide for ourselves. They have decided what they will show us and what they won't so that we will soon desire the ushering in of their New World Order and one-world currency (soon to be cashless) and a slave state!

To those who hasten to their daily newspaper or their favorite news station for accurate information it will be difficult to accept the fact that our "free press" has forced its own agenda on the American people! If at the present time you don't receive your news via a private source, newsletter, or listen to private (e.g., Christian) radio and TV, you and yours are becoming slowly ingrained with one of the most insidious plots since the downfall of Troy. If any of the previous bears out, we should see some evidence of it in the ownership of our "free media." What does the documentation show?

In 1896 the *New York Times* was bought by Alfred Ochs with backing from J.P. Morgan (CFR), Rothschild agent August Belmont, and Jacob Schiff of Kuhn, Loeb banking. It has been passed on to Arthur Ochs Sulzberger of—guess who?—the Council on Foreign Relations. The *Washington Post* was purchased in 1933 by Eugene Meyer. Meyer had joined the CFR in 1929. Today the *Post* is run by Katherine Graham (CFR), Meyer's daughter. *Washington Post* owns *Newsweek,* a descendent of *Today,* founded by Averill Harriman, CFR member since 1923. *Time* was founded by Henry Luce (CFR). Time Inc., which also publishes *People, Life, Fortune, Money,* and *Sports Illustrated,* has several CFR members on its board of directors.

In 1987 CBS had 11 of 14 board members enlisted in the CFR. Its chairman and CBS news anchor Dan Rather are both members of the CFR. The father of George Bush, Prescott Bush, was one of the early developers of CBS. CBS helped finance the Trilateral Commission. NBC is a subsidiary of RCA which was started by David Sarnoff CFR. Actually Sarnoff started ABC and CBS as well. Sarnoff had financial backing from Kuhn, Loeb and other Rothschild banking firms. NBC's chairman of the board is a member of the CFR as well as Marvin Kalb, John Chancellor, and Irving R. Levine. ABC obviously has CFR members on its board of directors as well. Two notables, who deliver the CFR gospel every night, are Ted Koppel and David Brinkley—both CFR. The CFR-Round Table message is delivered through the *Wall Street Journal, Los Angeles Times, Associated Press, PBS, Chicago Tribune,* and many, many others. Book publishers associated with the CFR include:

MacMillan	Random House
Simon and Schuster	McGraw-Hill
Harper Brothers	IBM Publishing
Xerox Corp.	Yale University Press
Little Brown and Co.	Viking Press
Cowles Publishing	Harper & Row

Since many of these publish textbooks, the CFR has and is sewing its secret philosophies into the fabric of our nation's children and college students as well. In his book *En Route to Global Occupation*, Gary Kah explains: "After finding out about the establishment's control of mass communication, I was even more appalled, but now, at least, I understand why I hadn't learned about the conspiracy any earlier. The Rockefellers controlled <u>every facet of the information industry</u>, from television to public education."[224]

It is a well-known fact that in the years 1900 to 1912, newspapers exposed the systematic bribery of government officials by banks and industries as well as abuses by monopolies and trusts. Thereby, J.P. Morgan and Rockefeller bought controlling interest in their meddling exposers' magazines (*Harper's, Scribners, Century...*) and set them in a new direction. With no genuinely diverse voices in the media, the result is an overemphasis on the world as seen by the financial powers; that is, the world as <u>they</u> wish it to be seen.

With textbooks, colleges and universities, day-care centers, TV, and every other element known to mankind spewing out the CFR-Round Table message, we have a guaranteed globalist, pro-socialist agenda being delivered daily to our door and we pay them for it! How many hours a week is your family watching TV? How long does it take to inculcate this Pravda-like brainwashing into your psyche?

By now it will not be a surprise to learn that the Chase Manhattan Bank and other Rockefeller institutions are among the largest holders of network stock with substantial interests in all three networks, ABC, CBS, and NBC. Ben Bagdikian, in *The Media Monopoly*, indicates the breadth of the tightening noose of control over our information: "There are 1000 television stations in the country and 3 national networks, but a person unacquainted with the personalities involved would have trouble distinguishing anything individual about any one station either in its entertainment, which is literally interchangeable among stations and networks, or in its news. The three networks it has been observed, are one network in triplicate."[225]

Even the wire services are CFR-Rockefeller controlled. Associated Press, UPI, Reuters, and CNN all have official ties to the CFR. Appropriately enough, it was not a psychologist nor a psychiatrist but a media man, C.D. Jackson, who was the deputy head of psychological warfare at Eisenhower's wartime headquarters. He was the publisher of *Fortune* magazine and director of Time-Life, well used to imposing psychological warfare on the American people. It was also under Eisenhower that Nelson Rockefeller ran the autocratic rule of the Rockefeller-humanism charged Department of Health, Education, and Welfare. Rockefeller created the department and ran it. Jackson's boss, Henry Luce, owner of *Time Life*, and other publications served for a time as trustee of the Institute for Pacific Relations (IPR). The IPR has been used by the CFR-controlled State Department to influence far eastern policies.

For decades, Rockefeller and Rothschild (CFR) have been shaping our children via secular humanism and continue to do so at an alarming rate. According to Gary Allen, author of *The Rockefeller File*, "The foundations (principally Carnegie, Rockefeller, and Ford) stimulated two-thirds of the total endowment funding of all institutions of higher learning in America during the first third of this century. During this period, the Carnegie-Rockefeller complex supplied twenty percent of the total income of colleges and universities and became in fact, if not in name, a sort of U.S. Ministry of Education."[226]

The Reece Committee (House of Representatives, 83rd congress 2nd session), when investigating foundation control over teacher training schools, learned: *"Research and experimental studies were established at selected universities, notably Columbia, Stanford, and Chicago. Here, some of the worst mischief in recent education was born. In these Rockefeller-and-Carnegie established vineyards worked many of the principal characters in the story of the suborning of American education. Here, foundations nurtured some of the most ardent academic advocates of upsetting the American system and supplanting it with a Socialist state."*[227] Now you understand why Johnny can't read. It was planned that way.

The Rockefellers have used their money to seize control of America's centers of teacher training and have spent millions to rewrite history and create texts which undermine patriotism and free enterprise. The California legislature refused to appropriate money for one series of Rockefeller-grant textbooks. These books called *Building America* were filled with so much Marxist propaganda that they were censored even in California. Nevertheless, Rocky financed them and the NEA promoted them. Rockefeller establishes his dictatorial control through the CFR. Today there is almost no school free of this draconian, socialistic propaganda. The lock on public education is virtually complete. Again, the fruit of the tree is evidenced by the teacher college heads who belong to the Council on Foreign Relations:

> Columbia University - Michael I. Sovern CFR
> Cornell University - Frank H.T. Rhodes CFR
> New York University - John Brademus CFR
> Sarah Lawrence College - Alice S. Ilchman CFR
> Notre Dame University - Theodore M. Hesburgh CFR/TC

Stanford University - Donald Kennedy CFR
Yale University - Benno C. Schmidt, Jr. CFR
University of Chicago - Hannah Holbom Gray CFR
Johns Hopkins University - Steven Muller CFR
Brown University - Howard R. Swearer CFR
University of Wisconsin - Donna E. Shalala CFR (now
    Secretary of Health and Human Services)
Washington and Lee University - John D. Wilson CFR[228]

The web of globalist intrigue dominates the faculties of the major training schools in the country. There are 69 CFR members on the faculty at the University of Chicago, 58 at Princeton, and 30 at Harvard.

Let's consider another item. How does the media select the news it reports? Is it by coincidence they leave out vital information? Is the fact that your child is no longer considered a ward of the family or of the state, but rather the UN, not newsworthy? It is intriguing that the media neglect to mention such constitutionally altering changes as the United Nations Convention on the "Rights of the Child."

In the midst of the Persian Gulf military buildup, George Bush went to New York to celebrate this event. Sadly, our Socialist Congress hurriedly passed resolutions calling on the president to sign the Convention and send it to the Senate for ratification before Bush attended the summit (The United Nations World Summit for Children).

Only Representative Thomas J. Bliley (R-VA) seemed to notice there had been no hearings on this treaty. His reading of the document convinced him "that the Convention represents a potential threat to our form of government."[229] He asked of his colleagues, "Have we resolved in our minds its inherent conflicts with the U.S. Constitution? I think not. Do we realize the great new powers Congress is taking away from the sovereign states, as well as giving up itself, to the judiciary?"[230]

The Convention on the Rights of the Child provides opportunity and authority for the United Nations, or the U.S. government acting under the UN Convention, to enforce its provisions *against state and local governments, and even against parents!* Similar to the UN Charter (written by Communists) and the Soviet Constitution, the Convention views rights not as God-given and unalienable, but as government-given and conditional. Stalin's chairman of the Soviet Supreme Court Andrei Vishinsky, proclaimed "The rights of human beings cannot be considered outside the prerogatives of governments, and the very understanding of human rights is a governmental concept."[231] Article 14, Section 1 of the UN Convention on the Rights of the Child states "Parties shall respect the right of the child to freedom of thought, conscience, and religion."[232] The trouble is, that right is nullified in Section 3 with a typical Soviet-style clause: "Freedom to manifest one's religion or beliefs may be subject only to such limitations as are prescribed by law..."[233] Since this convention is in the form of a treaty, under currently prevailing jurisprudence, all treaties—regardless of their constitutionality—are the "supreme law of the land."

In Article 28, the treaty recognizes a "right of the child to education." Who could argue with that? There's just one problem; that is, private schools, like public schools, must teach "the principles enshrined in the Charter of the United Nations...."[234]

Speaking of shrine, this is the same United Nations whose Meditation Room has a magnetite block, a metal altar, which symbolizes the ancient pagan form of stone worship in the Old Testament.

To continue, it has been argued that this treaty would amount to a whole new Socialist Manifesto for America. Where is the media? Where are the opposing sides debating over the true intrinsic value to our children of this all-encompassing treaty? The answer, as usual, is nowhere! They do not want us to know that this document exists, much less that it completely annihilates the U.S. Constitution. At last vote, we were only two states away from voting in an amendment to alter the Constitution anyway, so why get everyone all excited now? Bliley concluded: "It finally becomes clear. Ratification is not about children; it is about power."[235] Similar to other UN treaties (environment, women's rights, animal rights, minority rights, drug trafficking, etc.), it is about the power to undermine and destroy our Constitution, our national sovereignty, and our God-given rights.

I have repeatedly tried to ignore the writings of many authors and save the reader and myself from delving into "uncharted territory." However, there have been certain undesirable links between my research on the media and that "C" word—outdated and not to be used anymore—communism. Of course, as the United States promotes the advancement of socialism, and the USSR develops a democracy, (which historically ends in socialism), the old term (communism) gets thrown out. Here are a few facts:

1.) David Sarnoff, founder of RCA, NBC, ABC, CBS was born in Russia. RCA has been a major contributor to the CFR. Sarnoff is a former British Intelligence agent.[236]

2.) William S. Paley's real name is Palinski. He is also a native Russian. Paley, chairman of the board of CBS, (which has 200 TV and 255 radio affiliates) is a CFR member and trustee of the Ford Foundation. He is also a former British Intelligence agent.[237]

3.) *Look* magazine (7,750,000 copies distributed per issue) was owned by Cowles Communications. Their publishing empire encompassed *Harper's,* trade journals, a string of newspaper and television stations, and Harper & Row. John and Gardner Cowles have been members of the Council on Foreign Relations. John Cowles was on the Advisory Council of the U.S. Committee for the UN and the ultra-leftist National Committee for an Effective Congress, which has operated a soft-on-Communists lobby in Washington. As far back as 1954, John Cowles along with others sent numerous telegrams to U.S. senators asking support for measures which would stifle all Congressional investigations of communism.

In 1959 a UPI dispatch reported: "John Cowles, publisher of *The Minneapolis Star and Tribune,* said today that the traditional American concept of national sovereignty is obsolete..." William Atwood CFR ran *Look* magazine for the Cowles and once wrote we could "thank our lucky stars that Castro is not a Communist."[238] The Time Corporation (CFR) is part owner of media in South America, West Germany, Hong Kong, and Australia. Whittaker Chambers was a member of the U.S. Communist Party. As a senior editor of *Time,* he exposed Alger Hiss (CFR) in 1949 as a Communist spy in the State Department. Hiss was the first chairman of the UN and had helped draft the National Recovery Act and the Agricultural Adjustment Act. Apparently Chambers went against Time-Life pro-Communist policy, as he was not welcomed back to Time-Life after he had testified against Alger Hiss.

When Chambers died in 1961, the Associated Press (CFR) used so many hate descriptions that one of the few truly free newspapers protested. The *Sentinel Star* of Orlando, Florida, (now the *Orlando Sentinel* and part of the *Chicago Tribune*) published an editorial of dissent: "The staid powerful Associated Press handled the news of Whittaker Chambers in a peculiar way....Chambers, you may remember, was a $30,000 a year senior editor of *Time,* who, in 1948, put the finger on Alger Hiss, the State Department spy, and lost his job, his reputation, and his health. The only reason we can think of is patriotism. He made a clean breast of everything; he wanted to atone for his mistake by warning the U.S. of its danger.

"The AP's handling tends to indict him for being loyal to the U.S. The AP calls him a 'turncoat Communist.' Turncoat is a despised appellation and the inference is that anyone who turns from communism should be despised. The AP says Chambers 'tattled.' Telling the truth is honorable, but, from childhood, we are taught that tattling is unworthy. The AP says Chambers 'recited' to a 'Congressional spy-hunting committee,' implying that he merely repeated a cooked-up story and that spy-hunting is not a serious matter.

"Whereas the AP calls Hiss 'brilliant,' it kisses off Chambers as being 'pudgy, short, and fat' and says 'he lived with a woman outside of marriage.' This was before he married a woman to whom he was devoted for 30 years until his death."

The Sentinel later concluded: "We are living in peculiar times, gentlemen of the Associated Press, when patriots are maligned."[239]

JFK's first secretary of labor was Arthur Goldberg. Goldberg had served a number of Communist causes and fronts. He had been president of the Chicago Chapter of the National Lawyers Guild, a guild officially cited by the House Committee on Un-American Activities as "the legal bulwark of the Communist Party." He had served as a sponsor of the Conference on Constitutional Liberties in America, a Communist front designated by the Attorney General. As Secretary of Labor, Goldberg appointed Walter Gellhorn of Columbia University to a high level government position. Louis Budenz, before the House of Representatives Select Committee to Investigate Tax-Exempt foundations, identified Gellhorn as a Communist. The point is, that since the press ignored all information to the contrary, even though Goldberg never denied Communist affiliation, he went on to be appointed a Supreme Court Justice! In 1920, it was another Supreme Court Justice, Felix Frankfurter, a member of the Council on Foreign Relations, who founded the ACLU! His compatriots were William Z. Foster once head of the U.S. Communist Party; Elizabeth Gurley Flynn, a top Communist Party official, and Dr. Harry F. Ward of Union Theological Seminary, a notorious Communist front.

Another media blackout occurred in 1962, during a Senate investigation regarding the special assistant to Defense Secretary Robert McNamara. His understudy, Adam Yarmolinsky, had admitted attending meetings of the Young Communist League. He said, "They believed and I was inclined to believe that a so-called Communist government was a desirable end."[240] Yarmolinsky had authored a vicious attack on congressional committees which investigate communism and also security agencies such as the FBI which attempt to protect the nation from Communist subversion. The only press coverage of these aspects of the background of a top Defense Department Official has been limited ridicule of those who call attention to them. Should we be surprised then, that Whittaker Chambers, an ex-member of the Communist Party of the United States, wrote, "There is probably no important magazine or newspaper in the country that is not communist-penetrated to some degree."[241] Sadly, the demise of the American political system appears to go back farther than most of us remember.

What is apparent, however, is that today, hardly any thinking American is unaware that our system is not working. I must submit to you that those men who are portrayed as our elected representatives on TV are nothing more than puppets of a world system. I submit to you that America has been surreptitiously invaded by known members of the Communist party and the Communist party has had ties to the CFR since its Round Table infancy. And naturally, the CFR-controlled media is not likely to expose its plan of one-world socialism to the American people. Although CFR membership in America's key mass media is rampant, it can hardly be by accident that so few people know about the CFR.

Another Communist cover-up by the mass communications media is the recent media manipulation of the truth when newly appointed African National Congress (ANC) head, Nelson Mandela, came to Washington, D.C. Certainly the federal government, Congress, and senators have as much access to the "truth" as I do. Therefore, I was astounded when our leaders gave Mandela a standing ovation in Congress. Then, with taxpayers' money, they sent him throughout the United States to all the major cities for ticker-tape parades. Nelson Mandela, I already had learned from a private newsletter source, was a Communist! His wife was a murderer. They kill their own black brothers in South Africa by "necklacing" them. That is, they fill a tire full of gasoline, place it over the head of blacks of opposing view and light a match to it. This ugly, unregenerate mode of killing is espoused by the ANC. What has happened to Washington? Perhaps we are beginning to find out.

Believe it or not, on March 13, 1948, President Truman "issued an order instructing all federal employees to withhold personnel loyalty and security information from members of Congress...."[242] This order obviously makes it extremely difficult to pursue any security or loyalty risks through government channels.

This is the same Harry Truman who promoted Harry Dexter White, then assistant secretary of the Treasury, to a high post on the International Monetary Fund. This was even after Truman had received White's complete record as a long-time Communist agent from J. Edgar Hoover. Later, in 1949, Senator McCarthy was shown a "one hundred page summary of Communist subversion in the United States, including serious penetration of the State Department."[243] The report had been prepared under the direction of J. Edgar Hoover. "It detailed the operations of spy networks operating in the U.S. government and involving a large number of State Department employees, some in very high positions."[244] Joe McCarthy saw that all the juxtapositioning of the State Department and government were the work of a giant conspiracy. He wrote: "How can we account for our present situation unless we believe that men high in government are concerting to deliver us to disaster? This must be the product of a great conspiracy, a conspiracy on a scale so immense as to dwarf any previous such venture in the history of man....What can be made of this unbroken series of decisions and acts contributing to the strategy of defeat? They cannot be attributed to incompetence....The laws of probability would dictate that part of...[the] decisions would serve this country's interest."[245]

However, you may remember McCarthy, after the media smeared him as a psychopath, the government later substantiated his charges in 1953 in a report called *Interlocking Subversion in Government Departments*, written by the Senate Internal Security Subcommittee. It read: "The Soviet International Organization has carried on a successful and important penetration of the United States Government, and this penetration has not been fully exposed. This penetration has extended from the lower ranks to top-level policy and operating positions in our government. Despite the fact that the Federal Bureau of Investigation and other security agencies had reported extensive information about this Communist penetration, little was done by the executive branch to interrupt the Soviet operatives in their ascent in government...."[246] Was McCarthy a lunatic?

The Senate Internal Security Subcommittee revealed on June 27, 1956, the State Department's own security chief, Scott McLeod, had drawn up a list of 847 security risks in the State Department! All of the 81 risks McCarthy identified were either dismissed or resigned. His major mistake seems to be that he underestimated the extent to which the State Department *had* been penetrated. As far back as 1938, Supreme Court Justice Frank Murphy met with Congressman Martin Dies, the chairman of the House Committee on Un-American Activities. Murphy told Dies: "We're doomed! The Communists have control completely. They've got control of Roosevelt and his wife as well."[247]

In 1949, when Murphy died, it was presumed he had been assassinated. The Dies committee had "compiled lists of thousands of Communists, agents, stooges, and sympathizers on the government payroll."[248] He took the revealing information to President Roosevelt personally. Furiously, Roosevelt responded, "I have never seen a man who had such exaggerated ideas about this thing. I do not believe in communism anymore than you do but there is nothing wrong with the communists in this country; several of the best friends I've got are communists."[249] Apparently this was so, since the New Deal's farm program was "laced" with lawyers like Alger Hiss, Adlai Stevenson, John Abt, Nathan Witt, Nathaniel Weyl, and Charles Kramer. All of them except Stevenson were identified as secret communist agents.

James Forrestal was America's first secretary of defense (1947–1949) He was asked to resign by Truman and did. It was thought by many that he too was secretly assassinated but not before he had written a number of letters to his pastor, Monsignor Sheehy. Sheehy is on record as saying: "Many, many times in his letters to me, Jim Forrestal wrote anxiously and fearfully and bitterly of the enormous harm that had been, and was unceasingly being done, by men in high office in the United States government to aid Soviet Russia and harm the United States."[250]

Edward R. Murrow, once vice president of CBS then head of the United States Information Agency, was an ardent defender of two Communist invaders in the State Department, Alger Hiss and Owen Lattimore. Murrow did a select job of film editing to perform a character assassination of anti-Communist Joseph McCarthy.

Apparently, no one was ever to know about the memorandum sent to Secretary of State George C. Marshall by the Senate Committee on Appropriations regarding the FBI report on Soviet espionage activities in the United States involving large numbers of high-level State Department employees. The memo stated, "There is a deliberate, calculated program carried out not only to protect Communist personnel in high places, but to reduce security and intelligence protection to a nullity. Should this case break before the Senate Department acts, it will be a national disgrace."[251] Marshall completely ignored the warning. Seemingly, he already knew of the deceit and was content with its purpose.

Recall that the CFR's favorite niche is the State Department. What does it all mean? Who cares about communism? Communism is dead. The great Soviet bear has run with his tail between his legs. The Berlin wall is down. The once Communist countries are free. Nonetheless, if what the FBI, the Senate Appropriations Committee, Murphy, Forrester, and McCarthy have said is true, then "communism" has taken on a new look. Communism no longer has the look of the outlandish Stalin regime. It now has the look of "business". It has the sound of environmentalism. The extrapolation of communism has reached its desired intent for the U.S.—more and more government centralization, more socialism, and more economic hardship and less private enterprise. America has entered not the capitalist period, but the super-capitalist period.

As mega-international corporations continue to concentrate ownership and control of property and resources and legislation through political power and media manipulation, there is a natural reduction in the number of private individuals who can begin ownership and compete. Although communism is over in name, the international masters of finance have found a new way of achieving control. That is, extreme poverty. Poverty and strife in all the ex-Communist countries have led to the same kind of debilitating weakness that communism enforced. The powers that are still there, silent unless asking for U.S. taxpayer money, allow the Soviets to have control through Socialistic economics; i.e., poverty. Since everyone is broke, no one is going anywhere. As history shows, this will result in anarchy and complete power in the hands of a few. I never meant to get into "Common-ism," but no one, especially the media, seems to realize that the very mention of a New World Order should bring about cries of "Impeachment!" from the people of this country. George Bush, Bill Clinton, Al Gore, and others who disdain the very document they were sworn to uphold should be immediately impeached.

Where is the media? The media is in bed with the Trilaterist Bush, the CFR's Clinton, and what investigation proves to be their Communist allies. There is no difference between godless communism and godless capitalism.

This book was not meant to prove that the media is Communist-controlled. Yet consider for a moment what is happening in

America.

Every Communist revolution's goal has been to destroy the middle class. This has been done traditionally by creating massive inflation. This tends to destroy people's savings and redistribute wealth.

This is exactly what is happening in America. It is notable that as we uncover the CFR, the Trilateral Commission, the private Federal Reserve Bank, and the biased media we also observe a declining American society and standard of living. One could suggest concurrently that there is less "ordered" government, private property, inheritance, patriotism, family, and religion. Isn't it a grand coincidence that these were the very tenets of the historic great secret order—the Illuminati, and Marxism as well?

Getting back to the media manipulation of American minds, if this one-world, one-government, one-currency system is what is taking place, how would we know? Always, we need to test the fruit of the tree to be sure of the true character of the tree. If the tree regularly grows rotten or destructive fruit, it is rotten and should be cut down. Anyone who currently operates in contemporary society knows we are under constant mental bombardment regarding "earth" issues, "global" issues, and "planetary" issues. Again, why does every major television network and every major media outlet push this on its viewer? Has anyone considered how the "seeds" of "we are all one planet" sow destructively into any form of nationalism and patriotism? Putting America first is bitter in the mouths of those in power. How can the media possibly tell us the truth if they are attached to the same ball and chain as the government? The fact is, they don't tell the truth—and they can't. Simply stated, the powers that control the media support and maintain allegiance to the New World Order, not to the people of the United States. Sad, but true, mass media has become the authority at any given moment for what is true and what is false, what is reality and what is fantasy, what is important and what is trivial. There is no greater force shaping the minds of the public. The authorities in power have long recognized that to control the public they must control the public's information. The few who control news and ideas have political power—the power to disclose or conceal, to announce some parts and not others, to hold back until opportunistic moments, to predetermine the interpretation of what is revealed.

In the 1960s and early 1970s Congressman Wright Patman of Texas was chairman of the House Banking Committee. He tried repeatedly to expose the plot of a takeover of the sovereignty of the

United States. He understood that Rockefeller and Rothschild and their subsidiaries literally loaned money made out of nothing to the American government and that the government (CFR) and Federal Reserve Bank (CFR) were in collusion against the American public. Yet, although he vehemently called for audits of the Federal Reserve and even tried to have the Federal Reserve Act repealed, he never attracted any attention at all from the media. Naturally, we now know why. The club is private, secret, and organized. They formed a private bank, taxed the citizen, legislated against the American people, started two world wars, assassinated the two Kennedys, and continually tell us how strong America is. Yet we never win a war! Moreover, they oppress the American citizen and insult his intelligence.

In frustration Patman exclaimed, "Our exposés of the Federal Reserve Board are shocking and scandalous, but they are only printed in the daily Congressional Record, which is read by very few people."[252] We have today a centralized, private Ministry of Public Information. Each citizen's fate is shaped by powerful forces in distant places. These people set the national agenda. They are shaping the consensus of society. Lord Acton's aphorism that power corrupts and absolute power corrupts absolutely could never be truer. And what could be a more fitting corruption than corrupting 247 million people all at the same time! That is the height of Luciferian dominance.

Thanks to monopoly we no longer have media accountability. This concentration of power over public information is inherently anti-democratic. Centralized control (not at all different from Pravda in the USSR) is totally incompatible with freedom! The idea that the public will reject the media conglomerate product has no strength when public choice is inoperative due to a monopoly. The Rockefellers through their control over public information can shape public opinion and actually determine whether politicians are elected or reelected. Issues can be promoted by the media, or at strategic times, ignored. On March 29, 1979, Lionel Van Deerlin, an ex-journalist and former chairman of the House Subcommittee on Communications made a historic announcement: a new bill would give commercial broadcasters what they had lobbied for—"semipermanent possession of their station licenses, cancellation of the requirement to provide equal access for political candidates, and no further need to present community issues or do it fairly."[253]

This bill proposed a fundamental change. Now, whole generations of American voters have not heard serious content in election campaigns and often have not even heard mention of all the men running. This has left voters starved for pertinent information and at the mercy of paid political propaganda. The central requirement of a democracy is that those who are governed give not only their consent but their *informed* consent (even more important for a Republic). James Britton, in *Language and Learning*, suggests that by removing significant context from human events, all we have left are isolated fragments of information. "We can make nothing of the present moment."[254] Thus, people tend to remain inactive, static, and bewildered, left at the mercy of whoever acts with power; that is, power without accountability.

Congressman Larry McDonald was one of the few patriots who fought against the New World Order in the 1970s and 1980s. In his introduction to the book *The Rockefeller File*, he wrote: *The Rockefeller File* is not fiction. It is a compact, powerful, and frightening presentation of what may be the most important story of our lifetime—the drive of the Rockefellers and their allies to create a one-world government combining super-capitalism and communism under the same tent, all under their control. For more than one hundred years, since the days when John D. Rockefeller, Sr. used every devious strategy he could devise to create a gigantic oil monopoly, enough books have been written about the Rockefellers to fill a library. I have read many of them. And to my knowledge, not one has dared reveal the most vital part of the Rockefeller story: that the Rockefellers and their allies have, for at least fifty years, been carefully following a plan to use their economic power to gain political control of first America, and then the rest of the world. Do I mean conspiracy? Yes, I do. I am convinced there is such a plot, international in scope, generations old in planning, and incredibly evil in intent."[255] McDonald was an ardent anti-Communist. He was equally pro-American. He was a member of the John Birch Society—a good law-abiding group of patriots who support American sovereignty and the Constitution but have been smeared as radical-right by the conspiratorial press. Like Patman, no one in the media would report his findings. Frustrated, he began to travel and speak out publicly on what was happening in our usurped government. On August 31, 1983, McDonald was shot out of the sky in Korean Airlines 007, a commercial jet, which "accidentally" strayed into Soviet airspace. Perhaps President Kennedy was in Soviet airspace when he was shot too.

Most recently, the Rodney King beating in Los Angeles received major media attention. Although I rarely watch secular TV, I couldn't get away from this short video of the King beating. It was on ABC, CBS, and NBC. It was on morning, noon, and night. It was on day after day and week after week. I have never seen such repetition on national media. At the time, I mentioned to a friend, "What are they trying to accomplish here?" He replied, "Man, that was a terrible thing!" I went on, "I know, but they are beating this news piece to death. Surely, they mean to do something with it." Many months later we witnessed the result. While I was still incensed over the jury's inability to rule on the obvious, the phone rang. "Did you watch CNN today?" "No." "Well, they showed a different part of the video—a part we haven't seen before, and it shows King not surrendering to the police, even after 50,000 volts!"

I realized I had been right from the outset. Whatever the rulers of TV want us to see, we see. If we miss it once and it's *really important,* they'll show it again and again and again. I do not agree with the beating King took from the police. Nor do I necessarily agree with any other part of this terrible transaction. However, what followed the verdict (the jury got to watch the entire tape) was exactly what the masters desired to have happen. It was bedlam. It was anarchy. It was white against black, black against white, black against black. The CFR masters got their way. The results were the disrepute of the mainstay judicial jury system, rioting in the streets, federal control over state jurisdiction, and a prototype for the next time they desire to create chaos.

The tentacles of media are long and sharp. They carve into our minds like water creates tributaries through rock in a stream over time. The onslaught is constant, stealthy, and pervasive! With a background in education, I know the value of repetition. It works! We and our children get only the message that the CFR masters desire us to have engraved into our value system.

The all-encompassing nature of the message from the "enlightened" ones is easily portrayed by the Gannett Corporation. In 1967 Gannett had 28 newspapers and $250 million in annual revenues. Financed by Wall Street, the Gannett Corporation (CFR) has since grown to 93 daily papers, 40 weeklies, 15 radio stations, 8 television stations, and 40,000 billboards. Gannett has taken over the Lou Harris Public Opinion Poll, TV productions, half-interest in McNeil-Lehrer Productions (CFR) for television and cable, satellite operation in 36 states and has more than $2 billion in annual revenues. This is no less subtle than surrounding the president with members of a secret society bent on the destruction of America, the American people, and American sovereignty. With one company controlling so many outlets of information, your sons and daughters are getting only the message that they are meant to receive from the financial masters. Are corporate newsmen interested in freedom of the press or telling the truth or educating the public?

When Allen Neuharth was asked about whether the corporate name was pronounced GAN-nett or Gan-NETT, Neuharth smiled and said the proper pronunciation was MONEY. Your hometown paper is like your local congressman. He alone is deserving of being voted back in, but none of the others. Your local paper is "truthful" because you know someone who works there and is a local member of the community! She is a wonderful person, a churchgoer, a loved one. Although this may be true, it does not change the message! Is your local paper a part of a monopoly? "Unfortunately, almost all of them are."[256]

By 1986, of all cities with a daily paper, 98 percent had only one newspaper management (in 1910 more than half of all newspaper cities had local daily competition, typically five or six papers). Without competition, it is not surprising that a *Journalism Quarterly* study said that more than 85 percent of chain papers have uniform political endorsements. Neuharth, like other chain operatives, insists in public that there are no monopolies. Yet, in private, Neuharth tells the truth. In 1976 he reported to Wall Street analysts, "No Gannett newspaper has any direct competition...in any community in which we publish."[257]

Bagdikian, in *The Media Monopoly*, states that Gannett Co. Inc. "is an outstanding contemporary performer of the ancient rite of creating self-serving myths, of committing acts of greed and exploitation but describing them through its own machinery as heroic epics. In real life Gannett has violated laws, doctrines of free enterprise, and journalistic ideals of truthfulness."[258] There is no way that I could explain better than Bagdikian how the press has turned honesty and truthfulness in reporting into mythology, and then, into their own brand of theology. Some call it secular humanism.

"Turning life's natural mixture of the noble and ignoble into unrelieved heroism is done by those, who, like editors of the Soviet Encyclopedia, believe it is their religious duty to mislead the public for its own good or who convince themselves that their heroes' sins are merely misunderstood philanthropy. Every culture has its official folklore. In ancient times medicine men transformed tribal legends to enhance their own status. The twentieth century is no different, but the high priests who communicate mythic dogmas now do so through great centralized machines of communication newspaper chains, broadcast networks, magazine groups, conglomerate book publishers, and movie studios. Operators of these systems disseminate their own version of the world. And of all the legends they generate, none are so heroic as the myths they propagate about themselves."[259] Media is now a vital instrument necessary for the Establishment to maintain their economic and political power over us, the serfs of their New World Order. When they raise enough media hype about gun control, (guns are our only defense against tyranny) and eventually obliterate our sacred U.S. Constitution, in the proverbial phrase, "we have had it!"

As we move on in this great conspiracy by George Bush, Bill Clinton, the Rockefellers, Henry Kissinger, and so on, add these names to your list of present and past CFR members:

CBS
Bill Moyers CFR
William Paley CFR
Dan Rather CFR
Harry Reasoner CFR

NBC/RCA
Tom Brokaw CFR
John Chancellor CFR
Marvin Kalb CFR
Irving R. Levine CFR

ABC
David Brinkley CFR
Ted Koppel CFR
Diane Sawyer CFR
John Scali CFR
Barbara Walters CFR

CNN
Daniel Schoor CFR

PBS
Hodding Carter III CFR
Jim Lehrer CFR
Robert McNeil CFR

If you value your ability to think clearly and scrutinize truth; if you love your family; if you desire good things for your children—turn off the TV! Stop reading the news!

You must seek out honest, reliable sources of information. Christian TV and news is generally one, newsletters are another, but guard yourselves against the "force of evil" in America and its mouthpiece—the national media.

Chapter 9

CALCULATED COVER-UPS

Alaskan Oil

In the process of searching out applicable information on the subject of the demise of the American people and the assassination of the U.S. Constitution, I uncovered a very interesting book titled *The Energy Non-Crisis* by Lindsey Williams. It is the lamentation of a Baptist minister who served as chaplain to the men who worked on the Trans-Alaskan Oil Pipeline. His opening sentence is: *"There is no true energy crisis...except as it has been produced by the Federal government for the purpose of <u>controlling</u> the American people."*[260]

He discusses a conversation he had with then Senator Hugh Chance of Colorado: "Lindsey, I was in the Senate of the State of Colorado when the Federal briefers came in to inform us as to why there is an energy crisis. Lindsey, what I have heard and seen today [Prudhoe Bay], compared with what I was told in the Senate of the State of Colorado, makes me realize that almost everything I was told by those Federal briefers was a downright lie!"[261] Senator Chance's first question to a high-level Atlantic Richfield executive was, "...How much crude oil is there under the North Slope of Alaska, in your estimation?" The response from the oil man, was, "In my estimation, from the seismographic work and the drillings we

145

have already done, I am convinced that there is as much oil under the North Slope of Alaska as there is in all of Saudi Arabia."[262]

The executive, Ken Fromme, explained to Lindsey Williams at a later date that the Prudhoe Bay oil field is one of the richest oil fields on the face of the earth. He said it could flow for over twenty years with natural artesian pressure, without even a pump being placed on it. He also said there was enough natural gas, as distinct from oil, to supply the entire United States of America for more than two hundred years![263]

Fromme is an expert in his field and has developed numerous oil fields for Atlantic Richfield. In speaking to Senator Chance he explained, "...if the government can control energy, they can control industry, they can control an individual, and they can control business. It is well known that everything relates back to crude oil." He furthermore explained, "Over a period of years the intention is that we will fall so far behind in production that we will not have the crude oil here in America and will be totally dependent on foreign nations for our energy. When those foreign nations cut off our oil, we, as Americans, will be helpless."[264]

When Senator Chance asked the ARCO executive what could happen if the entire North Slope of Alaska were developed, the answer came back, "...In five years the United States of America could be totally energy free and totally independent from the rest of the world as far as energy is concerned. What is more, sir, if we were allowed to develop this entire field as private enterprise, within five years the United States of America could control balance payments with every nation on the face of the earth...."[265]

When Senator Chance invited Ronald Reagan to visit the North Slope of Alaska and make the energy crisis a major platform in his campaign, the president wrote back to say, "Sir, I'd like to, but I don't have the time—my schedule will not permit." Williams contends, "This scandal I am exposing is something that leads to the bureaucratic controls behind—and yet beyond—government political leaders, as such."[266]

As Williams watched the Pipeline escapade over two and a half years, he learned that there had been discoveries not only at Prudhoe Bay, but also at Gull Island (four times the size of Prudhoe—estimated as the richest oil field on the face of the earth) and at Kuparuh (an area sixty miles long and thirty miles wide) which contains again as much as Prudhoe Bay! Regarding the Gull Island find, Williams says, "...the government had ordered the oil company to seal the documents, withdraw the rig, cap the well, and not release the information...."[267]

Realizing that the American people could be free of debt and free of tyranny but were instead being deceived, Williams struggled with the why of the issue.

He discovered that even though the oil industry has been superlative in its protection of the Alaskan frontier, much to-do has been made about protecting the ecology. Yet, regarding a typical Sierra Club radio editorial crying out the woeful disturbance to the tender Alaskan ecology, he states, "...I could not find a single accusation in that Sierra Club editorial that was true—not one. It made me realize that the American people were being brainwashed."[268]

In his book, Williams contends that the government has deliberately determined that the oil and gas of Alaska will not reach the people of America. As prices increase, there are more regulations, more taxes, more cutbacks, more energy control, and the household god becomes "conservation."

To make absolutely certain the energy stays locked up, Morris Udahl sponsored the D-2 land bill turning Alaska into a wilderness area where most of its natural resources can never be produced—not even if America goes broke, and, according to nationally known accountant Larry Burkett, it will in 1995 or 1996.

Why, Williams asks himself, would the American government do this to its own people? William's theory is that we will eventually become so disgruntled with the oil companies that we will actually request the federal government to take them over and nationalize them. The ultimate objective, therefore, is to motivate the American people to accept—nay, to beg—for socialization. This is exactly what has been done in moving America toward full blown socialized medical care.

Lastly, how was the energy crisis concocted in America? In 1973 the federal government literally ordered the oil companies to shut down certain cross-country pipelines to reduce the output of refineries at certain strategic points in America. This was specifically to create an energy crisis.[269] Yet in 1973 the crisis was only in the East. This was the prototype to test how far the government could twist gullible TV-watching sponges called Americans. When, finally, everyone was getting heated up, bingo! No more shortage in the East. Suddenly there was a shortage in California. Then, just as suddenly, not in California, but in the Midwest. It was a nice experiment to see how far people can be pushed before they rebel.

We are dependent upon energy. Virtually everything is based on the control of oil and gas and other fuel sources. Whoever controls energy controls us.

Williams summarizes, "Neither did I ever think that our own Federal government would go this far in producing an energy crisis....Of one thing I am convinced. *Somewhere, some place, there definitely appears to be a conspiracy.*"[270]

MNCs and the Genocide of the American Indian

Apparently, Lindsey Williams, prior to becoming a missionary in Alaska, had no knowledge of the history of our own American Indian. Every treaty made by the American government with the Indian has been broken, and nearly every acre of Indian land which had verified oil, coal, or uranium deposits has been usurped or taken back despite all promises to the contrary.

Incredibly, to the average American, the government is just plain stupid. They don't do anything well. Don't allow them to get involved in private enterprise because they'll just make a mess of it. Yet, their true plan, covert though it is, succeeds most effectively, but never to the benefit of the citizens of this country. And as it turns out, never to the benefit of any other country either!

Our true foreign policy plan has worked fine. We are not any longer a sovereign nation; we are a member of the planet. Our economic plan, although listing to the absurd side of indebtness and failure, has worked out fine. Why? Because in order to transform hard-working, God-fearing, family-loving patriotic Americans into world citizens, the entire country will have to fall into a severe depression. Then we will seek what "they" have for us. Why else would the government plan for its own destruction?

In 1973, under the cloud of media hype regarding the national energy crisis, Project Independence was born. Here we have the government lying through the CFR-controlled media that we have no oil left (you have just read the contrary) in order for the energy conglomerates to move into the West and rape the natural resources held on Indian-reserved lands. In August 1979 John Sawhill, a member of the Trilateral Commission, was appointed deputy secretary of energy. He is the coauthor of the Trilateral Commission report *Energy, Managing the Transition*. From late 1973 to early 1975, Sawhill was administrator of the U.S. Federal Energy Administration, an agency created in the wake of the oil embargo and a forerunner of the current Department of Energy, according to the Trilateral Commission.

The Energy Mobilization Board (EMB) was proposed by Carter in 1979 to "cut through the red tape, the delays, and the endless roadblocks to completing key energy projects." Again, this is after the government told Atlantic Richfield not to disclose its findings of an oil reserve in Alaska that would make Americans the richest people on earth. This "fast track" bill empowered the EMB to override federal environmental conservation and other substantive laws with the approval of the president and Congress. In November 1980 Congress voted final approval of a massive $19 billion synthetic fuel program (because we're out of the real stuff). Yet they voted only $1 billion for solar energy and conservation programs. But, oh, we are saving the earth now at the Earth Summit in Brazil. We are, only in that the same masterminds that wreaked havoc on the earth from raping it for money now want to save it and own it for more money. Let's take a look at how the MNCs have cared for the earth and its inhabitants so far.

The coal industry is monopolized by a few select oil companies. Production has shifted from underground mining in Appalachia to strip-mining in the Great Plains and Rocky Mountains. In strip-mining, output per day is 100 percent greater and operating costs 30 percent lower than underground mining. More than 90 percent of U.S. low-sulphur coal reserves are found in the western United States, specifically Wyoming, Montana, New Mexico, and North Dakota.

Through a number of "Leasing Acts," the federal government through the secretary of the interior and the Bureau of Indian Affairs has been authorized to lease public and Indian lands and mineral rights to private corporations (MNCs). By 1973 the federal government had leased 680,854 acres of public land and 258,754 acres of Indian land, containing over 20 billion tons of coal to approximately fifteen multinational oil companies.

Through the Dawes Allotment Act of 1887, 38 million acres were stolen outright from the North American Indians by the government. As if that wasn't enough, Indian landowners were forced to sell an additional 23 million acres between 1887 and 1934 because of inability to pay their taxes and mortgage payments. By 1934 the Indians had lost nearly two-thirds of their land or 90 million acres![271]

When the MNCs lease Indian land, they use a system called a trusteeship. This is similar to how the transnational corporations work in Third World nations; that is, the end result is pressing economic needs, high unemployment, and basically a *dependency syndrome*. This is what the IMF has provided for all of its recipients.

All the leases follow a similar pattern. They are let at fixed prices and valid as long as the mineral being extracted is found in the ground in sufficient quantity. Naturally, Indian nations are not allowed to tax the corporations. That the vast quantities of energy resources in the West hold future hope of economic and social recovery is a false promise. Housing, sewers, roads, lighting systems, schools, teachers, and so forth are grossly inadequate. MNCs assume none of the social and physical infrastructure costs. They are borne by residents through bonds and property taxes. Local residents are never involved in the planning phases of pending energy development and are grossly misinformed of the human, social, fiscal, and environmental costs. These are the same MNCs who are pushing the Earth Summit.

The estimated population of the North American Indian at the time of Columbus's arrival was 8 to 12 million. Today it may be 1 million. Along the way, the government has had a 145-year-old policy of "terminating" the Indian nations. This means that sovereign Indian nations are decreed to no longer exist whether or not they exist in reality.[272] The actual purpose is to terminate the Indian nations' treaty rights. What does this have to do with this book? In fact, your constitutional rights are being torn up today not at all unlike what happened to the Indian nations. Moreover, our Judeo-Christian culture, like the Indian culture, is meant to be destroyed as well.

The policy of termination forces the members of the heretofore sovereign nation to seek a place in the mainstream of white society as individuals rather than as a coexisting, separate national cultural group. With termination, government assistance for education, health, welfare, and taxes ceases.

As if things aren't bad enough, Michael Garitty, in his treatise *The U.S. Colonial Empire as Close as the Nearest Reservation: The Pending Energy Wars,* announces: "Genocide is not a thing of the past. Hundreds of Indian activists have been murdered. Hundreds of Indian women are being sterilized against their wishes or entirely unbeknownst to them in public health service clinics each year; full-blooded Indian women are the special target of the doctors. From colonial times through the present, Indian children have been forcibly separated from their families and shipped off to boarding schools and foster homes to be raised as whites."[273]

It was the privately owned railroads which initially worked with the government to steal Indian land and water. Now it's the privately owned oil conglomerates and agribusinesses. In the Four Corners area of Arizona, what is left today of the Navajo reservation leased to energy development is an environmental and health disaster. The five generating plants in this area emit 40 tons of particulates a year—100 times the emissions allowable in Los Angeles County.

In New Mexico, where Anaconda (Rothschild-Rockefeller) has operated the largest open-pit mine in the United States, the Rio Paguate's waters have turned green due to discharged effluent. This is the water the people of the Laguna Pueblo must drink and give to their livestock. The mine has produced 80 million tons of uranium-308, devastating 2,800 acres of the Pueblo. Of the total labor force of 970, only 447 work in the mines. According to a staff member on the Senate Committee on Indian Affairs, more than one hundred Lugana babies have been born with some birth defect. In a paper titled *Uranium Mining and Lung Cancer Among Navajo Indians,* Dr. Gerald Buker stated that the risk of lung cancer had increased by a factor of 85 among Navajo miners. One of the companies which hired the Indians as miners and didn't explain the dangers associated with uranium mining was Kerr-McGee. When asked about its responsibility to the Indian miners, Kerr-McGee representative Bill Phillips told a Washington reporter, "I couldn't tell you what happened at some small mines on an Indian Reservation. We have uranium interests all over the world."[274] Small mines, indeed! In 1976, 25 percent of all U.S. uranium-308 was produced from Indian lands. As of 1978, 1,185,000 acres of Indian land were under lease for uranium exploration and development. New Mexico's Grants Mineral Belt is the largest uranium-producing area in the world. Over half of Grant's Mineral Belt is on Indian land. One of the energy companies leasing hundreds of thousands of acres of Navajo and Pueblo land is Anaconda Copper (ARCO), the same company that was "forced" to cap and not disclose its oil finds in Alaska! The president of Kerr McGee Corporation just happened to have been elected to the directorship of the Federal Reserve Bank in 1972.

Do the Indians actually receive a lease-payment? Sure they do. The Navajos received less than $1 million in total royalty payments for leasing their Red Rock reservation in New Mexico. Typically, there are no corporate taxes, no regulations regarding mining activities, and a ready population of cheap labor, ignorant of radioactivity and its dangers. After the Atomic Energy Commission discontinued its price supports and incentive program, the price of uranium dropped. The corporations closed their mines, threw hundreds of miners out of work, left millions of tons of radioactive waste, and left for higher profits in other countries. Cleanup cost to the Navajo nation—$21 million!

Garitty presents us with what we have begun to understand as an understatement. "Uranium miners—Indian and non-Indian—are part of the great national sacrifice to corporate wealth...reports indicate irradiation through uranium mining has resulted in the premature death of one out of every six uranium miners from lung cancer or radiation related illnesses. The primary goal of the energy-exploiting corporations is profit maximization. Through government subsidies, paid for by the taxpayers, even the financial costs of uranium exploration and development are socialized while the profits are monopolized."[275]

When the Indians have tried to make a stand for their rights, for example at Wounded Knee, South Dakota, in 1973, the U.S. Government has responded with armored personnel carriers, helicopters, automatic rifles, and a blockade of food, fuel, and medical supplies even though the Fort Laramie Treaty of 1868 was to last forever: "For as long as the grass shall grow." Twenty-seven MNCs operate in the western counties of South Dakota. One of them, Union Carbide, has as its vice president a man who was former head of the EPA—Russell Train. John D. Rockefeller, IV was chairman of President Carter's Commission on Coal.

The conclusion, in Garitty's opinion, is that "Successive U.S. governments have chosen to violate, rather than enforce, the treaties which forever guarantee sovereignty over these resources." Today, as the United States seeks a referendum on the U.S. Constitution, the president, Congress, the unelected CFR and Trilateralists prove that they are no respecters of national sovereignty either. Yet Garitty declares: "Native people have never ceased their struggle for self-determination. The survival of us all—Indian, White, Black, Hispanic, Asian, American—is being threatened by the men who control the transnational corporations and have organized the Trilateral Commission. It is time to decide which side we will be on."[276]

Nicaragua: America Supports Communism—Again

Anastasio Somoza was the president of Nicaragua from 1967 to 1979. He was educated at St. Leo School in Florida, LaSalle Military Academy in Long Island, New York, and the U.S. Military Academy at West Point. His father had been elected as president of

Nicaragua in 1937 and served three terms: 1937–1941; 1941–1947; 1950–1956. His father was assassinated in 1956 by Communist Sandinistas. Anastasio Somoza was constitutionally elected by the people in election laws patterned after the laws of the United States. Due to his devotion to American ideals, he was strongly pro-Western and was always considered to be the staunchest supporter of the United States and Western ideology in all of Latin America. His book *Nicaragua Betrayed* is one of the saddest books I have ever read. Here is a man who, although born in Latin America, was educated in the United States and loved its citizens, its freedom, and its constitutional government. He patterned his own government on the American system.

So it comes as a complete surprise to him when Jimmy Carter, Henry Kissinger, and Cyrus Vance decide to join forces with the Communist countries of South America, Latin America, and even Cuba to remove his democratic government from power and replace it with a Communist regime. Over and over he tries to come to grips with why Carter would do such a thing. Why would the media tell blatant lies to the American people? Why would they allow horrible persecution of his people yet claim in the name of "human rights" that Somoza had to go? He says: "Mr. Carter lied about Nicarauga; he lied about Iran; he lied about Israel; he lied about the Republic of China...."[277] Jimmy Carter, it has been shown, was concerned about human rights in only the small and militarily weak countries which were all *anti*-Communist! Examples are not only Nicaragua, but Chile, Argentina, and Paraguay. President Somoza knows what our own government has already done in the name of "rights" in our own country. He clarifies: "To observe gross human rights violations, all one has to do is visit any Indian reservation in the United States."[278]

Where are the human rights issues after the powers have had their way? Since the fall of the Somoza government on July 17, 1979, some three thousand men, women, and children have been slaughtered and buried in mass graves. Yet, now that the Communists are in control, the human rights issue is buried as well.

When the United States and its behind-the-scenes leaders desire a country to fall, they now have a pattern they know will work every time.

1. Due to interference from the United States, credit was not obtainable from the International Monetary Fund.
2. Because of international political influence, Nicaragua could not export its coffee. No shipping company would

come into the ports.

3. Weapons captured by the Nicaraguan Army proved to have originated from the United States!

4. The opposing army had been trained in the pattern of PLOs from the Middle East (remember, backed by the United States).

5. All sources of weapons and ammunition were cut off. Somoza says: "We finally found a source in Europe that agreed to sell us a limited supply of ammunition. When the airplane went to Portugal to pick up the shipment, the plane was picketed. This clearly indicated the depth of the international conspiracy."[279]

6. Media propaganda

Somoza considers the destruction of his good name by the American media:

"The conclusion one has to reach is that the power of the press is awesome. It makes no difference who you are or what you are; if this sector of our professional society wants to destroy you, it can be done."[280] He says that Jack Anderson was one of the most blatant in his lies at this time and eventually the U.S. Congress and public opinion was turned against Somoza.

Although Somoza knew better, he allowed an interview by CFR's Dan Rather. In retrospect he exclaims, "I didn't realize what the power of film editing really meant. With that power, Rather cast me in any role he chose. Everything good I said about Nicaragua was deleted. Any reference to Carter's effort to destroy the government of Nicaragua was deleted. Every reference to the Communist activity and Cuba's participation was deleted."[281]

"Rather depicted a situation that didn't exist in Nicaragua. That show did irreparable harm to the government of Nicaragua and to me. Such massive misinformation also does harm to the American people."[282]

"The power of television is frightening. I have felt its strength and know firsthand of its destructive capability...the Leftist cause, which is the cause supported by so many in this field, will one day prevail. If that day should come, a Dan Rather would not be licensed to shape, form, and mold a story according to his personal preconceived notions. That decision would be made for him, and who knows, in my case it might have been."[283]

For other government leaders the facts which Somoza came to understand are not new. As we have discussed in previous chapters, our so-called representative government represents something quite different from what it says publicly. What it *doesn't* say is equally diabolical.

This is supported by a statement of testimony made before Congress by General Gordon Sumner. General Sumner had been chairman of the Inter-American Defense Board in Washington. On June 7, 1979, this is what he said: "Unfortunately, the facts of Panamanian involvement in supporting leftist/communist terrorist groups in Central America have been denied the American people. I saw a great deal of this when I was chairman of the Inter-American Defense Board. There was a blackout of this particular subject, not only in the media, but also, I felt, in the U.S. Government....

"I have watched this over three years' experience as chairman of the Inter-American Defense Board; and [have experienced] the frustration of being unable to get this [through], to the American people [and] also to the officials of the Federal Government. That is one reason I retired from active military duty."[284] "When I met with General Torrijos, I brought this up (Sandinista support funneled from Panama), and I expected him to give me a denial. Well, much to my surprise, he not only did not deny it, but as I say, he said he would continue the support, and defended the Sandinistas....He told me at that time, he said, 'You people on the Board get too worried about these Communists. This is not really a problem.' He said, 'You know there is a lot going on, <u>socialism is the way of the future, and you people are behind the power curve on this</u>'. He had quite a lot to say about this...."[285]

"We divided up all of Latin America into good guys and bad guys. They are being designated as 'human righteous.' This is all being done by a very small group in the White House and State [Department]. The fact that these 'Good Guys,' the guys with the white hats, are supplying arms, which you see here, they are supplying the training, money, support, a lot of this is coming out of the U.S. taxpayers' pockets, perhaps indirectly, to murder and maim as General Noriega did in Nicaragua, without discrimination. As far as I'm concerned, that makes a mockery out of the president's human rights policy."[286]

What have been the effects of the deposed government in Nicaragua?

Early in the sporadic raids on smaller communities, the Sandinistas murdered 80 justices of the peace. To the rebels, these were local representatives of the government. Three thousand men, women, and children have been slaughtered and buried in mass graves. Over 8,000 men and women are political prisoners. Many of these are the officers of the Nicaraguan Army, nearly 1,000 who have been educated and trained in the United States! Although Alan Riding, an admitted "socialist" of the *New York Times*, and Karen De Young of the *Washington Post* did a day-to-day hatchet job on Somoza, they have been eerily quiet concerning the bloodbath that has taken place since the "leftist" Sandinistas came to power. Although we have every possible description of mayhem in our "free press," these news items are routinely left out:

The Sandinistas captured, tortured, and shot Lieutenant Juan Ocon. While he was still alive his head was cut off. His family could not find his head, so they buried him with a plaster head attached to the body.

Alvaro Sanchez was taken out of his home and shot in the presence of his mother and children.

Pedro Pablo Espinoza, newspaperman and member of the Liberal Party, was captured by the Sandinistas in El Dorado. He was tortured, had his eyes gouged out, and was then shot.

In Leon, thirteen young members of the Guardia Nacional surrendered to the Sandinistas. They were taken to the football stadium in Leon where they were all shot.

While Lieutenant Rene Silva, a member of the Guardia Nacional from Matagalpa, was at the battlefront, the Sandinistas went to his home and murdered his wife and two young children, four and two years old.

Dr. Rafael Saavedra, general director of customs, was burned alive by the Sandinistas, and his two sons were killed.

Two female police students were captured. One of them was four months pregnant. They opened her up and pulled the fetus out. According to sworn testimony given to the U.S. House of Representatives and which appears in the February 26, 1980, Congressional Record, this group was under the command of an American by the name of Clifford Scott.

Major Domingo Gutierrez and six of his men were captured. They were placed in a hole, sprayed with gasoline, and burned alive.

Sergeant Edwin R. Ordonez of the infantry training school was captured and burned alive.

Dr. Cornelio Hueck, former president of the congress, was captured at his ranch near Rivas. He was taken to the town square of Tola where he was shot several times in non-vital areas. Then, with the people of the town present, he was placed on a table and, while he was still alive, his heart was cut out.

Major Pablo Emilio Salazar, better known as "Commandante

Bravo," was captured by the Sandinistas in Honduras after the war was over and tortured to death. His face was beaten beyond recognition, his arms broken, his ears cut off, his genitals severed, strips of his skin peeled from his body, and finally, he was shot in the head.[287]

Discussing high-level political assignments which have gone to known Communists, Somoza writes. "The most gross appointment I have saved until last, because a single line would not suffice. This was the appointment of Nora Astorga to be special prosecutor for the new Marxist government against the political prisoners, which includes eight thousand former members of the Army. These men and women are being tried at this time, and they are subject to thirty years imprisonment at hard labor. Thus far, some three hundred have been tried and very few have been found innocent. I repeat, Nora Astorga is the chief prosecutor and I would like for her name to be remembered. She is a young woman known to all adults and most children in Nicaragua.

"Astorga became famous—infamous would be a better word—by setting a sexual trap for General Reynaldo Perez Vega, my number two man in the military, and participating in his atrocious murder.

"Unfortunately for General Vega, he had been having an affair with this young woman for some time. For this relationship he would pay with his life. On the night of the murder, General Vega went to Astorga's house and, on the allegation by Astorga that she had no liquor, he sent his driver and bodyguard away to get some. This, of course, was planned. General Vega had no way of knowing that secluded in the house was a group of Sandinista cohorts of Astorga's. What happened to Vega should not happen to any human being. First, he was beaten into a bloody pulp. Then his eyes were gouged out, his throat cut, his body burned with cigarettes, and as a final act of torture, his genitals were cut off and stuffed in his mouth. Attending doctors estimated it took several hours for the general to die.

"This murderess now dispenses justice in Nicaragua. This female vampire now sits in judgment of those eight thousand surviving members of the Guardia Nacional of their country.

"There were countless other vicious atrocities, but I thought Nora Astorga deserved special attention. It may be recalled that this is the same Nora who came in for special praise by Karen De Young of the *Washington Post*."[288]

This is a non-fiction book for a non-fiction world. I read non-fiction because what is happening in real life is more amazing than anything the science fiction writers could dream up.

Yes, Carter, with U.S. taxpayers' money financed a Marxist government in Nicaragua. Lenin stated it well: "Americans will sell us the rope with which we will hang them."[289] This time the Marxists didn't buy the rope, we gave it to them.

President Somoza concludes: "This financial aid to a proven Marxist government indicates a State Department situation even worse than lunacy. It could indicate that <u>the U.S. now has Communists and Communist sympathizers in most sensitive positions in the State Department</u>."[290]

He says to the few patriots left in America: "No longer can we afford the luxury of silence. In revealing truths as I am so sincerely trying to do, in speaking of events which heretofore have been whispered but not spoken or written publicly, I realize fully well that I place myself in even more jeopardy. But the people of the United States and the free world must know what is happening, events that sooner or later will affect them.

"With my many years in government, with my military training and background, with my close association with governmental leaders throughout the world, and with intelligence information, I come to one startling conclusion: <u>there is a planned and deliberate conspiracy in the United States of America to destroy that republican form of government</u>. I know that this is being done in the name of peace. Peace to me, the good people of Nicaragua, the solid American citizen, and freedom-loving people everywhere means the absence of armed hostility. To the dedicated Communist, peace has a diametrically opposite meaning. To the Communists, peace clearly means that point in time or space when and where there will be <u>no opposition</u> to Communism."[291]

Somoza was assassinated in Paraguay only months after publishing his book. The disbelievers will argue that it's not true. But if anyone will go to their city library, the facts are all there. An excerpt from the Congressional Record, June 23, 1977, reads:

(Mr. Charles Wilson of Texas) "Mr. Chairman, this amendment is very simple. It simply reinstates Nicaragua as a recipient of U.S. military assistance.

"First of all, the most important point which needs to be made is that, in my judgment, Nicaragua is not a gross violator of human rights. Nicaragua's main sin seems to me to be that it is friendly to the United States...."[292]

What would the American people think if they knew the president was directly interfering in the internal affairs of another republic?

Are the American people entitled to know why Carter joined forces with Castro and the Communists to bring down a long-time friend, ally, and supporter of U.S. policy?

You say, "Nothing of the sort could ever happen in our country!" I say, "Turn off the TV set! Begin to look analytically at the fruit of the tree."

At a Joint Chiefs of Staff session in Nicaragua, General Sumner reported: "At the meeting in Managua, just prior to my meeting with General Torrijos, I had prepared a one-page statement. I was there as an observer. The Conference of the American Armies is a very powerful political forum in Latin America. The armies run Latin America, not the Air Force or the Navy, but the armies. They always invite the chairman to be there.

"I prepared a one-page statement which I cleared with the Joint Chiefs of Staff. The night before the meeting was to convene, I gave the senior American delegate, General Kerwin, the Vice Chief of Staff of the U.S. Army, my statement. He told me that I could not use the statement; and the statement was a very simple explanation of what the Cubans were doing in Africa, and the implications of their action in Africa for this hemisphere; and I was, in effect—but not in effect—I was flat muzzled. I was told 'you cannot use that statement.'

"I told General Kerwin that I did not want to get into a confrontation with him. As it turned out, one of the other chiefs of a delegation, chief of the army, I believe it was the Brazilian, asked me a question which allowed me then to give the statement, but I could not go in and give that statement. It was the policy of the Government at that time, the U.S. Government, not to mention Cuban intervention in Africa. 'Do not, for God's sake, mention anything about Fidel Castro'; and this to me was just unacceptable. And it was that particular incident, along with a string of other things that have happened, that made me decide I could no longer be a part of the administration...."[293]

General Sumner apparently agreed with Somoza's depiction of unelected rulers in the American government. The Nicaraguan leader had stated, "Under the guise of human rights, Mr. Carter brought into the Federal Government a retinue of radicals. These are not elected officials who must answer to the voters of the United States. These are handpicked subordinates CFR who answer to Mr. Carter. With this group of appointees, Mr. Carter is changing the socioeconomic structure of the U.S. They may call it something else, but the new economic plan is socialism. The actors are radical, their plan is radical, and the capitalistic free enterprise system that made the United States the productive wonder of the world is undergoing radical surgery."[294]

Many Americans now are beginning to realize this is so. The New World Order espoused by President George Bush is the same plan that the Illuminati of 1776 had for the Bavarian government—the overthrow of that sovereign government in favor of a one-world government. Somoza was just a piece of the puzzle, another link in the chain.

The problem is, the American people are so greedy they will vote a known Communist into power as long as he promises to give their district jobs, housing, etc. Shame, America, shame!

As to Nicaragua, we are now fifteen years and 150,000 refugees later. On September 5, 1978, Hodding Carter (CFR), U.S. State Department spokesman, was quoted as saying: "Our policy remains one of nonintervention in the domestic politics of other countries....We are not in the position of suggesting the overthrow or downfall or anything else of any government."[295]

Remember that name. Hodding Carter was blatantly lying to the American public. Prove it? His own fellow CFR conspirator proved it for him: On August 13, 1979, U.S. Secretary of State Henry Kissinger left no doubt. He said, "The Jimmy Carter Administration actively participated in the overthrow of the Somoza government."[296]

During the 1992 election many disgruntled American people looked for a savior in H. Ross Perot. Yet, as expected, he hired the same team of professional liars that have served government for years and years. Two of the most famous were Hodding Carter and Hamilton Jordan—both members of the Council on Foreign Relations.

According to an ex-contra now living in Florida, the contras are returning to the jungle in preparation for a new Nicaraguan war. Now that they are nearly weaponless, they must fight again or the Sandinistas will continue to assassinate them all.

Chapter 10

WHO ARE THE BILDERBERGERS?

The Bilderbergers (The name stems from the first meeting place in Oosterbeek, Holland, 1954.) are a group of American and European government leaders, bankers, heads of state, top government officials, royalty, scholars, businessmen, politicians, and ruling elites who gather together in complete secrecy twice a year to discuss the world's agenda. These leaders take care of "world" business. Since this has been going on since the end of World War II, they have had considerable practice. Actually, even the decision to divide Germany into East and West was made by men who later proved to be Bilderbergers.[297]

Even though many prominent journalists have attended the Bilderberg meetings, virtually no word has appeared in the public press about the gatherings despite the "elite" credentials of the guest list. The original chairman of the Bilderbergers, Prince Bernhard, German-born (a former Nazi SS storm trooper) but now of the Netherlands, made it clear to the participants that those who deal with the press are not welcome back. He said, "The purpose of the conference is that eminent persons in every field get the opportunity to speak freely without being hindered by the knowledge that their words and ideas will be analyzed, commented upon, and eventually criticized in the press."[298] For example, although heads of state, luminaries, and reporters from all the wire services representing every newspaper in the world attended the 1972 meeting at Woodstock Inn in Vermont, owned by Laurence Rockefeller, all major newspapers in the United States suppressed the story, including the *New York Times, Washington Post and Tribune, Arizona Republic, Nashville Banner, National Review, Human Events,* etc.

The Bilderbergers' existence is generally denied. A media blackout has been in place for nearly forty years! Press Baron Cecil King, chairman of the International Publishing Corporation (accounted for the largest daily circulation press in Britain) and chairman of the Newspaper Proprietors Association, requested his fellow proprietors make certain that "on no account should any report or even speculation about the content of the conference be printed."[299]

Essentially, then, what we have here is an undercover group of world multinational global elitists who own and control the public press and disclose to the citizens of each country that which they desire us to know—and little else. Participants at these meetings make decisions affecting the American economy and politics and strategize world events. They are not bothered with worrying about "little things" like national interest, the U.S. Constitution, or the individual American citizen.

Almost all Americans refuse to believe their free country is no longer free. Our country has not been free for almost a century! To be certain, let us review the Congressional Record, Sept. 15, 1971, and Senator John R. Rarick as he disclosed the secret workings of the Bilderbergers to the House of Representatives:

"Mr. Speaker, on several occasions during recent months, I called the attention of our colleagues to activities of the Bilderbergers—an elite international group comprised of high government officials, international financiers, businessmen, and opinion-makers....

"This exclusive international aristocracy holds highly secret meetings annually or more often in various countries. The limited information available about what transpires at these meetings reveals that they discuss matters of vital importance which affect the lives of all citizens. Presidential Advisor Henry Kissinger, who made a secret visit to Peking from July 9 to July 11, 1971, and arranged for a presidential visit to Red China, was reported to be in attendance at the most recent Bilderberg meeting held in Woodstock, Vermont, April 23 to April 25, 1971. The two points reportedly discussed at the Woodstock meeting were 'the contribution of business in dealing with current problems of social instability' and 'the possibility of a change of the American role in the world and its consequences.'

"Following these secret discussions, which are certainly not in keeping with the Western political tradition of 'open covenants openly arrived at,' the participants returned to their respective countries with the general public left uninformed, not withstanding the attendance of some news media representatives, of any of the recommendations and plans agreed upon as a result of the discussions—or for that matter even the occurrence of the meeting itself."[300]

Rarick exposed the clandestine nature of the American press: "The key media of mass communications have been well represented at the Bilderberg meetings. The major newspaper of record, the *New York Times,* has sent several prominent individuals to the conferences. The list included the late Arthur Hays Sulzberger, C.L. Sulzberger, James Reston, Max Frankel, and Thomas Wicker. The chairman of the board of the *Washington Post,* Frederick S. Beebe, has attended one meeting. C.D. Jackson of Time, Inc. played an important role in the early Bilderberg meetings, Gardner Cowles of Cowles Publication (*Look* magazine) has been at several, and in addition, such newsmen as Joseph Kraft and Joseph C. Harsch have attended."[301]

The steering committee of the Bilderbergers is laced with the likenesses of:

David Rockefeller
    Chairman emeritus of the board-CFR
    Trilateral Commission executive committee member
Edmond de Rothschild
    French banker
William Bundy
    Longtime editor of CFR's *Foreign Affairs*
    Top Vietnam War planner
Giovanni Agnelli
    Head of Italy's FIAT
    Trilateral Commission executive committee member
Otto Wolff
    Top German industrialist
    Trilateral Commission executive committee member
    (his father had been a substantial contributor to Hitler)
Theo Sommer CFR
    Top German columnist

Arthur Taylor CFR
 Former chairman of CBS
Niel Norlund CFR
 Chief editor of Denmark's *Berlingske Tindende*[302]

It becomes evident that what is beneficial for the media is printed and exposed. Subjects meant to be concealed and uninspected remain covert so that the machinations of global mammonism can continue at the expense of God, the family, education, private enterprise, and the U.S. Constitution. This is tyranny!

Who attends these meetings? Please permit me to again quote the Honorable John R. Rarick from the Congressional Record: "All the Americans on the Steering Committee are members or officers of the Council on Foreign Relations in New York City, an organization that has a more than symbiotic relation with the Rockefeller-Standard Oil empire....

"The best represented industry at Bilderberg is banking...."[303]

Represented are:
Chase Manhattan Bank
 President, David Rockefeller
Manufacturers Hanover Trust
 President, Gabriel Hauge
First National City Bank
 Chairman, James Rockefeller
Morgan Guaranty Trust
Chemical Bank
New York Trust Company
Continental Illinois Bank
 Former chairman of the board, David Kennedy CFR
 (also past secretary of the treasury under Nixon)
Banque de France
Banque de Bruxelles
Dillon, Read and Co.
 President, C. Douglas Dillon CFR
 (also former secretary of the treasury under Eisenhower)
Toronto Dominion Bank
World Bank
 President, Robert McNamara CFR (former secretary of defense under Kennedy)
Bank of Canada
House of Rothschild
 Baron Edmond de Rothschild

Stockholmes Enskilda Bank
Vice-chairman, Marcus Wallenberg
Industrialists represented:
General Motors
Standard Oil
Ford
General Electric
DuPont
Alcoa
Allied Chemical
Royal Dutch Shell
Fiat
Pirelli
Unilever
Beers Consolidated Mines, Ltd.[304]

One might notice the seeming disparity of a meeting with so-called international "competitors".

Obviously, with the power elites listed, once Bilderberg participants reach a form of consensus, they have at their disposal powerful transnational institutions for bringing about what they want to pass. When they run into difficulty, they register the traditional elitest complaint: "Political decisions of such magnitude are rarely understood by the public at large."[305]

Bilderbergers in American government? Certainly! President Kennedy "virtually staffed the State Department with Bilderberg Alumni"—Secretary of State Dean Rusk, Under Secretary of State George W. Ball, George McGhee, Walter Rostow, McGeorge Bundy, Arthur Dean, and Paul Nitze at the Pentagon.[306]

Carter administration Trilateral Commissioners who were also Bilderbergers:
Vice President Walter Mondale
Secretary of State Cyrus Vance
National Security Advisor Zbigniew Brzezinski
Secretary of Treasury Michael Blumenthal
Deputy National Security Advisor David Aaron

Funding

Since 1955 the Carnegie Endowment for International Peace has administered funds provided by the Ford Foundation and other sources for the Bilderbergers. The noted British authority on international groups, A.K. Chesterton, in *The New Unhappy Lords*, asserts "...it will be seen that the proper study of political mankind is the study of power elites, without which nothing that happens can be understood...."[307] Financial support received from the big three American foundations—Rockefeller, Carnegie, and Ford—provides an infallible means of recognizing who these elites are.

Joseph E. Johnson, past secretary general of the American Bilderberg Group, former chief of international security affairs in the State Department, and director of the Council on Foreign Relations, became president of the Carnegie Endowment for International Peace (CEIP). The earnings of CEIP, the Foreign Policy Association, and the Brookings Institution have all supported the Bilderberg group. The Brookings Institution, renowned for "expertise" on CBS, NBC, and ABC has been represented substantially at the Bilderberg meetings. The institute takes special delight in advising the State and Defense Departments and the CIA.[308] Brookings chairman Eugene R. Black (1971), although not a household name, was naturally enough—president of the World Bank. Other titles this unknown has held are:

> Trustee of the Ford Foundation
>
> Director of Chase Manhattan Bank (Rockefeller-CFR)
>
> Director of American Express, ITT, Communications Satellite Corporation, Royal Dutch Petroleum, and the Atlantic Council.

Black was also a member of the boards of both Harvard and Johns Hopkins universities.

Joseph E. Johnson, whose CEIP is tax-exempt, has claimed that the reason the Bilderberg meetings are private is to permit an official to "give an explanation of policy that he would not give in public."[309] These meetings are paid for by taxpayer-subsidized grants from the Ford and Rockefeller foundations through the CEIP.[310] Costs include transportation for dignitaries, including private planes and chartered airlines. When meeting in the United States, taxpayers directly foot the bill for hundreds of FBI and Secret Service agents and state and local police who are always around to guard participants and maintain complete secrecy. We, the American people, subsidize a secret elite of transnational bankers and secret society luminaries. They who are slaves of greed and power plan against our personal and financial interests as we finance them! The war goes on. The war is secret. The war is against our freedom, our children's freedom, and our Constitution, and we fund the enemy!

166

What do the Bilderbergers meet about?

"As soon as the Bilderbergers got home from their April 1971 meeting in Woodstock, Vermont, billions of dollars started mysteriously flooding out of America."[311] Four months later the dollar was no longer convertible into gold, and thereafter the administration let the dollar float (i.e., no fixed value against gold or any other reserve asset). The increasing flow of dollars out of America and into Europe continued until just before the devaluation. On December 14, 1971, President Nixon met French President Pompidou in the Azores. Pompidou was a former employee of the Rothschilds. Jointly, they announced the devaluation of the dollar. On December 18, 1971, the dollar was devalued 8.5 percent. For those who converted their dollars into European currencies or sold the dollar short, fabulous fortunes were made. Could it be that an American Bilderberger would realize enormous profit at the expense of the American people? The Manchester, New Hampshire, *Union Leader* on Nov. 12, 1971 reported: "At a top-secret conference held last April in Woodstock, Vt., a presidential advisor leaked information on the proposed economic freeze to a select group of national and international figures enabling them, according to a Washington source, to profit to the tune of $15 to $20 billion."[312] This devaluation, although benefiting the banking elites, signaled the end of American financial independence. At the June 1991 Bilderberger meeting in Baden-Baden, Germany, a few of the notable attendees were:

> David Rockefeller
> Bill Clinton
> Michael Boskin, Chairman of the Bush's Council of Economic Advisors
> Nicholas Brady, Bush's Treasury Secretary
> Theodore L. Elliot, Jr., Previous U.S. Ambassador to Afghanistan
> Emilio Collado, Executive Vice President of Exxon (Rockefeller)
> Katherine Graham, *Washington Post*
> John Reed, Chairman of Citicorp (Rothschild)
> Senator John Chaffee, Republican - Rhode Island
> Governor Doug Wilder, Virginia
> Vice President Dan Quayle

One question which has surfaced is: Have the American officials who have attended the Bilderberger meetings violated the Logan

Act? This is the same act with which the corrupt Congress tried desperately to hang Oliver North. The Logan Act prohibits any American citizen without proper authority from "commencing or carrying on any correspondence or intercourse with any foreign government or officer or agent, thereof, with intent to influence the measures or conduct of any foreign government or officer or agent thereof, in relation to any disputes or controversies with the U.S. or to defeat the measure of the U.S...."[313]

When one considers that the Bilderbergers' goal is one-world government, which necessitates American sovereignty's demise, attendance at such a meeting is automatically a crime. Apparently, Congressman Rarick agrees: "Because the American people have a right to know of any projections for a change in America's role in the world and because Henry Kissinger and other government officials and influential Americans met with high government officials and other powerful foreign leaders, I sought to have more information about the recent Bilderberg meeting made public by raising the question to the U.S. Attorney General of a possible violation of the Logan Act by American participants and asked if the Justice Department anticipated taking any action in the matter.

"The reply from the Justice Department, in effect, was that all of the elements constituting a violation of the Logan Act were present...."[314] The Justice Department attempted no action.

A little research will aptly demonstrate that most economic policy, whether in Washington, Singapore, Indonesia, or Chile, emanates from a relatively small circle of interested parties. A.K. Chesterton stated: "I affirm that the influences behind the European movement which made use of Retinger's (secretary general, Bilderberg meeting, Buxton, Derbyshire, 1958) idealism are, from a national and Christian point of view, thoroughly unwholesome and indeed evil in that what they seek is a monopoly of political and financial power. Evil, too, is the method."[315]

What we are coming to learn then is that we have a group of men (women excluded) similar in interest and outlook shaping events from invulnerable positions behind the scene. Chesterton continues, "...I propose to designate them as the chosen lackeys of the New York Money Power charged with the task of plotting to bring into being a One World tyranny."[316] How is it, then, that the most powerful men in all the world can meet in various parts of the world for nearly forty years and cause not a stir in the media? Even though the publisher of *Time,* Henry Greenwald and his supposed competitor, Osborn Elliott of *Newsweek,* have attended, the free press have been silent.

Since it becomes apparent that the Bilderberg group has control over its underling publishers, there is no explanation save that of conspiracy for the complete suppression of news on this group and its activities. To think America is a truly free nation is a dream born in yesteryear, no longer valid, held only by those in denial. Professor Carrol Quigley, author of *Tragedy and Hope*, referred to an extremely influential Anglo-American economic, political, and academic combine standing as a shadow or secret trans-Atlantic government with worldwide connections, and whose name, he said, is the Round Table, of which the Bilderbergers are a part and the American front is the Council on Foreign Relations.

"There does exist, and has existed for a generation, an international network which operates, to some extent, in the way the radical right <u>believes</u> the Communists act. In fact, this network, which we may identify as the Round Table groups, has <u>no aversion to cooperating with the Communists, or any other groups, and frequently does so</u>."[317]The ruling dignitaries of Communist countries routinely travel quietly and discreetly to CFR headquarters at the Pratt House, 58 East 68th Street, New York City, to receive their marching orders before they attend the big media events thereafter at the White House for the benefit of American Propaganda.

As a matter of fact, the Establishment made up of the Bilderbergers, the Trilateral Commission, the CFR, and the inner core group of the super-secret Round Table are a very real power structure affecting life across the board, not only in the United States but throughout the world. Carroll Quigley states conclusively in *Tragedy and Hope* the true nature of the deceit:

"It is <u>this power structure</u> which the Radical Right in the United States has been attacking for years <u>in the belief</u> that they are attacking the Communists. This is particularly true when these attacks are directed, as they so frequently are, at 'Harvard socialism' or at 'left-wing newspapers' like the *New York Times* and *The Washington Post*, or at foundations and their dependent establishments...."[318] The public reacts to such charges as time to change political parties, yet <u>has not realized the power structure controls them both</u>!

The latest personalities that the "power structure" controls are Bill and Hillary Clinton. Their agenda is not their own.

If the CFR and Bilderbergers were about national pride and conservatism, morality, and justice that is what the puppet, Clinton, would be speaking from the White House. But because the CFR-Bilderberger beast speaks totalitarianism, immorality, injustice, and one-world government, that is what the Clintons will preach. Woe to the churches and woe to the middle class. Only lies can be expected from the CFR-controlled White House, the CFR-controlled State Department and the CFR-controlled media.

The *Chicago Tribune* on December 9, 1950, wrote: "The members of the Council [on Foreign Relations] are persons of more than average influence in the community. They have used the prestige that their wealth, their social position, and their education have given them to lead their country toward bankruptcy and military debacle. They should look at their hands. There is blood on them—the dried blood of the last war (World War II) and the fresh blood of the present one (Korea)."[319] That was written forty-three years ago. Extrapolate that out to the history of the sufferings of the world's people through 1993.

Now let's look at the CFR power chart on pages 172 and 173 for Mr. Bill Clinton.

What is the Destiny of the Nation which turns its back on God's Law?

When the people of Israel came to Samuel demanding a leader to organize and protect their nation, Samuel delivered to them God's warning:

> He said, "This is what the king who will reign over you will do: He will take your sons and make them serve with his chariots and horses, and they will run in front of his chariots. Some he will assign to be commanders of thousands and commanders of fifties, and others to plow his ground and reap his harvest, and still others to make weapons of war and equipment for his chariots. He will take your daughters to be perfumers and cooks and bakers. He will take the best of your fields and vineyards and olive groves and give them to his attendants. He will take a tenth of your grain and of your vintage and give it to his officials and attendants. Your menservants and maidservants and the best of your cattle and donkeys he will take for his own use. He will take a tenth of your flocks, and you yourselves will become his slaves. When that day comes, you will cry out for relief from the king you have chosen, and the Lord will not answer you in that day." – 1 Samuel 8:11-18.

We find ourselves today in the same state as that of our ancestors, the Israelites at the time of Nehemiah, when he recorded that the people called out to God, recounting their own transgressions and disobedience and concluded:

> "Our kings, our leaders, our priests and our fathers did not follow your law; they did not pay attention to your commands or the warnings you gave them. Even while they were in their kingdom, enjoying your great goodness to them in the spacious and fertile land you gave them, they did not serve you or turn from their evil ways. But see, we are slaves today, slaves in the land you gave our forefathers so they could eat its fruit and the other good things it produces. Because of our sins, its abundant harvest goes to the kings you have placed over us. They rule over our bodies and our cattle as they please. We are in great distress. In view of all this, we are making a binding agreement, putting it in writing, and our leaders, our Levites and our priests are affixing their seals to it....", and he here lists the signatories of the covenant. – Nehemiah 9:34 - 10:1.

Good Times - Bad Times
Recession - Depression

Influence or control of money, mail, media, military, IRS, tax courts, commerce, energy, unions, domestic and foreign policy, etc. provides an apparent opportunity for massive fraud, robbery, and control of the American people!

THE CFR / TRILATERAL

MEDIA

CBS

Laurence A. Tisch, CEO	CFR
Roswell Gilpatric	CFR
James Houghton	CFR/TC
Henry Schacht	CFR/TC
Dan Rather	CFR
Richard Hottelet	CFR
Frank Stanton	CFR

NBC/RCA

John F. Welch, Jr., CEO	CFR
Jane Pfeiffer	CFR
Lester Crystal	CFR/TC
R. W. Sonnenfeldt	CFR/TC
John Petty	CFR
Tom Brokaw	CFR
David Brinkley	CFR
John Chancellor	CFR
Marvin Kalb	CFR
Irving R. Levine	CFR
Herbert Schlosser	CFR
Peter G. Peterson	CFR
John Sawhill	CFR

ABC

Thomas S. Murphy, CEO	CFR
Barbara Walters	CFR
John Connor	CFR
Diane Sawyer	CFR
John Scali	CFR

PUBLIC BROADCAST SERVICE

Robert McNeil	CFR
Jim Lehrer	CFR
C. Hunter-Gault	CFR
Hodding Carter III	CFR
Daniel Schorr	CFR

ASSOCIATED PRESS

Stanley Swinton	CFR
Harold Anderson	CFR
Katharine Graham	CFR/TC

REUTERS

Micheal Posner	CFR

BALTIMORE SUN

Henry Trewhitt	CFR

WASHINGTON TIMES

Arnaud de Borchgrave	CFR

CHILDREN'S TV WORKSHOP (Sesame Street)

Joan Ganz Cooney, Pres.	CFR

CABLE NEWS NETWORK

W. Thomas Johnson, pres.	TC
Daniel Schorr	CFR

U. S. News & World Rep.

David Gergen	TC

NEW YORK TIME CO.

Richard Gelb	CFR
William Scranton	CFR/TC
John F. Akers	Dir. CFR
Louis V. Gerstner, Jr.	" CFR
George B. Munroe	" CFR
Donald M. Stewart	" CFR
Cyrus R. Vance	" CFR
A.M. Rosenthal	CFR
Seymour Topping	CFR
James Greenfield	CFR
Max Frankel	CFR
Jack Rosenthal	CFR
John Oakes	CFR
Harrison Salisbury	CFR
H.L. Smith	CFR
Steven Rattner	CFR
Richard Burt	CFR
Flora Lewis	TC

TIME, INC.

Ralph Davidson	CFR
Donald M. Wilson	CFR
Henry Grunwald	CFR
Alexander Heard	CFR
Sol Linowitz	CFR/TC
Thomas Watson, Jr.	CFR
Strobe Talbott	TC

NEWSWEEK/WASH. POST

Katharine Graham	CFR
N. deB. Katzenbach	CFR
Robert Christopher	CFR
Osborne Elliot	CFR
Phillip Geyelin	CFR
Murry Marder	CFR
Maynard Parker	CFR
George Will	CFR/TC
Robert Kaiser	CFR
Meg Greenfield	CFR
Walter Pincus	CFR
Murray Gart	CFR
Peter Osnos	CFR
Don Oberdorfer	CFR

DOW JONES & CO. (Wall St. Journal)

Richard Wood	CFR
Robert Bartley	CFR/TC
Karen House	CFR

NATIONAL REVIEW

Wm. F. Buckley, Jr.	CFR

READERS DIGEST

George V. Grune, CEO	CFR
William G. Bowen, Dir.	CFR

SYNDICATED COLUMNISTS

Georgie Anne Geyer	CFR
Ben J. Wattenberg	CFR

GENERAL MOTORS CORP.

Marina v.N. Whitman, VP	CFR/TC
Anne L. Armstrong	Dir. CFR
Marvin L. Goldberger	" CFR
Edmund T. Pratt, Jr.	" CFR
Dennis Weatherstone	" CFR
Leon H. Sullivan	" CFR
Thomas H. Wyman	" CFR

FORD MOTOR COMPANY

Clifton R. Wharton	Dir. CFR
Roberto C. Goizueta	" CFR

GE / NBC

John F. Welch, Jr. Chmn.	CFR
David C. Jones	CFR
Lewis T. Preston	CFR
Frank H.T. Rhodes	CFR
Walter B. Wriston	CFR

ENERGY COMPANIES

EXXON CORPORATION

Lawrence G. Rawl, Chmn.	CFR
Lee R. Raymond, Pres.	CFR/TC
Jack G. Clarke, Sr. VP	CFR
Randolph W. Bromery, Dir.	CFR
D. Wayne Calloway, Dir.	CFR

TEXACO

Alfred C. DeCrane, Jr. Chmn.	CFR
John Brademas Dir.	CFR/TC
Willard C. Butcher "	CFR
William J. Crowe, Jr. "	CFR/TC
John K. McKinley "	CFR
Thomas S. Murphy "	CFR

ATLANTIC RICHFIELD - ARCO

Hannah H. Gray, Dir.	CFR
Donald M. Kendall, Dir.	CFR/TC
Henry Wendt, Dir.	TC

SHELL OIL CO.

Frank H. Richardson, CEO	CFR
Rand V. Araskog, Dir.	CFR/TC

MOBIL CORP.

Allan E. Murray, Chmn. & Pres.	CFR/TC
Lewis M. Branscomb, Dir.	CFR
Samuel C Johnson, "	TC
Helene L Kaplan, "	CFR
Charles S. Sanford, Jr. "	CFR

TENNECO, INC.

James L. Ketelsen, Chmn.	CFR
W. Michael Blumenthal, Dir.	CFR
Joseph J. Sisco, "	CFR

INDUSTRY

DEERE & CO.

Hans W. Becherer, Chmn & CEO	CFR

IBM

John F. Akers, Chmn.	CFR
C. Michael Armstrong, Sr. VP	CFR

AMTRAK (National RR Passenger Corp.)

William S. Norman, Exec. VP	CFR

AMERICAN TELEPHONE & TELEGRAPH CO. (AT&T)

Robert E. Allen, Chmn. & CEO	CFR
Randall L. Tobias, Vice Chmn	CFR
Louis V. Gerstner, Dir.	CFR/TC
Juanita M. Kreps, "	CFR
Donald F. McHenry "	CFR
Henry B. Schacht "	CFR
Michael I. Sovern "	CFR
Franklin A. Thomas "	CFR
Rawleigh Warner, Jr. "	CFR
Thomas H. Wyman "	CFR

CHRYSLER CORPORATION

Joseph A. Califano, Jr. Dir.	CFR
Peter A. Magowan "	CFR

AMERICAN EXPRESS CO.

James D. Robinson, CEO	CFR
Joan Edelman Spero	TC
Anne L. Armstrong	CFR
William G. Bowen	CFR
Charles W. Duncan, Jr.	CFR
Richard M. Furlaud	CFR
Vernon E. Jordan, Jr.	CFR/TC
Henry A. Kissinger	CFR/TC
Frank P. Popoff	CFR
Robert V. Roosa	CFR
Joseph H. Williams	CFR

"The Council on Foreign Relations is the American Branch of a society which originated in England...(and)...believes national boundaries should be obliterated and one-world rule established...

"The Trilateral Commission is international ...(and)... is intended to be the vehicle for multinational consolidation of the commercial and banking interests by siezing control of the political government of the United States." WITH NO APOLOGIES.
Senator Barry Goldwater

Peter G. P
CHAIRMAN
COUNCIL ON
RELATI
58 E. 68th St. New
Phone (212)
FAX (212) 8

Dick Thornburgh **CFR**
ASST. SEC. FOR ADMINISTRATION
UNITED NATIONS

Anthony Lake CFR — NATIONAL SECURITY ADVISOR

Albert Gore, Jr. CFR — VICE PRESIDENT

Warren — SECRET

Laura Tyson CFR — CHAIRMAN, COUNCIL OF ECONOMIC ADVISORS

Lloyd Bentsen BILDERBERG, Former CFR — TREASURY SECRETARY

JUDICIARY

Sandra Day O'Connor, Asso. Justice, U. S. Supreme Court	CFR
Steven G. Breyer, Chief Judge US Court of Appeals, First Circuit, Boston	CFR
Ruth B. Ginsburg, US Court of Appeals, Wash., DC Circuit	CFR
Laurence H. Silberman, US Court of Appeals, Wash., DC Circuit	CFR

U.S. INSTITUTE FOR PEACE

John Norton Moore, Chairman	CFR
Elspeth Davies Rostow, Vice Chmn	CFR
Samuel W. Lewis, President	CFR
John Richardson, Counselor	CFR
David Little, Senior. Scholar	CFR
William R. Kintner, Dir.	CFR
W. Scott Thompson, Dir.	CFR

OFFICE OF U. S. TRADE REP.

Gary R. Edson, Ch. of Staff & Counselor	CFR
Joshua Bolten, Gen. Counsel	CFR
Daniel M. Price, Dep. Gen. Counsel	CFR

TREASURY DEPA

Roger Altman, Deputy Sec.
Robert R. Glauber, Under
Finance
David C. Mulford, Under Se
Intntl Affairs
Robert M. Bestani, Dep. As
Sec., Intntl. Monetary Af
J. French Hill, Dep. Asst. S
Corp. Finance
John M. Niehuss, Dep. Ass
Sec., Intntl. Monetary A

OFFICE OF TECHNOLOG

Joshua Lederberg, V. Chm
John H. Gibbons, Director
Lewis M. Branscomb, Adv

ENVIRONMENTAL PROT

James M. Strock, Asst. Adr
Enforcement & Complianc

AFRICAN DEVELOPM

Leonard H. Robinson, Jr.,

DEP

Madeleine Albright, UN Ambassador	CFR
Clifton Wharton, Jr., Deputy Sec.	CFR
Lynn Davis, Under Sec. For International Security Affairs	CFR/TC
Brandon H. Grove, Dir. Of Foreign Service Institute	CFR
H. Allen Holmes, Asst. Sec. Bureau of Politico - Military Affairs	CFR
John H. Kelly, Asst. Sec. Near East - South Asian Affairs	CFR
Alexander F. Watson, Dep. Rep. United Nations	CFR
Jonathan Moore, UN Mission	CFR
Joseph Verner Reed, Chief of Protocol	CFR
Dennis B. Ross, Dir. Policy Planning Staff	CFR
Edward Perkins, Dir. of Personnel	CFR
Abraham David Sofaer, Legal Advisor	CFR

Peter Tarnof
Brian Atwoo
Joan E. Spe
George E. M
Strobe Talb
Thomas R.
Morton I. Ab
Michael H. A
Shirley Tem
Julia Chang
Henry E. Cat
Frances Co
Edward P. D
George E. M

UNI

SENATORS

David L. Boren (D), OK	CFR
William Bradley (D), NJ	CFR
John H. Chafee (R), RI	CFR/TC
William S. Cohen (R), ME	CFR/TC
Christopher J. Dodd (D), CT	CFR
Dianne Feinstein (D), CA	TC
Bob Graham (D), FL	CFR
Joseph I. Lieberman (D), CT	CFR

George J. Mitchell (D), ME
Claiborne Pell (D), RI
Larry Pressler (R), SD
Charles S. Robb (D), VA
John D. Rockefeller, IV (D
William Roth, Jr. (R), DE

REPRESENTAT

Howard L. Berman (D), CA
Thomas S. Foley (D), WA

"The People are entitled to know who controls their government."
Johnny Stewart, Founder of F.R.E.E.

BUSINESS & INDU

Richard D. Wood	CEO, Eli Lily & Co.	CFR
Richard M. Furlaud	CEO, Bristol-Myers Squibb Co.	CFR
Frank Peter Popoff	CEO, Dow Chemical Co.	CFR
Charles Peter McColough	Chmn Ex. Comm, Xerox	CFR
Rozanne L. Ridgeway	Dir., 3M, RJR Nabisco, Union Carbide	CFR
Ruben F. Mettler	former CEO, TRW, Inc.	CFR
Henry B. Schacht	CEO, Cummins Engines	CFR
Edmund T. Pratt, Jr.	CEO, Pfizer, Inc.	CFR
Rand V. Araskog	CEO, ITT Corp.	CFR/TC
W. Michael Blumenthal	Chmn, UNISYS Corp.	CFR
Joseph John Sisco	Dir., GEICO, Raytheon, Gilette	CFR

J. Fred Bucy	former Pres, (
Paul A. Allaire	Chmn, CEO,)
Dwayne O. Andreas	Chmn, CEO, /
James E. Burke	Chmn, CEO E
D. Wayne Calloway	Chmn, CEO, I
Frank C. Carlucci	Vice Chmn., T
Lynn E. Davis	VP, Dir. RANI
Stephen Friedman	Sr. VP, Co-Ch
Louis V. Gerstner, Jr.	Chmn, CEO, I
Joseph T. Gorman	Chmn, Pres, (
Maurice R. Greenberg	Chmn, CEO, /

Sources:

1. *The United States Government Manual 1991/92*, Office of the Federal Register - National Archives and Records Administration
2. *Standard & Poor's Register of Corporations, Directors and Executives 1991*
3. *Annual Report 1991/92*, The Council on Foreign Relations, Pratt House, New York City

★ ★ ★ ★ ★ ★ ★ ★ ★ ★ ★ ★ ★ ★ ★

Non-copyrighted educational material: Order or re-print for distribution to local/state/federal officials, law enforcement officers, ministers, friends, relatives, students, teachers, and citizens from every walk of life. It may be reprinted, and reproduced in newspapers, newsletters, books and magazines. Large quantities may be obtained from F.R.E.E.
PLEASE GIVE CREDIT TO Fund To Restore An Educated Electorate

★ ★ ★ ★ ★ ★ ★ ★ ★ ★ ★ ★ ★ ★ ★

100 copies shipped postpaid for a contribution of $25.00. Fifty copies for $15; 25 for $10. State quantity wanted when larger contributions are made.

★ ★ ★ ★ ★ ★ ★ ★ ★ ★ ★ ★ ★ ★ ★

Fund to Restore an Educated Electorate
★ ★ ★ ★ **P.O. BOX 33339 KERRVILLE, TX 78029** ★ ★ ★ ★

WORLD ORDER CONNECTION

★ CFR Indicates membership in the Council on Foreign Relations.
★ TC Indicates membership in the Trilateral Commision.

r

Paul Volker
MERICAN CHAIRMAN OF
TERAL COMMISSION
th St. New York, NY 10017
one (212) 661-1180

NCIL

FEDERAL RESERVE SYSTEM
(Past & Present) - Partial Listing

Alan Greenspan, Chairman	CFR/TC
E. Gerald Corrigan, V. Chmn. Pres., NY Fed. Res. Bank	CFR
Richard N. Cooper, Chmn. Boston	CFR
Sam Y. Cross, Mgr. Foreign Open Market Acct.	CFR
Robert F. Erburu, Chmn., San Fran	CFR
Robert P. Forrestal, Pres. Atlanta	CFR
Bobby R. Inman, Chmn., Dallas	CFR/TC
Robert H. Knight, Esq.	CFR
Steven Muller	CFR
John R. Opel	CFR
Anthony M. Solomon	CFR/TC
Edwin M. Truman, Staff Dir. International Finance	CFR
Cyrus R. Vance	CFR
Paul Volcker	CFR/TC

The Federal Reserve System and Bank is a privately owned corporation established by act of Congress. By its control of the money supply and the interest rate, it effectively controls the economy of the United States.

s Aspin — CFR — CRETARY DEFENSE

Colin L. Powell — CFR — CHAIRMAN JOINT CHIEFS OF STAFF

James Woolsey — CFR — DIRECTOR CENTRAL INTELLIGENCE AGENCY

Henry Cisneros — CFR — SECRETARY OF HOUSING & URBAN DEVELOPMENT

Donna Shalala — CFR/TC — SECRETARY OF HEALTH & HUM. SER.

R

WHITE HOUSE STAFF

Stephanopoulos, Director, Communications	CFR
J. Crowe, Chief eign Intelligence Advisory Bd.	CFR/TC
Soderberg, Staff Director onal Security Council	CFR
R. Berger, Deputy Advisor ional Security	CFR
man Cutter, Deputy Assistant tional Economic Council	CFR

E OF MANAGEMENT & BUDGET

vlin, Deputy Director	CFR

EXPORT-IMPORT BANK

Macomber, Pres. & Chmn	CFR
K. Lawson, 1st VP & Vice Chmn	CFR
Rodriguez, Director	CFR
senden, General Council	CFR

E OF SCIENCE & TECHNOLOGY

R. Graham, Jr., Advisor To President & Director	CFR

LIBRARY OF CONGRESS

James H. Billington, Librarian, Chmn. Trust Fund Board	CFR
Ruth Ann Stewart, Asst. Librarian National Programs	CFR

NATIONAL SCIENCE FOUNDATION

Frank H. T. Rhodes, Bd. of Directors	CFR
James B. Holderman, Bd. of Directors	CFR
D. Allen Bromley, Bd. of Directors	CFR

U.S. ARMS CONTROL & DISARMAMENT AGENCY

Thomas Graham, Jr., General Council	CFR
William Schneider, Chmn., General Advisory Council	CFR
Richard Burt, Negotiator on Strategic Defense Arms	CFR
David Smith, Negotiator, Defense & Space	CFR

FEDERAL JUDICIAL CENTER

William W. Schwarzer, Director	CFR

E

CFR/TC	Winston Lord, Asst. Sec. East Asian & Pacific Affairs	CFR/TC
CFR		
CFR	Stephen A. Oxman, Asst. Sec. Europ. Affairs	CFR
CFR	Timothy E. Wirth, Counselor	CFR

AMBASSADORS

r CIS) CFR	John D. Negroponte,	(Mexico)	CFR
CFR	Edward N. Ney,	(Canada)	CFR
CFR	Robert B. Oakley	(Pakistan)	CFR
CFR	Robert H. Pelletreau, Jr.	(Tunisia)	CFR
CFR	Christopher H. Phillips	(Brunei)	CFR
CFR	Nicholas Platt,	(Phillipines)	CFR
CFR	James W. Spain,	(Maldives & Sri Lanka)	CFR
CFR	Terence A. Todman,	(Argentina)	CFR
CFR	Frank G. Wisner II,	(Egypt)	CFR
CFR	Warren Zimmerman,	(Yugoslavia)	CFR

RESS

son (D), CT	CFR	Dave K. McCurdy (D), OK	CFR
ephardt (D), MO	CFR	Eleanor Holmes Norton (D), DC	CFR
ingrich (R), GA	CFR	Thomas E. Petri (R), WI	CFR
ton (D), IN	TC	Charles B. Rangel (D), NY	TC
hton, Jr. (R), NY	CFR	Carlos A. Romero-Barcelo (D), PR	CFR
ohnson (R), CT	CFR	Patricia Schroeder (D), CO	CFR
), IA	TC	Peter Smith (R) VT	CFR
(D), GA	CFR	Olympia J. Snow (R) ME	CFR
tsui (D), CA	CFR	John M. Spratt (D), SC	CFR
		Louis Stokes (D), OH	CFR

Robert D. Haas	Chmn, CEO, Levi Strauss	TC
David J. Hennigar	Chmn, Crownx, V-Chmn, Crown Life	TC
Robert D. Hormats	V. Chmn, Goldman Sachs Int.	TC
James R. Houghton	Chmn, CEO. Corning Inc.	TC
Donald R. Keough	Pres, CEO, The Coca Cola Co.	TC
Henry A. Kissinger	Chmn, Kissinger Assoc.	TC
Whitney MacMillan	Chmn, CEO, Cargill, Inc.	TC
Robert S. McNamara	Former Pres, The World Bank	TC
William D. Ruckelshaus	Chmn, CEO, Browning-Ferris Ind.	TC
David Stockman	Gen Ptnr, The Blackstone Group	TC
Henry Wendt	Chmn, SmithKline Beecham	TC

CHASE MANHATTAN CORP.

Thomas G. Labrecque, Chmn. & CEO	CFR/TC
Robert R. Douglass, V. Chmn.	CFR
Willard C. Butcher, Dir.	CFR
Richard W. Lyman "	CFR
Joan Ganz Cooney "	CFR
David T. McLaughlin "	CFR
Edmund T. Pratt, Jr. "	CFR
Henry B. Schacht "	CFR

CHEMICAL BANK

Walter V. Shipley, Chmn.	CFR
Robert J. Callander, Pres.	CFR
William C. Pierce, Exec. Off.	CFR
Randolph W. Bromery Dir.	CFR
Charles W. Duncan, Jr. "	CFR
George V. Grune "	CFR
Helen L. Kaplan "	CFR
Lawrence G. Rawl "	CFR
Michael I. Sovern "	CFR
Richard D. Wood "	CFR

CITICORP

John S. Reed, Chmn.	CFR
William R. Rhodes, V. Chmn.	CFR
Richard S. Braddock, Pres.	CFR
John M. Deutch Dir.	CFR
Clifton C. Garvin, Jr. "	CFR
C. Peter McColough "	CFR
Rozanne L. Ridgeway "	CFR
Franklin A. Thomas	CFR

FIRST CITY BANCORP, TEXAS

A. Robert Abboud, CEO.	CFR

MORGAN GUARANTY

Lewis T. Preston, Chmn.	CFR

BANKERS TRUST NEW YORK CORPORATION

Charles S. Stanford, Jr., Chmn	CFR
Alfred Brittain III, Dir.	CFR
Vernon E. Jordan, Jr., "	CFR
Richard L. Gelb, "	CFR
Patricia Carry Stewart, "	CFR

FIRST NATIONAL BANK OF CHICAGO

Barry F. Sullivan	TC

MANUFACTURERS HANOVER DIRECTORS

Cyrus Vance	CFR
G. Robert Durham	CFR
George B. Munroe	CFR
Marina V. N. Whitman	CFR/TC
Charles J. Pillod, Jr.	CFR

BANK AMERICA

Andrew F. Brimmer Dir.	CFR
Ignazio E. Lozano, Jr. "	CFR
Ruben F. Mettler "	CFR

SECURITIES & EXCHANGE COMM.

Michael D. Mann, Dir. Intntl. Aff.	CFR

No one escapes when freedom fails.
The best men rot in filthy jails, and those who cried,
"Appease, appease!"
Are hanged by those they tried to please

U.S. MILITARY

DEPARTMENT OF DEFENSE

Les Aspin, Secretary of Defense	CFR
Frank G. Wisnerll Under Sec. for Policy	CFR
Henry S. Rowen, Asst. Sec. International Security Affairs	CFR
Judy Ann Miller, Dep. Asst. Sec. for Manpower	CFR
Franklin C. Miller, Dep. Asst Sec. Nuclear Fcs & Arms Control	CFR
W. Bruce Weinrod, Dep. Asst.Sec. Europe & NATO	CFR
Adm. Seymour Weiss, Chmn, Defense Policy Bd.	CFR
Charles M. Herzfeld, Dir. Def. Research & Eng.	CFR
Andrew W. Marshall, Dir. Net Assessment	CFR
Michael P. W. Stone, Secretary of the Army	CFR
Donald B. Rice, Secretary of the Air Force	

JOINT CHIEFS OF STAFF

Gen. Colin L. Powell, Chmn.	CFR
Gen. Carl E. Vuono, Army	CFR
Gen. John T. Chain, CO SAC	CFR
Gen. Merrill A. McPeak, CO Pac AF	CFR
Lt. Gen. George L. Butler, Dir. Strat Plans & Policy	CFR
Lt. Gen. Charles T. Boyd, Com. Air Univ.	CFR
Lt. Gen. Bradley C. Hosmer AF Inspector General	CFR

SECRETARIES OF DEFENSE

57-59	McElroy	CFR
59-61	Gates	CFR
61-68	McNamara	CFR/TC
69-73	Laird	CFR
73-75	Richardson	CFR/TC
75-77	Rumsfeld	CFR
77-80	Brown	CFR/TC
80-88	Weinberger	CFR/TC
88-	Carlucci	CFR
88-	Cheney	CFR

ALLIED SUPREME COMMANDERS

49-52	Eisenhower	CFR
52-53	Ridgeway	CFR
53-56	Gruenther	CFR
56-63	Norstad	CFR
63-69	Lemnitzer	CFR
69-74	Goodpaster	CFR
74-79	Haig	CFR
79-87	Rogers	CFR/TC

SUPERINTENDENTS U.S. MILITARY ACADEMY AT WEST POINT

60-63	Westmoreland	CFR
63-66	Lampert	CFR
66-68	Bennett	CFR
70-74	Knowlton	CFR
74-77	Berry	CFR
77-81	Goodpaster	CFR

CFR MILITARY FELLOWS, 1991

Col. William M. Drennan, Jr. USAF
Col. Wallace C. Gregson, USMC
Col. Jack B. Wood, USA

CFR MILITARY FELLOWS, 1992

Col. David M. Mize, USMC
Col. John P. Rose USA

ADDITIONAL MILITARY

MG R.C. Bowman	CFR
BG F. Brown	CFR
LT COL W. Clark	CFR
ADM Wm. Crowe	CFR
COL P. M. Dawkins	CFR
V.ADM Thor Hanson	CFR
COL W. Hauser	CFR
MAJ R. Kimmitt	CFR
GEN W. Knowlton	CFR
V. ADM J. Lee	CFR
COL D. Mead	CFR
M G Jack Merritt	CFR
GEN E. Meyer	CFR
COL Wm. E. Odom	CFR
COL L. Olvey	CFR
COL Geo. K. Osborn	CFR
MG J. Pustay	CFR
LG E.L. Rowny	CFR
CAPT Gary Sick	CFR
MG De Witt Smith	CFR
BG Perry Smith	CFR
LTG Wm. Y. Smith	CFR
COL W. Taylor	CFR
ADM S. Turner	CFR
MG J. Welch	CFR
GEN J. Wickham	CFR

LABOR UNION LEADERS

Jay Mazur, International Ladies' Garment Workers Union	CFR/TC
Jack Sheinkman, Amalgamated Clothing & Textile Workers Union	CFR
Albert Shanker, Pres., American Federation of Teachers	CFR/TC
Glenn E. Watts, Communication Workers of America	CFR/TC

UNIVERSITY PROFESSORS

Graham Allison, Prof. of Gov., Harvard Univ.	TC
Zbigniew Brzezinski, Prof. Johns Hopkins	TC
Gerald L. Curtis, Prof, Pol. Sci., Columbia Univ.	TC
Martin S. Feldstein, Prof. Econ., Harvard Univ.	TC
Richard N. Gardner, Prof. Law, Columbia University	TC
Joseph S. Nye, Jr., Prof. Intntl Affrs., Harvard Univ.	TC
Robert D. Putnam, Prof. Politics, Harvard Univ.	TC
Henry Rosovsky, Prof. Harvard Univ.	TC
George P. Shultz, Hon. Fellow, Stanford Univ.	TC
Lester C. Thorow, Dean, SloanSchool of Mgmt., MIT	TC
Paul Volcker, Prof. Intnl Econ., Princeton Univ.	TC

COLLEGE & UNIVERSITY PRESIDENTS

Robert H. Edwards, Bowdoin College	CFR
Vartan Gregorian, Brown University	CFR
Hanna Holborn Gray, University Of Chicago	CFR
Joseph S. Murphy, City Univ.of NY	CFR
Michael I. Sovern, Columbia University	CFR
Frank H.T. Rhodes, Cornell University	CFR
James T. Laney, Emory University	CFR
Rev. Joseph A. O'Hare, Fordham Univ.	CFR
Thomas Ehrlich, Indiana University	CFR
Steven Muller, Johns Hopkins University	CFR
Alice S. Ilchman, Sarah Lawrence College	CFR
Edward T. Foote, II, University Of Miami	CFR
S. Frederick Starr, Oberlin College	CFR/TC
Joseph Duffey, Chans., Univ. of Mass.	CFR
John M. Deutch, Institute Professor, MIT	CFR/TC
Lester C. Thurow, Dean, Sloan Sch.., MIT	CFR
Bernard Harleston, City College of New York	CFR
John Brademus, New York University	CFR/TC
Wesley W. Posvar, University Of Pittsburg	CFR
Harold T. Shapiro, Princeton University	CFR
Charles W. Duncan, Jr., Chmn, Rice University	CFR
Dennis O'Brien, Univ. of Rochester	CFR
David Baltimore, Rockefeller University	CFR
Donald Kennedy, Stanford University	CFR
Richard Wall Lyman, Pres. Em., Stanford	CFR
Hans M. Mark, Chans, Univ. of Texas	CFR
Robert H. Donaldson, Univ. of Tulsa	CFR
Stephen J. Trachtenberg, Geo. Washington Univ.	CFR
William H. Danforth, Washington University St. Louis	CFR
John D. Wilson, Washington & Lee University	CFR
Nannerl O. Keohane, Wellesley University	CFR

Chapter 11

UNHOLY ALLIANCES ARE
KILLING AMERICA

For many years I have wondered what is going on in our government. There were enough years of horrible "life experiences" to cause me to ask questions. This book is the end result of a quest to learn why the winds of change blow as they do. Almost every thinking American, by now, must be asking himself what is going on. What can they possibly be thinking? The problem is our rose-colored glasses. The American people have been the dupes of a ferocious and single-minded plan of brainwashing which results first in socialism, then total dictatorship by the elite.

Argue, debate, prove the material wrong if you can, but I pray that those who cling to their denial will be delivered before the curtain opens for the final act of the New World Order. Otherwise, it will be a rude awakening indeed.

In this book I have attempted to show who some of the players are and the "unholy alliances" that have been operating entirely unexposed to the American people. The media is completely sold out to this secrecy; that is why you do not know what is going on.

It wasn't until I moved to Boston that I was forced to realize the dishonesty of the media. It became apparent that the *Boston Globe* twisted the news any way it wanted to present its own version of "what really happened." Later I learned that this was standard operating procedure since their objective was to manipulate the state's masses rather than to truthfully report the news. And, from what I could make of Massachusetts, they had done a fine job indeed.

Still later I learned that this "little conspiracy" was just part of a worldwide scheme to manipulate the masses. I believe many people are becoming painfully aware of this today. Why wouldn't a fair and honest press tell us the "real" news? The answer is that no one in the upper levels of ruling hierarchy believes you would go along with their plan if you really knew what is going on.

Although most Americans are either completely asleep or in denial, other countries have been aware of our demise from within for some time. A.K. Chesterton, commenting from Great Britain stated, "Even if the United States were on our side, as over and over again she has shown herself *not* to be, this [abandoning British power of nuclear deterrence and turning it over to the United States] would be shameful—indeed a traitorous—abandonment of the power to survive as a nation in our own right. The United States is not on our side for the simple reason that she is not even on her own side, but a cat's paw for alien interests to use as they please. Many American patriots are aware of this truth and do their best to make it known. Many have been smashed in the process."[320]

In his book *Propaganda* Edward Bernays helps us understand what is really going on. He explains:

"Propaganda is the executive arm of the invisible government."[321]

"The conscious and intelligent manipulation of the organized habits and opinions of the masses is an important element in democratic society. Those who manipulate this unseen mechanism of society constitute an invisible government which is the true ruling power of our country...."[322]

"We are governed, our minds are molded, our tastes formed, our ideas suggested, largely by men we have never heard of...."[323]

"It is they who pull the wires which *control the public mind*, and who harness old social forces and contrive new ways to bind and guide the world...."[324]

"To deplore the existence of such a mechanism is to ask for a society such as never was and never will be. To admit that it exists, but expect that it shall not be used, is unreasonable."[325]

The first editor to read this book called me to indicate that Bernays's material was "too futuristic." He was flabbergasted to learn *Propaganda* was published in 1928!

It is difficult to imagine the power of those who control secret unholy alliances like the Council on Foreign Relations, the Trilateral Commission, and the Bilderbergers. Yet these are only a few of the groups which make up a complex web of subterfuge and cause treason to be a normal turn of events in individual nations. What could possibly be more treasonous than President George Bush calling for a New World Order? The media not only blacks out the true nature of the unholy alliances but makes something good out of the New World Order.

Here, from a professional intelligence officer, Dr. John Coleman, is what the New World Order is really about:

"A One World Government and one-unit monetary system under permanent non-elected hereditary oligarchists who self-select from among their numbers in the form of a feudal system as it was in the Middle Ages..."(Self-selection is presently through the CFR.)

"There will be no middle class, only rulers and servants. All laws will be uniform under a legal system of world courts practicing the same unified code of laws, backed up by a One World Government police force and a One World unified military to enforce laws in all former countries where no national boundaries shall exist..."(The American Bar Association is promoting an international court system.)

"Only one religion will be allowed and that will be in the form of a One World Government Church, which has been in existence since 1920... Satanism, Luciferianism, and Witchcraft shall be recognized as legitimate One World Government curricula with no private or church schools. All Christian churches have already been subverted and Christianity will be a thing of the past in the One World Government." (Satanism and witchcraft are already recognized as "true religions." Presently, satanic church services are being held on military bases in the United States.)

"To induce a state where there is no individual freedom or any concept of liberty surviving, there shall be no such thing as republicanism, sovereignty, or rights residing with the people. National pride and racial identity shall be stamped out and in the transition phase it shall be subject to the severest penalties to even mention one's racial origin." (This is being propelled by the "Hate Crimes Bill", but ultimately all will be slaves so it won't matter.)

"Each person shall be fully indoctrinated that he or she is a creature of the One World government with an identification number clearly marked on their person so as to be readily accessible, which identifying number shall be in the master file of the NATO computer in Brussels, Belgium, subject to instant retrieval by any agency of the One World government at any time...."(Hypodermic needles to insert bar-coded implants have already been developed.)

"Marriage shall be outlawed and there shall be no family life as we know it. Children will be removed from their parents at an early age and brought up as state property...."(HRS has been accused of doing this. Ross Perot suggested on national TV we develop a "society of winners" by taking infants out of the home for "training" at an early age. Hillary Clinton advocates such programs.)

"Self-abortion shall be taught and practiced after two children are born to a woman; such records shall be contained in the personal file of each woman in the One World Government's regional computers. If a woman falls pregnant after she has previously given birth to two children, she shall be forcibly removed to an abortion clinic for such an abortion and sterilization to be carried out." (China presently allows only one child per family and practices forced abortion. The abortion pill is being marketed presently.)

"Pornography shall be promoted...showing in every theater or cinema, including homosexual and lesbian pornography. The use of 'recreational' drugs shall be compulsory, with each person allotted drug quotas which can be purchased at One World Government stores throughout the world. Mind control drugs will be expanded and usage become compulsory. Such mind control drugs shall be given in food and/or water supplies without the knowledge and/or consent of the people...."(Fluoride was used by Germany and the Soviet Union to reduce resistance to mind control. Presently, bars in New York City sell a drink that heightens a person's sexual instincts and keeps them high for hours.)

"The economic system shall be based upon the ruling oligarchical class allowing just enough foods and services to be produced to keep the mass slave labor camps going. All wealth shall be aggregated in the hands of the elite members...." (Recession, loss of jobs, lack of necessities, lack of food, and so forth keep the masses "in line.")

"Euthanasia for the terminally ill and the aged shall be

compulsory...."(Euthanasia was on the California ballot—1992.)

"At least 4 billion 'useless eaters' shall be eliminated by the year 2050 by means of limited wars, organized epidemics of fatal rapid-acting diseases, and starvation. Energy, food, and water shall be kept at subsistence levels for the non-elite, starting with the populations of Western Europe and North America and then spreading to other races. The population of Canada, Western Europe, and the United States will be decimated more rapidly than on other continents, until the world's population reaches a manageable level of 1 billion, of which 500 million will consist of Chinese and Japanese races, selected because they are people who have been regimented for centuries and who are accustomed to obeying authority without question." (Somalia, abortion, and the AIDS cover-up. Why do you think, for the first time ever there is no testing and no contact tracing of those infected during a world-wide epidemic, if this is not a planned and enforced world "depopulation?" Moreover, why would our schools and our government be encouraging sex and immorality while promoting the use of condoms when they know that the research shows that almost all condoms leak? Abstinence isn't even discussed because it would promote a moral, up-right society rather than a decadent, easily-manipulated society. Recently the House [U.S. Congress] rejected a provision of an AIDS funding bill which would have mandated that States receiving federal money require health officials to notify the spouses of HIV carriers. Congress refuses to protect unsuspecting legitimate spouses from being notified that their mates are infected.)

"The United States will be flooded by peoples of alien cultures who will eventually overwhelm America, people with no concept of what the United States Constitution stands for and who will, in consequence, do nothing to defend it, and in whose minds the concept of liberty and justice is so weak as to matter little. Food and shelter shall be the main concern." (Legislation has already been passed to open the floodgates. Haitians with AIDS are currently entering the country in droves. It's becoming necessary to be bilingual to work in Miami.)

"No central bank, save the Bank of International Settlement and the World Bank, shall be allowed to operate.

Private banks will be outlawed. Remuneration for work performed shall be under a uniform predetermined scale throughout the One World Government. There shall be no wage disputes allowed, nor any diversion from the standard uniform scales of pay laid down by the One World Government. Those who break the law will be instantly executed." (National central banks are privately owned, primarily by the Rothschilds. Examples are the central banks of the United States, Italy, England, France, Germany, and Austria.)

"There shall be no cash or coinage in the hands of the non-elite. All transactions shall be carried out by means of a debit card which shall bear the identification number of the holder. Any person who in any way infringes the rules and regulations...shall have the use of his or her card suspended for varying times according to the nature and severity of the infringement." (Why do you think they push credit so much? Is it for your benefit?)

"Such persons will find, when they go to make purchases, that their card is blacklisted and they will not be able to obtain services of any kind. Attempts to trade 'old' coins, that is to say silver coins of previous and now defunct nations, shall be treated as a capital crime subject to the death penalty. All such coinage shall be required to be surrendered within a given time along with guns, rifles, explosives, and automobiles. Only the elite and One World Government high-ranking functionaries will be allowed private transport, weapons, coinage, and automobiles." (Weapons are being outlawed little by little each month. You never hear about the good they do, only the bad. At least four laws have been crafted to control gold. More are expected. In his book, *Earth in the Balance*, Al Gore promotes the elimination of the internal combustion engine, i.e., cars, trucks, and motorcycles.)

"If the offense is a serious one, the card will be seized at the checking point where it is presented. Thereafter that person shall not be able to obtain food, water, shelter and employment, medical services, and shall be officially listed as an outlaw..."(In a no-money system, when the machine loses your number—you are out of luck!)

"Rival factions and groups such as Arabs and Jews and African tribes shall have differences magnified and be

179

allowed to wage wars of extermination against each other under the eyes of NATO and UN observers. The same tactics will be used in Central and South America. These wars of attrition shall take place before the takeover of the One World Government and shall be engineered on every continent where large groups of people with ethnic and religious differences live, such as the Sikhs, Moslem Pakistanis, and the Hindu Indians. Ethnic and religious differences shall be magnified and exacerbated and violent conflict as a means of 'settling' their differences shall be encouraged and fostered." (Examples are Nicaragua and Yugoslavia. Radical Moslems are attempting to overthrow the Moderate government of Egypt. China and North Korea are supplying fundamentalist Arabs with sophisticated weaponry.)

"All information services and print media shall be under the control of the One World Government. Regular brainwashing control measures shall be passed off as 'entertainment' in the manner in which it was practiced and became a fine art in the United States."[326] (Virtually all media is under *centralized* control and is indeed brainwashing at a subtle, subconscious level.)

National security advisor as well as Trilateral Commission founder Zbigniew Brzezinski authored a book blandly titled *Between Two Ages, America's Role in the Technetronic Era*. It was commissioned by another dubious society, the Club of Rome. Brzezinski proposed that the United States was moving "into an era unlike any of its predecessors; we were moving toward a technetronic era that could easily become a dictatorship."[327]

Brzezinski goes on to say that our society "is now in an information revolution based on amusement focus, spectator spectacles (sporting event saturation) which provide an opiate for an increasingly purposeless mass." (Why so much emphasis and money on sports; yet so little on important issues—you pick the topic.)

Since he assumes that the TV watchers will never awaken to hear the alarm of the dawning of the New Age, he clarifies what this period of history will be like:

"At the same time the capacity to assert social and political control over the individual will vastly increase. It will soon be possible to assert almost continuous control over every citizen and to maintain up-to-date files, containing even the most personal details about health and personal behavior of every citizen in addition to the more customary data.

"These files will be subject to instantaneous retrieval by the authorities. Power will gravitate into the hands of those who control information. Our existing institutions will be supplanted by pre-crises management institutions, the task of which will be to identify in advance likely social crises and to develop programs to cope with them."[328]

The government creates legislation it desires to implement. Then it plans an "emergency" or "war" by which to implement that legislation previously created. It always appears necessary because of media propaganda. We are forced to believe we need it. The new legislation always leads to more government control and power over American citizens' lives.

An answer waiting to be "needed" at just the right "emergency" is the implementation of the Federal Emergency Management Act (FEMA). This act was originally developed during the Kennedy administration, but was solidified under Nixon and polished under Jimmy Carter.

Given a planned and created and propagandized "international crisis" or "economic crisis," Executive Order 12148 would be called into action. Suddenly, the government would:

1. Take over all communication media.
2. Seize all sources of power: petroleum, gas, electrical, nuclear, etc.
3. Seize all food resources, farms, ranches, and timberland.
4. Take over all transportation travel on highways and seaports by air and rail.
5. Force citizens into work forces under bureaucratic supervision.
6. Take over all health, welfare, and education.
7. Register all citizens nationwide using the postmaster general.
8. Relocate communities.
9. Freeze all wages and prices.
10. Regulate the amount of your own money you can withdraw from your bank account.
11. Close all banks and stock exchanges.
12. Institute extraordinary measures said to be essential to national survival.

Using almost any planned and staged pretext, the president can declare an emergency and take all Americans' rights away.

Brzezinski goes on, "In the technetronic society the trend seems to be toward aggregating the individual support of millions of unorganized citizens, *who are easily within the reach of magnetic and attractive personalities,* and effectively exploiting the latest communication techniques to manipulate emotions and control reason."[329] In order to do this Brzezinski alludes to "the possibility of biological and chemical tampering with what has until now been considered the immutable essence of man."[330] He says, "speaking of a future at most only decades away (written in 1970), an experimenter in intelligence control asserted, 'I foresee the time when we shall have the means and therefore, inevitably, the temptation to manipulate the behavior and intellectual functioning of all the people through environmental and biochemical manipulation of the brain.'"[331]

Brzezinski predicts the upcoming depersonalization of economic power. He claims that "as economic power becomes inseparably linked with political power, it becomes more invisible and the sense of individual futility increases."[332] This frustration will increase as americans are manipulated into a cashless money system.

The military and all government employees are already moving into a cashless system. Presently, an imaginary amount of money is signaled to their accounts which they can then spend. Soon they will receive an I.D. card or credit card, and the imaginary money will be signaled to it for use.

We now have the ability to deduct money from our accounts automatically with a card at the grocery store. So both ends will soon be complete. The next thing you know—cashless. But of course we will be sold on its "convenience;" what we're really talking about here is control.

Note already that the prototype for an implanted chip is being experimented with routinely on pets in California. And there is a satellite already in place to monitor these California animals. Do you seriously think our government has spent millions on a satellite for the surveillance of pets?

These things are spoken about in Revelation 13:16–18.

Many thinking people today have begun to realize there is something very wrong in America. They know that whether they vote for Bush or Clinton, they are sunk. They are absolutely right—because either way they get the Trilateral Commission, the CFR, and a one-world government philosophy.

The net is too intricately woven for us to do much about it. Our senators and congressmen have deceived us. Those who know have not even bothered to warn us about the overthrow of the American government. "Even if the congressmen know the details of the plot...there is nothing they can do to stop it. The international bankers can inflict their will on any country and the United States is as helpless as any other."[333]

It is time to get your family in order. It is time to make certain that your loved ones are purchased by the blood of Jesus Christ. It is time to reach out to those you love and pray for those whom you have concerns about.

It is time to witness to your friends and family that these difficult times ahead are part of God's plan for a rebellious world. It is time to "get tough" for Christ and those you love.

It is time to get out of debt and become self-sufficient. It is time to remove yourself from the "world system" to whatever degree possible. It is time to store provisions for harder times. It is time to pray. Pray not only for your own, but for those who are duped by money and power and greed. There are even those who believe they are serving some righteous cause, who with proper understanding might come out of this mystery Babylon and join ranks with the only truth and freedom there is—that found not in a religion, but in a relationship with Jesus Christ.

We are at the precipice. Only God Himself can deter America from going over the brink. I urge you to consider carefully the implications of these truths and begin to seek God and ask Him for forgiveness. Seek God's forgiveness (John 3:16) and begin anew to wash daily in His counsel (Psalm 32:8). The men who seduce you are described in 2 Peter 2. But we understand the truth described in 1 John 1:8 that if we claim to be without sin, we deceive ourselves and the truth is not in us. If we confess our sins, He is faithful and just and will forgive us our sins and purify us from all unrighteousness. He [Jesus Christ, the Righteous One] is the atoning sacrifice for our sins, and not only for ours but also for the sins of the whole world (1 John 2:1–2). This is nothing new to Him, since it is written:

With cunning they conspire against your people; they plot against those you cherish (Psalm 83:3).

In his arrogance the wicked man hunts down the weak, who are caught in the schemes he devises (Psalm 10:2).

With one mind they plot together; they form an alliance against you (Psalm 83:5).

The wicked freely strut about when what is vile is honored among men (Psalm 12:8).

Why do the nations rage and peoples plot in vain? The kings of the earth take their stand and the rulers gather together against the Lord and against his Anointed One... (Psalm 2:1).

The One enthroned in heaven laughs...The Lord laughs at the wicked, for he knows their day is coming (Psalm 2:4, Psalm 37:13).

"Because of the oppression of the weak and the groaning of the needy, I will now arise," says the Lord. "I will protect them from those who malign them" (Psalm 12:5).

Though they plot evil against you and devise wicked schemes, they cannot succeed (Psalm 21:11).

Many are the woes of the wicked, but the Lord's unfailing love surrounds the man who trusts in him (Psalm 32:10).

Cast your cares on the Lord and he will sustain you; he will never let the righteous fall (Psalm 55:22).

Do not be afraid or discouraged because of this vast army. For the battle is not yours, but God's (2 Chronicles 20:15).

Yours, O Lord, is the greatness and the power and the glory and the majesty and the splendor, for everything in heaven and earth is yours. Yours, O Lord, is the kingdom; you are exalted as head over all (1 Chronicles 29:11).

To him who loves us and has freed us from our sins by his blood, and has made us to be a kingdom and priests to serve his God and Father—to him be glory and power for ever and ever! Amen (Revelation 1:5–6).

APPENDIX

For greater truth in news, try these resources:

1. Focus on the Family *Citizen*
   Colorado Springs, CO 80995
   719–531–3400

2. The New American
   P.O. Box 8040
   Appleton, WI 54913
   800–341–1522

3. Newswatch Magazine
   3706 Dax
   Bridgeton, MO 63044
   314–739–4490

4. Committee to Restore the Constitution
   P.O. Box 986
   Ft. Collins, CO 80522
   303–484–2575

5. Point of View Radio Talk Show (Christian Radio)
   P.O. Box 30
   Dallas, TX 75221
   800–347–5151

6. Insider Report
   P.O. Box 467939
   Atlanta, GA 30346–9989
   800–728–2288

7. McAlvany Intelligence Advisor
   P.O. Box 84904
   Phoenix, AZ 85071–9965
   800–528–0559

8. Christian Coalition
   1801-L Sara Drive
   Chesapeake, VA 23320
   800–325–4746

9. The Spotlight
   300 Independence Ave., S.E.
   Washington, D.C. 20003
   800–522-6292

10. Midnight Messenger
    9205 S.E. Clackamas Rd. #1776
    Clackamas, OR 97015
    503–824–2050

11. Concerned Women for America
    P.O. Box 65453
    Washington, D.C. 20035–5453

12. 700 Club (Christian TV)

13. Youth Action News
    P.O. Box 312
    Alexandria, VA 22313

14. U.S. Veteran News and Report
    P.O. Box 1713
    Kinston, NC 28501

15. Ultrasound, "A Window to the Womb"
    Sound Wave Images–VM6
    P.O. Box 199
    Birmingham, MI 48012
    313–360–0743 or 313–347–9439

All reading should be done with discrimination. However, even at their worst, any of these newsletters carry more truth and are more honest than any local newspaper. No endorsement is necessarily given for any particular publication or its contents.

The Planned Destruction of America

NOTES

1. Robert L. Preston, *Wake Up America* (Hawkes Publishing Inc., 1972).
2. J.R. Church, *Guardians of the Grail* (Oklahoma City, OK: Prophecy Publications, 1989), p. 206.
3. Frank Vanderlip, "Farm Boy to Financier," *Saturday Evening Post*, 8 February 1935.
4. Church, *Guardians of the Grail*, p. 203.
5. Charles A. Lindbergh Sr., *Lindbergh on the Federal Reserve* (Costa Mesa, CA: Noontide Press, 1923), p. 70.
6. *Ibid.*, p. 71.
7. *Ibid.*, p. 74.
8. *Ibid.*, p. 85.
9. *Ibid.*, p. 88.
10. Louis T. McFadden, *Collective Speeches as Compiled from the Congressional Record* (Hawthorne, CA: Omni Publications, 1970), p. 239.
11. *Ibid.*, p. 298.
12. *Ibid.*, p. 309.
13. Archibald E. Roberts, *Bulletin–Committee to Restore the Constitution*, February 1989, p. 6.
14. *Ibid.*, p. 5.

15. McFadden, *Collective Speeches*, p. 326.
16. *Ibid.*, chap. XVII, p. 342.
17. Archibald E. Roberts, Lt. Col., *The Most Secret Science* (Ft. Collins, CO: Betsy Ross Press, 1984), p. 32.
19. *Ibid.*, p. 32.
18. *Ibid.*, p. 31.
20. John R. Rarick, "Deficit Spending," *Congressional Record*, 1 February 1971.
21. 102nd Congress, 1st Session, H.R. 1468.
22. Jerry Voorhis, *Out of Debt, Out of Danger* (Washington, Populist Action Committee, 1943), p. 98.
23. Martin Larson, *Tax Revolt* (Greenwich, CT: Devin-Adair, 1985), p. 128.
24. *Ibid.*, p. 135–136.
25. *The Occult Technology of Power* (Dearborn, MI: Alpine Enterprises, 1974), p. 22.
26. Arthur M. Schlesinger Jr., *The Age of Jackson* (New York: Mentor Books, 1945), pp. 6–7.
27. Robert J. Donovan, *The Assassins* (New York: Harper & Brothers, 1952), p. 83.
28. Church, *Guardians of the Grail*, p. 201.
29. Eustace Mullins, *The Secrets of the Federal Reserve*, (Staunton, VA: Banker Research Institute, 1991), p. 168.
30. *Ibid.*, p. 34.
31. Elisha Ely Garrison, *Roosevelt, Wilson and the Federal Reserve Law* (Boston, MA: Christopher Publications, 1931).
32. Alfred Aldrich, *The Independent*, July 1914.
33. Mullins, *The Secrets of the Federal Reserve*, p. 64.
34. Mullins, *The Secrets of the Federal Reserve*, p. 59.
35. Roberts, *Bulletin–Committee to Restore the Constitution*, p. 2.
36. *Ibid.*
37. Ralph Epperson, *The Unseen Hand* (Tucson, AZ: Publius Press, 1985), p. 273.
38. Mullins, *The Secrets of the Federal Reserve*, p. 120.
39. Mullins, *The Secrets of the Federal Reserve*, p. 87.
40. Mullins, *The Secrets of the Federal Reserve*, p. 137.
41. Mullins, *The Secrets of the Federal Reserve*, p. 136.
42. Roberts, *The Most Secret Science*, p. 69.
43. *The Nation*, 11 December 1982.
44. William Guy Carr, *Pawns in the Game* (Palmdale, CA: Omni Publications), p. 155.
45. Roberts, *Bulletin–Committee to Restore the Constitution*, p. 5.

46. Roberts, *The Most Secret Science*, p. 93.
47. Christopher Weber, *"...Good as Gold"? How We Lost Our Gold Reserves and Destroyed the Dollar* (Berryville, VA: The George Edward Durrell Foundation, 1988), p. 3.
48. *Ibid.*, pp. 90–94.
49. McFadden, *Collective Speeches*, p. 304.
50. Roberts, *The Most Secret Science*, p. 93.
51. *The Federal Reserve System, Its Purposes and Functions* (Hawthorne, CA: Omni Publications, 1958), p. 23.
52. Roberts, *The Most Secret Science*, p. 82.
53. *Ibid.*
54. *The Federal Reserve System, Its Purposes and Functions*, Appendix, p. C.
55. Mullins, *The Secrets of the Federal Reserve*, p. 163.
56. Roberts, *The Most Secret Science*, p. 93.
57. Mullins, *The Secrets of the Federal Reserve*, p. 154.
58. Theodore R. Thoren and Richard F. Warner, *The Truth in Money Book*, (Chagrin Falls, OH: Truth in Money, Inc., 1986), p. 194.
59. *Ibid.*, p. 194.
60. *Ibid.*, p. 192.
61. "Federal Reserve Directors: A Study of Corporate and Banking Influence," Staff Report of the Committee on Banking, Currency, and Housing, House of Representatives, 94th Congress, 2nd Session, p. 120.
62. Carroll Quigley, *Tragedy and Hope* (London: The Macmillan Company, 1966), p. 131.
63. *Ibid.*, p. 133.
64. *Ibid.*, p. 953.
65. Laurence H. Shoup, "Jimmy Carter and the Trilateralists: Presidential Roots," in Holly Sklar, *Trilateralism* (Boston: South End Press, 1980) Part IV, Chapter 1, p. 202.
66. Quigley, *Tragedy and Hope*, p. 147.
67. Frederick Howe, *Confessions of a Monopolist* (Chicago: Public Publishing Co., 1906), p. 157.
68. William P. Hoar, *Architects of Conspiracy* (Belmont, MA: Western Islands, 1984), p. 92.
69. "Ronald Reagan," *American Opinion*, September 1980, p. 99.
70. James Perloff, *The Shadows of Power* (Belmont, MA: Western Islands, 1988), p. 169.
71. *Ibid.*, p. 157.
72. *Foreign Affairs*, Fall 1984.

73. Richard N. Gardner, "The Hard Road to World Order," *Foreign Affairs*, April 1974, p. 558.
74. Perloff, *The Shadows of Power*, p. 159.
75. Zbigniew Brzezinski, *Between Two Ages* (New York: Penguin Books, 1976), p. 300.
76. *Ibid.*, p. 304.
77. Perloff, *The Shadows of Power*, p. 143.
78. Richard Nixon, "Asia After Vietnam," *Foreign Affairs*, October 1967, p. 113.
79. Henry Kissinger, *White House Years* (Boston: Little, Brown, 1979), p. 4.
80. J. Robert Moskin, "Advise and Dissent," *Town & Country*, March 1987, p.156.
81. *New York Times*, 31 January 1971, p. E13.
82. Perloff, *The Shadows of Power*, p. 148.
83. *Ibid.*
84. J. Anthony Lukas, "The Council on Foreign Relations: Is It a Club? Seminar? Presidium? Invisible Government?", *New York Times Magazine*, 21 November 1971, p. 126.
85. Perloff, *The Shadows of Power*, p. 111.
86. David Halberstam, *The Best and the Brightest* (New York: Random House, 1972), p. 60.
87. Rene A. Wormser, *Foundations: Their Power and Influence* (New York: Devin-Adair, 1958), pp. 304–305.
88. Report–Special House Committee to Investigate Tax-Exempt Foundations, 1954, pp. 176–177, in John Stormer, *None Dare Call It Treason* (Florissant, MO: Liberty Bell Press, 1964), p. 210.
89. Walter Isaacson and Evan Thomas, *The Wise Men: Six Friends & the World They Made* (New York: Simon and Schuster, 1986), p. 19.
90. Curtis B. Dall, *FDR: My Exploited Father-In-Law* (Washington, DC: Action Associates, 1970), p. 185.
91. Perloff, *The Shadows of Power*, p. 61.
92. Laurence H. Shoup and William Minter, *Imperial Brain Trust: The Council on Foreign Relations and U.S. Foreign Policy* (New York: Monthly Review Press, 1977), p. 119.
93. Robert W. Lee, "Still in the Saddle," *The New American*, 14 December 1992, p. 14.
94. Quigley, *Tragedy and Hope*, p. 73.
95. Gary Allen, "Who They Are, The Conspiracy to Destroy America," *American Opinion*, October 1972, p. 65.
96. *The Review of the News*, 9 April 1980, pp. 37–38.

97. Medford Evans, "Waking up to the Conspiracy," *American Opinion*, June 1980, p. 38.
98. Charles W. Eliot, "The Next American Contribution to Civilization," *Foreign Affairs*, 15 September 1922, p. 59.
99. Edith Kermit Roosevelt, "Elite Clique Holds Power in U.S.," *Indianapolis News*, 23 December 1961, p. 6.
100. United Nations Charter, Chap. VII, "Actions with Respect to Threats to the Peace, Breaches of the Peace, and Acts of Aggression," art. 43.
101. "Freedom From War: The United States Program for General and Complete Disarmament in a Peaceful World," State Department Publication Number 7277, September 1961.
102. "Freedom From War," p. 11.
103. *Ibid.*
104. *Ibid.*
105. Roberts, *The Most Secret Science*, p. 131.
106. James B. Utt, Congressman, *Washington Report*, 14 February 1963.
107. Roberts, *The Most Secret Science*, p. 133.
108. *Ibid.*, p. 134.
109. Perloff, *The Shadows of Power*, p. 183.
110. Council on Foreign Relations, Annual Report, 1986–1987, p. 13.
111. Perloff, *The Shadows of Power*, p. 202.
112. Donald L. Robinson, ed., *Reforming American Government: The Bicentennial Papers of the Committee on the Constitutional System* (Boulder, CO: Westview Press, 1985), p. 149.
113. *Atlantic Magazine*, October 1987.
114. Zbigniew Brzezinski, "U.S. Foreign Policy: The Search for Focus," *Foreign Affairs*, July 1973, p. 723.
115. Richard Cooper, Karl Kaiser and Masataka Kosaka, "Towards a Renovated International System," *The Trilateral Commission: Triangle Paper 14*, 1977, p. 32.
116. C. Fred Bergsten, Georges Berthoin and Kinhide Mushakoji, "The Reform of International Institutions", *Trilateral Commission: Triangle Paper 11*, 1976, p. 6.
117. Cooper, Kaiser and Kosaka, "Towards a Renovated International System," 1977.
118. Brzezinski, *Between Two Ages*, p. 74.
119. Barry Goldwater, *With No Apologies* (New York: William Morrow, 1979), p. 299.

120. Michael J. Crozier, Samuel P. Huntington and Joji Watanuki, "The Crisis of Democracy: Report on the Governability of Democracies," *Trilateral Commission: Triangle Paper 8* (New York: New York University Press, 1975), p. 98.
121. Ralph Epperson, *The Unseen Hand*, (Tucson, AZ: Publius Press, 1985), p. 245.
122. Goldwater, *With No Apologies*, p. 297.
123. Jeremiah Novak, "Trilateralism and the Summits," in Sklar, *Trilateralism*, Part III, Chap. 3, pp. 194–195.
124. The Trilateral Commission, *The Trilateral Commission* (New York, 15 March 1973), p. 4.
125. Shoup, "Jimmy Carter and the Trilateralists," in Sklar, *Trilateralism*, Part IV, Chap. 1, p. 208.
126. Goldwater, *With No Apologies*, p. 280.
127. Larry Abraham, *Insider Report*, January 1992, p. 2.
128. David Rockefeller, "Foolish Attacks on False Issues," *Wall Street Journal*, 30 April 1980, p. 26.
129. Michael Collins Piper, "Spotlighters Not Surprised at Eastern European Events," *Spotlight Reprint*, February 1990, p. 9.
130. Epperson, *The Unseen Hand*, pp. 231–232.
131. *Ibid.*, p. 239.
132. *Washington Post*, 16 January 1977.
133. Zbigniew Brzezinski, *Power & Principle: Memoirs of the National Security Advisor, 1977–1981* (New York: Farrar, Straus, Giroux, 1983), p. 289.
134. *U.S. News and World Report*, 21 February 1977.
135. Goldwater, *With No Apologies*, p. 286
136. *The Humanist Manifesto I and II*, pp. 13–31.
137. Brzezinski, *Between Two Ages*, p. 300.
138. *Ibid.*
139. Epperson, *The Unseen Hand*, p. 241.
140. Larry Abraham, *Call It Conspiracy* (Seattle, WA: Double A Publications, 1985), p. 201.
141. *Ibid.*, p. 205.
142. *American Opinion*, September 1980, p. 6.
143. Victor Marchetti, *Inside the CIA* Video, "On Company Business," Part 2, "Assassination," (Maljack Productions Inc., 1987).
144. Abraham, *Call It Conspiracy*, p. 211.
145. *U.S. News and World Report*, 7 February 1983.
146. Abraham, *Call It Conspiracy*, pp. 226-227.
147. *New York Times*, 25 January 1981.

148. Abraham, *Call It Conspiracy*, p. 214.
149. *Ibid.*
150. David A. Broder, *Washington Post*, 23 March 1983.
151. James J. Drummey, *The Establishment's Man* (Appleton, WI: Western Islands, 1991), p. 143.
152. "Red China Chief Urges World to 'Defeat US,' " *The Oregon Journal*, 20 May 1970.
153. Gary Allen, "Betraying China," *American Opinion*, October 1971, p. 23.
154. Epperson, *The Unseen Hand*, p. 219.
155. *Time*, 30 December 1973, p. 51.
156. David Rockefeller, "From a China Traveler," *New York Times*, 10 August 1973, p. L-31.
157. Norman Giwan, "Economic Nationalists vs. Multinational Corporation," in Sklar, *Trilateralism*, part VII, Chapter 1, p. 450.
158. *American Opinion*, July-August 1980, p. 113.
159. *Arizona Daily Star* (Tucson), 17 December 1978, p. A-11.
160. *The Review of the News*, 10 January 1979, p. 7.
161. David B. Funderburk, *Betrayal of America* (Dunn, NC: Betrayal of America, 1991), p. 23.
162. *Ibid.*, p. 23.
163. *Ibid.*, p. 24.
164. *Ibid.*, p. 25.
165. Larry Abraham, *Insider Report*, May 1990, p. 5.
166. Alan Stang, "The Tsar's Best Agent," *American Opinion*, March 1976, p. 4.
167. Frank Capell, "The Kissinger Caper," *The Review of the News*, 20 March 1974, p. 31.
168. Funderburk, *Betrayal of America*, Chap. 2, "Appeasement of Deng Xiaoping—The Butcher of Beijing" and Drummey, *The Establishment's Man*, Chap. 8, "The Obscurantist."
169. Drummey, *The Establishment's Man*, p. 150.
170. *Ibid.*
171. *New York Times*, 24 December 1989.
172. Funderburk, *Betrayal of America*, p. 33.
173. Drummey, *The Establishment's Man*, p. 155.
174. George J. Church, "Bush the Riverboat Gambler," *Time*, 25 December 1989, pp. 32–33.
175. Gary Allen, "Too Much of the Wrong Stuff," *American Opinion*, February 1984.

176. Richard Falk, "A New Paradigm for International Legal Studies," *The Yale Law Review*, 84:5, April 1975.
177. "International Debt, the Banks and U.S. Foreign Policy," Staff Report of the Subcommittee on Foreign Economic Policy of the Senate Committee on Foreign Relations, August 1977, p. 66.
178. "The Importance of the Atlantic Connection," *International Finance*, 17 November 1975.
179. Dr. John Coleman, *Conspirators' Hierarchy: The Story of the Committee of 300* (Carson City, NV: America West Publishers, 1992), p. 218.
180. *Ibid.*, p. 219.
181. Sklar, *Trilateralism*, "Overview," p. 48.
182. Axel Madsen, *Private Power, Multinational Corporations for the Survival of Our Planet* (New York: William Morrow and Co., 1980), p. 11.
183. George Ball, "Cosmocorp: The Importance of Being Stateless," *Columbia Journal of World Business*, 2:6, November-December 1967, p. 26.
184. Sklar, *Trilateralism*, "Overview," p. 28.
185. *Ibid.*, p. 29.
186. Raymond Vernon, *The Economic and Political Consequences of Multinational Enterprise: An Anthology* (Boston: 1972), p. 19.
187. Donald L. Barlett and James B. Steele, *America: What Went Wrong* (Kansas City, MO: Universal Press Syndicate Company, 1992), p. 19.
188. *Ibid.*, p. 49.
189. *Ibid.*, p. 98.
190. James "Bo" Gritz, *Called to Serve* (Sandy Valley, NV: Lazarus Publishing Company, 1991), p. 488.
191. *Ibid.*, p. 559.
192. *Ibid.*
193. Sklar, *Trilateralism*, Part VI, Chap. 3, "Trilateralism and the Rhodesian Problem: An Effort at Managing the Zimbabwean Liberation Struggle," p. 399.
194. Philip Agee, *Inside the CIA* Video, Part 2, 1987.
195. Eustace Mullins, *The World Order* (Staunton, VA: Ezra Pound Institute of Civilization, 1985), pp. 72–73.
196. *Ibid.*, p. 74.
197. *Ibid.*, p. 76.
198. Mullins, *The Secrets of the Federal Reserve*, p. 91.
199. Mullins, *The World Order*, p. 81.
200. *Ibid.*, p. 71.

201. *Ibid.*, p. 84.
202. *Ibid.*
203. Antony C. Sutton, *America's Secret Establishment*, (Billings, MT: Liberty House Press, 1986), p. 214.
204. Congressional Record, Volume 54, 9 February 1917, pp. 2947–2948.
205. Perloff, *The Shadows of Power*, p. 181.
206. Herman Dinsmore, *All the News That Fits* (New Rochelle, NY: Arlington House, 1969), pp. 13, 167.
207. Jesse Helms, "An Examination of U.S. Policy Toward POW/MIAs," Staff Report by the U.S. Senate Committee on Foreign Relations, Prologue to Part II, p. i.
208. *Ibid.*, "Accountability," p. 8-4.
209. *Ibid.*
210. *Ibid.*, p. 8-5.
211. *Ibid.*, "The Second Indochina War," p. 5-8.
212. *Ibid.*, p. 5-9.
213. *Ibid.*, "The AEF and World War I," p. 2-1.
214. *Ibid.*, "The Korean War," p. 4-2.
215. *Ibid.*, Memorandum, National Security Council, "To: Zbigniew Brzezinski, From: Michael Oksenberg," 21 January 1980, p. 4–10.
216. *Ibid.*, "World War II," p. 3-1.
217. *Ibid.*, Office of Strategic Services, Report No. EES/18645/1/22 USSR - General, p. 3-13.
218. *Ibid.*, Cable, SECRET PRIORITY, "To: AGWAR, From: SHAEF MAIN, SIGNED EISENHOWER, REF. No: S-88613," 19 May 1945, p. 3-19.
219. *Ibid.*, Cable, "To: AGWAR, From: SHAEF FORWARD, SIGNED EISENHOWER, REF. No. FWD-23059," 1 June 1945, p. 3-20.
220. *Ibid.*, "10,000 Ex-Captives Coming by Week-End; Army Sees All in Europe Accounted For," *The New York Times*, 1 June 1945, p. 3–21.
221. *Ibid.*, "Prologue to Part I," p. i.
222. *Ibid.*, "Epilogue: The Peck Memo," p. 10-4.
223. *Ibid.*, p. 10-5.
224. Gary Kah, *En Route to Global Occupation*, (Lafayette, LA: Huntington House, 1992), p. 62.
225. Ben Bagdikian, *The Media Monopoly* (Boston: Beacon Press, 1987), p. 132.

226. Gary Allen, *The Rockefeller File* (Seal Beach, CA: '76 Press, 1976), p. 45.
227. Wormser, *Foundations: Their Power and Influence*, pp. 142–143.
228. Kah, *En Route to Global Occupation*, pp. 61-62.
229. William F. Jasper, "Child Grab: Why Does The United Nations Want To Control Our Kids?", *The New American*, Vol. 7, No. 13, 18 June 1991, p. 5.
230. *Ibid.*
231. *Ibid.*, p. 7.
232. *Ibid.*
233. *Ibid.*
234. *Ibid.*, p. 8.
235. *Ibid.*, p. 9.
236. Coleman, *Conspirators' Hierarchy*, p. 69.
237. *Ibid.*, p. 50.
238. Allen, *The Rockefeller File*, p. 71.
239. Stormer, *None Dare Call It Treason*, p. 151.
240. Hearing, Military Cold War Education and Speech Review Policies, Senate Armed Services Committee, 87th Congress, Part IV, p. 1491.
241. Whittaker Chambers, *Witness* (New York: Random House, 1952), p. 475.
242. William F. Buckley Jr. and L. Brent Bozell, *McCarthy and His Enemies* (Chicago: Henry Regnery Company, 1954), p. 20.
243. Frank A. Capell, "McCarthyism," *American Opinion*, January 1973, p. 63.
244. *Ibid.*
245. David Brion Davis, *The Fear of Conspiracy* (Ithaca, NY, and London: Cornell Paperbacks, 1971), p. 4.
246. Capell, "McCarthyism," p. 69.
247. *American Opinion*, February 1971, p. 14.
248. Congressional Record, 22 September 1950, p. A6832.
249. *Ibid.*
250. Cornell Simpson, *The Death of James Forrestal* (Boston; Los Angeles: Western Islands, 1966), p. 84.
251. Epperson, *The Unseen Hand*, p. 309.
252. Dr. John Coleman, *The Federal Reserve Bank: Greatest Swindle in History*, pp. 26–27.
253. Bagdikian, *The Media Monopoly*, p. 93.
254. James Britton, *Language and Learning* (London: Penguin, 1970).

255. Allen, *The Rockefeller File*, "Introduction."
256. Bagdikian, *The Media Monopoly*, p. 74.
257. *Ibid.*, p. 75.
258. *Ibid.*, p. 68.
259. *Ibid.*, pp. 67–68.
260. Lindsey Williams, *The Energy Non-Crisis* (Worth Publishing Co., OR, 1980), p.13.
261. *Ibid.*, pp. 15–16.
262. *Ibid.*, p. 16.
263. *Ibid.*, p. 32.
264. *Ibid.*, p. 38.
265. *Ibid.*, p. 39.
266. *Ibid.*, p. 43.
267. *Ibid.*, p. 178.
268. *Ibid.*, pp. 86-87.
269. *Ibid.*, p. 31.
270. *Ibid.*, p. 61.
271. Michael Garitty, "The U.S. Colonial Empire is as Close as the Nearest Reservation: The Pending Energy Wars," in Sklar, *Trilateralism*, by Part IV, Chap. 3, p. 251.
272. *Ibid.*, p. 250.
273. *Ibid.*, p. 251.
274. *Ibid.*, p. 258.
275. *Ibid.*, p. 259.
276. *Ibid.*, pp. 265-266.
277. Anastasio Somoza, *Nicaragua Betrayed* (Belmont, MA: Western Islands, 1980), p.58.
278. *Ibid.*, p. 64.
279. *Ibid.*, p. 260.
280. *Ibid.*, p. 200.
281. *Ibid.*, p. 206.
282. *Ibid.*, p. 207.
283. *Ibid.*, p. 208.
284. *Ibid.*, p. 97.
285. *Ibid.*, p. 98.
286. *Ibid.*, p. 99.
287. *Ibid.*, pp. 198–199.
288. *Ibid.*, p. 293.
289. *Ibid.*, p. 287.
290. *Ibid.*
291. *Ibid.*, p. 291.
292. *Ibid.*, p. 68.

293. *Ibid.*, p. 308.
294. *Ibid.*, p. 66.
295. *Ibid.*, p. 412.
296. *Ibid.*, p. 421.
297. Peter Thompson, "Bilderberg and The West," in Sklar, *Trilateralism*, Part III, Chap. 2, p. 160.
298. *News Herald*, (Borger, TX), 21 June 1974, Excerpt from "Spotlight on the Bilderbergers: Irresponsible Power," (Washington DC, Liberty Lobby), p. 34.
299. Robert Eringer, "The West's Secret Power Group," *Verdict* (a former British monthly), November 1976.
300. John R. Rarick, Congressional Record, 92nd Congress, 1st Session, Wednesday, Volume 117, No. 133, 15 September 1971, pp. E9615–E9624.
301. *Ibid.*, p. E9619.
302. Sklar, *Trilateralism*, pp. 179–180.
303. Rarick, Congressional Record, p. E9617.
304. *Ibid.*
305. Sklar, *Trilateralism*, p. 163.
306. *Ibid.*, p. 177.
307. A.K. Chesterton, excerpt from *The New Unhappy Lords, An Exposure of Power Politics*, in *Liberty Lowdown: A Confidential Washington Report* (Washington DC:, Liberty Lobby), p. 9.
308. Rarick, Congressional Record, p. E9618.
309. "Lame Excuses," *Washington Observer Newsletter*, No. 123, 1 August 1971.
310. *Ibid.*
311. *Liberty Lowdown*, (Washington DC Liberty Lobby, July 1974).
312. Authur C. Egan Jr., "Freeze Was 'Leaker' at Vermont Talks Those in Know made Billions, Source Asserts", *Union Leader* (Manchester, NH), 12 November 1971.
313. *Liberty Lowdown*, No. 132, August 1974, pp. 47–48.
314. Rarick, Congressional Record, p. E9615.
315. A.K. Chesterton, The New Unhappy Lords, An Exposure of Power Politics (Hawthorne, CA: Christian Boys Club of America, 1969).
316. *Ibid.*
317. Quigley, *Tragedy and Hope,* referred to in "Cooperators With Reds' Dominate Bilderbergers," *Orlando Sentinel Star*, 30 June 1974.
318. *Ibid.*, p. 956.
319. *Chicago Tribune*, 9 December 1950.

320. Chesterton, *The New Unhappy Lords*, (3rd Edition, 1970), p. 164.
321. Edward Bernays, *Propaganda* (London: Kennikat Press, 1928), p. 20.
322. *Ibid.*, p. 9.
323. *Ibid.*
324. *Ibid.*, p. 10.
325. *Ibid.*, p. 18.
326. Coleman, *Conspirators' Hierarchy*, pp. 161–166.
327. Brzezinski, *Between Two Ages*.
328. Coleman, *Conspirators' Hierarchy*, p. 28.
328. Brzezinski, *Between Two Ages*, p. 13.
329. *Ibid.*, p. 15.
330. *Ibid.*
331. *Ibid.*, p. *13*.
332. Mullins, *The Secrets of the Federal Reserve*, p. 132.

To order additional copies of *The Planned Destruction of America*, by James Wardner use the handy order form below.

Please send me the following copies of *The Planned Destruction of America* @ $12.95 per copy.

Qty.	Title		Total
_____	*The Planned Destruction of America*	$	_____
	Tax (Florida residents add 6% sales tax)	$	_____
	Shipping and handling ($2.50 per book)	$	_____
	Total:	$	_____

Payment of $ _____ is enclosed (check or money order).

Ship to:

Name: _____

Address: _____

City:_____State: _____Zip: _____

Make check or money order payable to "The Planned Destruction of America" and mail this form to:

James W. Wardner
P.O. Box 533438
Orlando, FL 32853-3438

or call 1-800-TYRANNY or 1-800-897-2669.

For special quotes on orders of 10 or more copies shipped to one address, write Mr. Wardner at the above address or Orlando residents call 898-2997.

✂ Cut out and Mail ☒

The Planned Destruction of America